She Is Cuba

SHE IS CUBA

A Genealogy of the Mulata *Body*

Melissa Blanco Borelli

OXFORD
UNIVERSITY PRESS

OXFORD
UNIVERSITY PRESS

Oxford University Press is a department of the University of
Oxford. It furthers the University's objective of excellence in research,
scholarship, and education by publishing worldwide.

Oxford   New York
Auckland   Cape Town   Dar es Salaam   Hong Kong   Karachi
Kuala Lumpur   Madrid   Melbourne   Mexico City   Nairobi
New Delhi   Shanghai   Taipei   Toronto

With offices in
Argentina   Austria   Brazil   Chile   Czech Republic   France   Greece
Guatemala   Hungary   Italy   Japan   Poland   Portugal   Singapore
South Korea   Switzerland   Thailand   Turkey   Ukraine   Vietnam

Oxford is a registered trademark of Oxford University Press
in the UK and certain other countries.

Published in the United States of America by
Oxford University Press
198 Madison Avenue, New York, NY 10016

© Oxford University Press 2016

Library of Congress Cataloging-in-Publication Data
Blanco Borelli, Melissa.
She is Cuba : a genealogy of the mulata body / Melissa Blanco Borelli.
   pages cm
Includes bibliographical references and index.
ISBN 978-0-19-996816-9 (cloth : alk. paper) — ISBN 978-0-19-996817-6 (pbk. : alk. paper)
1. Racially mixed people—Cuba—History.   2. Women—Cuba—History.
3. Stereotypes (Social psychology)—Cuba—History.   I. Title.
HT1523.B54 2015
305.80097291—dc23
2015008909

9 8 7 6 5 4 3 2 1
Printed in the United States of America
on acid-free paper

Para Elba y Carmen, Para Carmen y María, el pasado
Para Teresita y Ramoncito, el presente
Para Sebastian y Sofia, el futuro

For my grandmothers and great-grandmothers, the past
For my parents, the present
For my nephew and niece, the future

Ellas: ¿quiénes serán? ¿O soy yo misma?
¿Quiénes son estas que se parecen tanto a mí,
no sólo por los colores de sus cuerpos
sino por ese humo devastador que exhala nuestra piel de res marcada
por un extraño fuego que no cesa?

Who are they, these women? Or are they me?
Who are they, who look so much like me
not only in the color of their bodies
but in the devastating smoke
that rises from our animal hides, branded
by a strange, unceasing fire?

—excerpt from Nancy Morejón, *"Persona" (2000),*
translated by David Frye

CONTENTS

ACKNOWLEDGMENTS

If it were not for the people I am about to thank, this book might still be in fragments, spread out among Dropbox, box, Google Drive, or some other virtual storage site. Virtuality seems less frightening a space to store ideas, feelings, and stories. On the page they glare back, asking for certainty, begging for one more rewrite. Yet, from virtuality I come back to the material reality of my book and the immaterial sentiments that feel overwhelmingly real as I write this section.

This project began as a doctoral thesis many years ago at the University of California, Riverside. My thesis adviser, Anna Beatrice Scott, helped me summon many of these ideas. Thank you, Anna, for encouraging me to let my hips loose, to think broadly and differently, and to move along with my writing. My professors at Riverside and UCLA consistently provoked and inspired: Susan Leigh Foster, Marta Savigliano, Jacqueline Shea Murphy, Alicia Arrizón, Linda Tomko and Jenny Sharpe. Alicia Arrizón and Deb Vargas published excerpts from chapter 3 in their special edition of *Women and Performance*. I think it was my first academic publication, and it went on to receive Honorable Mention for the Gertrude Lippincott Award at the Society of Dance History Scholars' June 2009 conference. I thank them for being early supporters of my work. Sections of chapter 3 and the introduction were originally published as "Y ahora qué vas a hacer, mulata?: Hip choreographies in the Mexican cabaretera film *Mulata* (1954)" *Women and Performance: A Journal of Feminist Theory* (2008) 18:3. Chapter 1 first appeared in a shorter form as "Hip Work: Undoing the Tragic Mulata" in Thomas F. DeFrantz and Anita Gonzalez's edited collection *Black Performance Theory* (Duke University Press, 2014). Nadine George Graves and Anthea Kraut invited me to do a keynote address at the joint ASTR/CORD 2010 conference. There, I presented what eventually became chapter 2. I am grateful for the opportunity they provided. Marta Savigliano came up to me after my talk, and she calmly asked, "Melissa, what if you can't find an *academia* dancer?" Little did I know that such a practical question would open up interesting methodological possibilities. A grant from Santander Bank allowed me to travel to Medellín, Colombia, to present at La Universidad de Antioquia and give the keynote address at the Segundo Congreso de Estudios Teatrales. I want to thank Anamaría Tamayo Duque for her help and determination in making this happen.

The Black Performance Theory group offered a space to share and discuss different stages of this work. I want to particularly thank Thomas DeFrantz, Anita González, Omi Jones, Hershini Bhana, and Jayna Brown for their intellectual generosity. Tommy has been a warm, guiding light. From our time together at MIT during my post-doctoral year, to working on conferences together, to FIRT/IFTR Choreographies and Corporealities Working Group, to late-night laughs and giggles, I am forever grateful for his constant encouragement, friendship, and compassion. As I struggled to complete the manuscript, I often heard his voice telling me, calmly and simply, to finish the book. The inimitable Diyah Larasati kept encouraging me, as well. The last time we saw one another was at a conference at Riverside, where she spoke to me about the urgency in completing the project as a way to honor my family. I think this was the last bit of motivation I needed. Ramón Rivera-Servera, Cindy Garcia, and Raquel L. Monroe have been supporters of my work for such a long time. Thank you for your friendship, intellectual curiosity, and for the silly conversations that make life so much more enchanting.

My editor at Oxford University Press, Norman Hirschy, has been patient, supportive, and genuinely invested in the project since its inception. Every time I received feedback from him, it was kind, encouraging, and demonstrated his passion for dance and its myriad scholarly possibilities. My anonymous readers offered rigorous yet supportive comments that I welcomed and relied on as I continued to shape the project.

In the UK, my colleagues and friends have been of enormous support. When Rachel Fensham was head of the dance department at the University of Surrey, she allowed me a short research leave to travel to Cuba to gather some information. She continues to encourage and inspire. Sherril Dodds offered wise counsel on how to make the most of short amounts of time to write. I consider her a queen of productivity and am always immensely grateful for any advice she offers. Helen Hughes made some astute observations about my project during one research afternoon; they were instrumental in rethinking the chapter on the *academias*. Other UK friends and colleagues provided sympathetic ears, hearts, and much-needed laughter over much more needed drinks: Stuart Andrews, Jyoti Argade, Claudia Brazzale, Kathrina Farrugia, Karen da Silva, Jennifer Jackson, Jean Johnson-Jones, Bella Honness-Roe, Bryce Lease, Churnjeet Mahn, Royona

Mitra, Clare Parfitt-Brown, Jen Parker-Starbuck, Bernadette Percebois, Tom Phillips, Efrosini Protopapa, Laura Saunders, Sabine Sörgel, Maria Salgado, and Lise Uytterhoeven.

My students from BA to PhD level consistently remind me why dance studies matters: Eva Aymamí-Reñe, Jinny Han, Kathy Milazzo, Manrutt Wongkaew, Dara Milovanovic, Celena Monteiro. An extra special thank-you goes to Celena Monteiro for helping out with the works consulted section.

In Cuba, I met many gracious and generous people, happy to spend time and share information. I want to first thank Raúl Fernández for his support and interest in my project and for putting me in contact with some of of these wonderful people: Rafael Lam, Radames Giro, José Galiño, Senén Suarez, Rosa Marquetti, Alfonsín Quintana, and Lázaro Montero. Every one them went above and beyond in providing information, photos, books, essays, music, and probably the greatest luxury, time.

A Targeted Research Grant from the American Society of Theatre Research (ASTR) helped fund an important trip to Havana in January 2011. Since 2004, I have been going regularly to Havana, and want to thank the Jiménez Rodríguez family, particularly Andrés, for his love and companionship during the dissertation stages of this project. Marta Vitorte always had a room and some rich conversation ready for me in her lovely apartment. Tony and Marina not only offered wonderful accommodations while I visited Cuba but also made me feel part of their family. At the University of Miami, Esperanza B. de Varona and Lesbia Orta Varona at the Cuban Heritage Collection were very generous with their help as I flipped through pages and pages of *Show* magazine.

Lalín Lafayette and Mayda Limonta invited me into their respective homes and kindly shared time, photos, and stories. Although I have not done their respective performance careers rich justice in this book, I do hope others take it upon themselves to write about these incredible women.

To my dear friends, some of whom I have known since the third grade, thank you for your unfailing presence in my life: Genevieve Gacula, Jeannine Lewis, Desmond D'Silva, Trinette Faint, Mario Johonson, Rosa Pérez, David Shepard, Suzanne Lieberman, Niurka Benavides, Ilaria Mazzoleni, Marisol Pérez, Ximena Schyfter, Lauren Greene, Craig Missler, Olga Baglay, Elena Jessup, and Nadia Ammar.

It has been difficult to pursue an academic career without my family nearby—without a family. Writing this made me feel close to them. My parents have always encouraged excellence and intellectual curiosity. My mother used to leave me with my brother at our local library while she ran errands. I always looked forward to those afternoons in the library because of the books and movie screenings. These are still some of my favorite things. My father used to make us read *National Geographic* and report back to him about something that interested us. I owe my love of knowledge to them. While in Los Angeles, my cousins the Victorio family took good care of me. Carmen, Vladimir, and Vanessa, thank you for your unwavering love and support. My family is quite a *matriarcado*, which might explain my commitment to writing about women's everyday histories. I want to thank my beloved cadre of kooky and caring *tías* for being in my fan club *sin dudas*: Anita García, Dulce Blanco, Rocío Borrero, Yamile Castillo, and Araceli Gil.

I finished this book in the summer of 2014, some of it while in Greece. Perhaps there is something about being near the sea that helps clear the mind—or perhaps it was a rather prophetic encounter that made so many things in my life clear. If I want to add a dose of magical realism to this story, I suppose I can say both Yemayá and Ochún were scheming with one another on that day. However I choose to tell it, I really just want to say thank you, Stratis Volanis, for bringing my heart a lovely sense of peace.

Prologue

Entre Familia(s), Entre Comillas

BETWEEN FAMILIES

When I was about three years old, family members would ask: "Melissa, where are you from?" I would look up, smile, and move my hips innocently from side to side, and answer proudly, "Cu-BAAA-naaa." My Colombian *abuela* loved to tell this story. Obviously, I do not remember doing this, yet I do remember the pleasure on my grandmother's face when she told the story countless times as I was growing up. Maybe she taught me that micro performance of identity—in fact, I think she did—but I can never fully know. It has become so ingrained in the stories of my family that, at this point, it exists as a type of truth. I do not know what makes me Cuban . . . or Colombian, for that matter. Nor do I know why my Colombian grandmother would show such pride in watching her first grandchild pronounce a national identity dissimilar to her own. Nevertheless, that would not be the first time I would be interpellated as Cuban.

When I was about ten years old, my Colombian aunt and uncle celebrated a significant wedding anniversary. I remember they hosted a large party in their home with a live band playing outside. I also remember the sense of awe I felt as I watched their backyard transformed into a dance floor. I watched the many bodies dancing: shoulders shimmying, legs twisting, hips moving from side to side. I hid against the stairs so that no one would notice my fascination, or worse, ask me to dance. I hated to dance back then, especially in public and definitely not in front of the family. Suddenly, my other Colombian aunt saw me. *"Ven, caramba, que tienes que bailar! Con papa cubano no es possible que no puedas bailar"*/Come here, you have to dance! With a Cuban father it's impossible that you cannot dance. There it was again: the imposition of Cuban identity. Reluctantly, I followed my *Tia* Nulvia onto the dance floor. She led, I followed. She tapped my stiff back and told me to relax. *"Echa tu pie izquierdo para atras cuando yo echo mi pie derecho hacia adelante. Deja que mi mano en tu espalda te dirija. Así es. Sí, sientes el ritmo. Mueve más tus caderas."*/Move your left foot back when I move my right foot forward. Let my hand resting on your back signal where I want you to turn. That's good. Yes, you feel the rhythm. Move your hips my more.

As the song progressed, I remember being more comfortable, but I still looked around or rolled my eyes, mortified that I would be assessed by any relatives. I can't remember who watched. I think my brother ran by and laughed at me the way younger brothers often do. He always seemed to be excused from the how-to-be-Latino lessons in the family. To this day, I think *Tia* Nulvia takes credit for teaching me how to dance (and my brother rarely dances in front of anyone).

In my late twenties, I started taking Afro-Cuban dance lessons. I had seen a performance at the Echo Park Cuban Festival in Los Angeles, and I wanted to learn how to move like that. Already versed in folkloric Colombian dance (*cumbia, mapale, bullerengue, currulao,* and *joropo*) by another Colombian aunt (yes, I have many Colombian *tias*), tango, and Hollywood salsa, I figured it would not hurt to learn one more Latin dance style. At that point, they were moves to add to my growing Latino dance repertoire—dance vocabulary to consume pleasurably and methodically.

The experience of learning the dances of the *orishas,* or deities, of the Afro-Cuban Lukumí or Santería spiritual tradition eventually led me to plan and make my first visit to Cuba in 2000. Not only would I learn how to dance by taking classes from well-established professional dance troupes, but I would meet my Cuban relatives. Displacement and disconnection often go hand in hand among members of a diasporic group, so even though I was born and raised in New York City, I was more comfortable asserting my identity as a Latina New Yorker than as Colombian and /or Cuban. (Sometimes I wonder how my identity might have been different if I had spent more time with the Cuban side of my family than the Colombian.)

Culture in my family is decidedly maternal, and sometimes even matrilineal. My father left Cuba in February 1959, yet his journey was not one of forced exile or politically motivated. His family was humble, working class, from a small town, Ranchuelo, near Santa Clara. My Cuban grandmother told him he needed to find his way, and sent him to New York City to be with his older brother, who had been living in New York for several years. Little did my father know that he would not return to Ranchuelo for more than fifty years. At the conclusion of my first trip to Cuba in 2000, I was on the plane to return "home" to Los Angeles, and I could not stop crying. My tears were a mixture of sadness, loss, uncertainty, and relief. I kept thinking of the privilege I enjoyed in being able to leave the country. *I am allowed to leave. I will always be allowed to leave. My aunt has never left. My father has not returned.*

I thought about my grandparents' grave in the Ranchuelo cemetery and the group of shirtless boys playing ball there on a humid late afternoon. I never knew my Cuban grandfather; he died the year I was born. I met my Cuban grandmother only once when she came to stay with us in New York. I cannot remember what time of year that was. I suppose I could just ask my father, but he may not remember, either. On my trip, I lingered in that cemetery for a long time. That I do remember.

It was during that first trip to Cuba that I realized how my corporeality signified within the Cuban context. I was "read" as Cuban until I opened my mouth and spoke my flavorful Caribbean Colombian–New York Latina bilingual Spanish. According to the Cubans I encountered at dance classes or during nights out, I was definitely not Cuban enough when I danced to the *orishas*, but could somewhat pass for Cuban when I danced *son*. The rationale: stiff hips and rigid torso. I began hearing a term called out to me, "*mulata blanconaza*," or "white-ish *mulata*."

I found it amazing that Cubans find ways of labeling one another according to their varying gradations of skin color seen on the island. What about me immediately signified that category? What did that label require in terms of successful representation? What was the history behind such a term? These questions would resurface later, when I began my graduate studies. I am drawn to Ruth Behar's statement in her beautifully written *The Vulnerable Observer* as a way to understand my rationale for this book. In her essay "Going to Cuba," she states: "We invent research projects for ourselves, but ultimately we go back to prove to ourselves that we're not afraid to go back."[1]

My unwillingness to confront specific aspects of my family history prolonged the completion of this book, I confess. Sometimes I felt I purposely delayed because of my fear in admitting my apprehension about endings. Even my own body rebels against the end (or the rear end). My hips were stiff. But, as this project took shape theoretically, I knew I could not avoid making it more personally relevant. That is, I could not write about *mulatas* in Cuba and their sexual relationships with Spanish men in the nineteenth and twentieth centuries without including my family history in that story.

I could not write about the pleasures of witnessing *mulatas* dancing in the flesh or on film without admitting my own pleasure in analyzing, learning, and enacting performances of *mulata*-ness. And, I could not write about how I finally allowed my stiff hips to soften, wriggle, and sway. In a way, I start this prologue from the end—the back, a return. That's quite fitting, as this book focuses on the hips of the *mulata* and how they take us back through the complex intersections of race, class, and gender in Cuba.

Why was I going back? What drew me to this project? The book begins with a glimpse of my family history to contextualize my obsession with the *mulata*. The introduction functions as a search for the self through a contextualization of family history relating to race, gender, and nation. But, more important, it is a search for ways in which identity is always a search, a process of sifting through a culture (often one's own, sometimes another's) for gestures, mannerisms, vocal inflections, and family and national histories. As Clifford Geertz says when speaking about culture, "You put yourself in its way and it bodies forth and enmeshes you."[2]

What does it mean to em*body* the Cuban *mulata*? Where does the movement and gestural vocabulary come from? How do these movements circulate? Why are some movements more valuable than others? What does the history of racialized gender and a libidinal economy borne of colonial paradigms of desire have to do with the em*body*ing of *mulata*? And lastly—and perhaps most important to this project—what do her hips have to do with all of this? This book makes a case for how identity can be analyzed and shaped through the living, dancing body. Ultimately, this is a project about the construction of subjectivity—the historical *mulata* and my own.

Introduction

Nineteenth-century Cuban doctor Benjamin de Céspedes wrote this about the *mulata*: "There is no such civility, culture, beauty or flattery in the semi-savage type of the ordinary mulata who only possesses the art of moving her hips acrobatically."[1] To move one's hips acrobatically? That does not seem like such a bad thing. However, in a nineteenth-century world that privileges mind over body, to relegate a woman—particularly a woman of color—to mere physicality was nothing new. Prompted by this doctor's dismissive generalization, I am going to start a rumor, spread some gossip. Then again, for some, this rumor is nothing new. I only repeat what has been either whispered or heralded throughout Cuba for over a century.

This has to do with the *mulata*, the mixed-race woman of European, African, and Native ancestry. They say her hips are bewitching, that those hips move with an agility, grace, and precision that, if you stare at them too long, you get hip-notized. It is *this* body and *those* hips that have been a Cuban siren call, beckoning admirers and would-be victims by their corporeal spell. I do not pretend to know who started this rumor, nor is it my objective to find out. I am more interested in how this rumor gets produced, reproduced, and circulated.

I take you on a journey, a genealogy of sorts, to uncover how the rumor gained traction. Rumor functions as a powerful device of informational exchange, in that it can circulate quickly and be quite persistent. In this study, the *mulata* body counters the rumors about her hips, through her consistent presence in Cuba: as a proprietor, performer, traveler, dancer, concubine, or cabaret entertainer. Her lived reality troubles the rumors that make claims about her racial and sexual identity, that commodify her body, and that associate her with tragedy, veneration, or vilification in the history and cultural imaginary of Cuba.

This book is about the Cuban *mulata* as laborer, professional perfomer, and brand in the twentieth century. It examines how the *mulata* choreographs her racialized identity through her hips and enacts an embodied theory I call *hip(g)nosis*. By focusing on her living and dancing body to flesh out her identity formation, I make a claim for how subaltern bodies negotiate a cultural identity that marks their bodies on a daily basis. Through this examination of the *mulata* and those venerated hips, I reveal the ways in which empire, nation, race, and gender affect how her body signifies and embodies history, religiosity, resistance, and pleasure. What options exist for the *mulata* in her enactment or em*body*ing of *mulata*? How does she find ways to construct a subjectivity within what Adrienne Rich would call a "politics of location"?[2]

My analysis is framed in three historical moments. The first is the nineteenth century, when Cuban *mulatas* danced in the homes of other *mulatas* as part of a libidinal economy, where white Cuban or European men in attendance specifically sought *mulata* mistresses. I compare the social-dance spaces in Havana and the quadroon balls in New Orleans to highlight the market for *mulata* flesh, and how it necessitated choreographies of race and gender by the *mulatas* for economic survival. The second frame is the mid-twentieth century, where again I inhabit the spaces of social dance. I piece together a history of the notorious *academias de bailes* of Havana nightlife, and I examine the circulation of the *mulata* as a brand in films that feature *mulata* dancing for both prayer and pleasure. Here, my interest is on how the *mulata* body—even the fictional filmic body—engages with the circulating ideas of said body and hips; Cuban social dance undergirds these histories. The last frame in the book is of Cuba from 1970 to the 1990s, leading to the *despelote* dance.

Within each of these time periods I align the *mulata* and her hips with specific Cuban dance forms: *danzón, rumba*, Afro-Cuban *orisha* praise dance, and *despelote*. In so doing, I demonstrate how the *mulata's* association with her hips sets up an embodied "habitus," which I am not just identifying but also critically unpacking so as to trouble the assumption of tragedy within the *mulata* subjectivity.[3]

Racialist discourses in Cuba constructed the *mulata* as a visceral, non-sentient, threatening object. As a visible representative of the miscegenation that Cuban elites were trying to contain, she needed placating. Furthermore, colonial racialist ideologies in the Americas created a hierarchal caste system based on skin color, where lighter skin and proximity to whiteness were more valuable. The *mulata*, depending on her phenotype, operated in the space between blackness and whiteness. This indeterminate status often created tragic encounters, as she was unable to dwell in either location. This liminal identity rendered her tragic, and this tragedy manifested in nineteenth-century plays, literature, and visual culture in the Americas, which also capitalized on the sentimentality and melodrama of the tragic *mulata* narrative.[4] Discursive practices may have rendered her mute, yet on this journey I carve out a space for the *mulata* body to dialogue with those practices, those "rumors." I argue that it is through those acrobatically skilled hips of hers that she finds an opportunity for self-authorship, pleasure, and discursive contestation. Through her embodiment and performances of what I call hip(g)nosis, the *mulata* can step outside the limits of tragedy.

LA MULATA AND HER ENUNCIATING HIPS: A BRIEF HISTORY

When I began this project as a dissertation many years ago, I read an essay by José Piedra, entitled "Hip Poetics." In it, he searches for a way to find language and agency for the woman of(f) color/*mulata* in the Caribbean by articulating how her hips speak. He focuses on the literary representations of the *mulata* in poetry and music lyrics. As a then dance scholar in training, I remember thinking that if that body were indeed speaking, he had not described what that particular body was doing *physically* with her hips. How did they move? What dance forms provide a language to speak the Cuban *mulata* story? How does the body achieve fluency with those hips? I knew those hips spoke, but what provided them with a history, a space, or a subjectivity from which to speak?

The genealogy of this research begins in the nineteenth century, during which time the Yorùbá presence in Cuba increased through the slave trade. The nineteenth century also trafficked in female potential, as many *mulatas* were independent economic agents, owning their own businesses. By the early 1900s, though, the *mulata* had been relegated to iconographic status, despite being discursively rendered as sexualized, tragic, and a threat to the Cuban social order. As part of the Cuban nationalist project, the *mulata* combined the racial history of Cuba in one neat and often aesthetically pleasing package.[5] Her body existed as the conflation of the violence of empire: the Spanish colonizer, the African and Indigenous colonized. The patron saint of Cuba, the Virgin of Charity of Copper (who remains syncretized with the Yorùbá deity Ósun or Ochún), is represented as a *mulata,* thereby offering virginal and spiritual imagery to the iconography. Thus, the disjunction between the *mulata* as aberrant product of taint and miscegenation and the *mulata* as the virginal, spiritual protector of the nation has lent a rich array of signifiers to the *mulata* body. These *mulata* signifiers that materialized by the end of the nineteenth century were widely circulated in twentieth-century Cuba. Such rich signifiers were set in motion on the *zarzuela* (comedic operas) stages, the *teatro bufo* (comedy stages), the cabaret spectacles (of the Sans Souci and the Tropicana nightclubs), the Cuban popular-dance forms (such as *son, danzón, cha-cha-chá,* and *rumba*) in and beyond Cuba, and the exchange of Cuban commodities, such as tobacco packaging (*mulata* iconography on lithographs), rum (the Ron Mulata label), and sugar (association of *mulata* with sweetness).

The active, living presence of the *mulata* wielding her hips to carve out, occupy, and mark her space becomes an embodied response to the textual narratives of tragedy that are embedded in the shared histories of the New World. Furthermore, the *mulata's* association with the Yorùbà/Afro-Cuban deified force of energy known as Òsun/Ochún provokes consideration of how the spiritual affects the secular through the body. The connection between the *mulata* and Ochún has indeed been discussed in Cuban and Cuban-American scholarly work, yet *how* that manifestation of Ochún, her veneration through the *mulata* signifier, and her folkloric dance practices inform the multiple readings of the *mulata* body stills lack scholarly attention. This partnering of the spiritual and the material is fleshed out in this book to suggest how this pairing influences our understandings of the racialized and gendered body of the *mulata*. Her ongoing relationship to blackness undergirds many of these claims, as well.

The Afro-*Cubanismo* movement (1927–late 1930s) instigated widely circulated interest in the African traditions of Cuba, spawning a *rumba* craze in the 1930s in Europe, the United States, Latin America, and other countries.[6] As Afro-Cuban rhythms "plagued" white middle- and upper-class Cuban ideas of moral and bodily pulchritude, the accompanying dances gained widespread notoriety as both enticing and inappropriate. One such rhythm, music and dance, the *rumba*, infiltrated the national consciousness and became inexorably linked with the *mulata*— specifically, her moving hips. While the pelvic area signifies moral abandon in Western cultural codes, it's a source of power and reverence in many African contexts.

These contrasting ideologies reverberated onto the dancing body executing the *rumba*, or *danzón* (what the nineteenth-century *danza* evolved into), or *son-guaracha* (rhythmic precursor to salsa), and Yorùbà ritual dances—dance vocabularies that structured the corporeality of the *mulata* in Cuba.[7] All of these dance forms necessitate certain pelvic movements to punctuate the complex rhythmic quality of the music; as such, they inform how the *mulata* enunciates with her hips. Notice what one eyewitness ascribed to a performance of a hip(ped) repertoire, vis-à-vis the *rumba*:

a dance . . . enveloped in a highly voluptuous atmosphere, reinterpreted with the elegance of [traditional] rumba communicated by the rhythmic shaking of the shoulders, the slow and gentle undulation of the hips, and the movement of the arms, flexible tentacles that hold and agitate the colored silk scarf, an inseparable complement of the female dancer.[8]

Lina Frutos, the *mulata* dancer described here, reportedly caused a scandal in Havana because she inserted "racey" pelvic movements in her performances, even though her body was hidden underneath a long dress covered in flounces. She performed on stage from the 1890s through the 1910s, when many of the "mulata" dancers of the time were white-in-brown-face and significantly trained in voice, dance, and theater.

As a dance genre, the Cuban *rumba* is a highly eroticized and heterosexual dance, evoking a precoital mating game.[9] In the dance, the man attempts to make contact—or, sometimes, merely a "penetrating" gesture—with hands, hips, or foot toward the woman's intimate area. The female constantly rejects the male's attempts at entering her feminine space. Nevertheless, aware of the power of her body, her sex, and his attraction for her, she invites him to continue his pursuit with his phallic jabs. (These pelvic thrusts or quick arm and leg gestures made by the man trying to attempt contact with the woman are called *vacunaos*.) Some of her movements involve languorously executed concentric circular movements of the hips, getting down on hands and knees, or miming some floor scrubbing while continually rotating what I like to call the butt/hip symbiotic complex. All of this, executed and improvised while never losing her focus on the male partner, intends to excite and entice the man to attempt contact again.

She gets close to him to dance, using one hand to fan in front of her pubic area, beckoning him into another attempt. He tries, but he fails again. She has avoided his *vacunao* by quickly dodging it (with a hand placed over the pelvic area, or a protective fold of the skirt pulled over it) and turning away from him. She pauses briefly, savoring her victory, and then her hips begin their in-sinew-ations again, never once refraining from marking two full circles to one side, then punctuating a slow circle pause to the other side.

There are many variations to the *rumba* and how the dancer fills the rhythm with her hip circles. The shift in weight and the bent knees and hip flexion that accompany the hip movements contribute to those variations. Also, the dancer's improvisatory skill can create many more variations.

As a dance stemming primarily from the Afro-Cuban working class, the *rumba* was somewhat sanitized by the *mulata* on the stage and in film productions of the late nineteenth and early twentieth centuries.[10] The dance, still coded as dark and underclass, gained a certain respectability when performed by a lighter skinned body, accentuating the erotics of the *mulata* while diluting or rendering impotent the perceived overt sexual antics of black bodies. To draw attention to the pelvic region while dancing was considered a moral faux pas, a projection of degenerate bodily vocabulary that signified poverty or, worse, "blackness." The Cuban *rumba* developed as a variation on West Central African or Kongo-Angolan rhythms and dances called *yuka* and *makuta*.[11] Thus, complex rhythms and body isolations (the pelvic area with hips as central movement axis) invoked the shock and ire of Cuban white bourgeoisie, who considered these dances and bodies explicit, yet who at the same time found the dances seductive and transgressive enough to learn and dance at *bailes de cuna* in the nineteenth century or *academias de baile* in the twentieth century. As with most transgressive dance forms, the *rumba* moved through a process to acceptability and respectability. It was the *mulatas* on stage who effectively enabled this process.

By the 1930s and '40s, *vedettes* (cabaret style entertainers), recognized for their *rumba* dancing ability and their hip-tivities, came from *mulato* (and occasionally white) working-class families, the majority of whom did not initially have any dance training. *Mulata* dancers such as Luz Gil, Lina Frutos, and Carmen Curbelo created frissons among the audience because of their pelvic pronunciations, coupled with their epidermal reality. Curbelo, who worked as a washerwoman before she secured work at an *academia de baile* in Havana, had no dance experience, for example. Her "attractive and light-skinned" body, however, enabled her to acquire the job, with those at the *academia* assuming she possessed some innate skill at dancing *son, danzón*, and *pasodoble*.[12]

All these dance forms require some form of pelvic/hip swivel coded as something other, either Spanish gypsy or African. Certain musicologists liken the *academias de baile* to *casas de cunas* (homes where *bailes de cuna* took place earlier), classifying them as houses of ill-repute, where men went to socialize or learn how to dance from *mulata* teachers, expecting to engage in some sort of sexual exchange afterwards. Robin Moore explains that "dance choreography in the *academias* frequently emphasized fancy *vueltas* (turns), as well as exaggerated hip movement and close physical contact deemed unacceptable in more "respectable' locations."[13] I am wary of immediately assigning disreputability to these places where the pedagogical exchanges occurred among *mulatas* and their students, however. Moore categorizes these women as prostitutes, yet if sexual relationships occurred as a result of dancing together, it becomes crucial to investigate the negotiations involved, as well as the relationships established between teacher and student.

Despite their imagined notoriety, the *academias* serve as sites of embodied knowledge production, drawing teachers and the subsequent male bodies eager to possibly press up against a *mulata* dance partner or instructor. With the instructor, he could learn the intricacies of the rhythmic *danzón* and later, the *son*; and through her corporeality, he could feel as though he were embracing Cuba, body and soul.

This brief overview of the *mulata* and her relationship to specific dances and places for dancing sets up how her dancing body and her hips are crucial to the national identity of Cuba. The dancing *mulata*, as performer more than as teacher, became the bodily signifier of Cuba. With the nationalization of *danzón*, *son*, and then *rumba*, the dancing *mulata* developed into a commodified, exportable Cuba.[14] This *mulata* moved from national Cuban symbol to international symbol by way of the *cabaretera* genre of film popularized in Latin American cinema, especially from Mexico, from the 1930s to the 1950s.[15] These *cabaretera* films featured Cuban *mulata*-cized moves by (white) bodies and characters ascribed with the *mulata* stereotypes: sexual, sinful, trickster, economically disadvantaged, and tragic. Despite these negative characteristics, the hip swaying, pelvic thrusts, and undulations by featured actresses and dancers contributed to the myth of the *mulata* and her rhythmic hips. In similar fashion, the Tropicana nightclub (since 1939) contributed to the commercialization of the *rumba*-dancing *mulata*, though "she" had already hip-notized audiences in other local musical revues.[16]

Thus, Cuba's *mulata* became a body that subsumed both rhythm and popular dance forms. The possibility of divorcing the Cuban *mulata* from hipped dance forms and vice versa disappeared at this point. Strikingly, that was almost inconsequential, as this body's value lay not just in its national function in Cuba but also in the modernist fascination with "blackness" throughout the Americas and beyond.

The shaking, rotating, revolving hips are transformed into the signifier of the *mulata*. It is through the hips—in essence, her dancing body and the enjoyment of that dancing body—that a *mulata* could both perform and assert her identity because she had had no official voice in the overarching colonial power structure and its visible economy. Her speech act or her enunciation emerged out of her body, notably her hips.

I briefly turn to José Piedra as a way to position the theoretical intervention of hip(g)nosis. Piedra insists that "the rumba hips, exaggerated, voyeuristic, exhibitionist, deified, and prostituted as they might appear to be, might also be a signifier of both acceptance of our bodies and defiance of foreign impositions, and even further: a substitute for the silenced or muffled voice, and not just for women or through women."[17] Influenced by Piedra's postulations, I nevertheless move away from his examples of the hips as a source of liberation for women, in that I don't read the hips as static text. The hips that I refer to belong to Cuban *mulatas* who are constantly moving them—through acts of sex, walking or peddling goods, and dancing. Following the example of Saidiya Hartman, I choose instead to begin "counter-investing in the body as a site of possibility."[18] If the *mulata* is incarcerated by its own cultural constructions, why not liberate the *mulata's* own pleasurable performance of those cultural constructions?

In a video distributed by the national tourist agency of Cuba, the Hotel Nacional's cabaret show, "Ajiaco Cubano" (Cuban Stew), tells the tale of Cuba's national identity by showing, through dance, the different cultures that have coalesced on the island and have developed into *Cubanidad*. In the show, a balletic duet between a black man (symbolizing Africa) and a white woman (signifying Spain) serves as the "mating ritual" that produces the approximately fifteen *mulatas* who subsequently appear on stage. They wear large headdresses, bikini tops and bottoms, and long ruffled trains cascading from their waists. Their bare legs are contoured by the high heels on their feet. The male singer calls out: *"Ya llegó la mulata!"*/The *mulata* has arrived; and these women begin their choreography of revolving, swaying, undulating, and popping hips. All of them smile, and in the film, the camera occasionally frames one or two of their posteriors in closeup. In their performance of "mulata," these bodies address the audience, mostly foreign, and Cuba with their hips. They are a real presence and, through their performance, they conflate as well as deflate the constructed nature of *mulata*. Their dancing "conveys both the cross-purposes and the circulation of various modes of performance and performativity that concern the production of racial meaning and subjectivity, . . . the forms of race(d) pleasure."[19] In their hips is a complex choreography of history, spectacle, race, gender, and embodied subjectivity. The *mulata* grapples with a colonized cultural construction, yet my theoretical intervention complicates both the witnessing and the embodying of her subjectivity. I consider how she works with her embodied experience to formulate a way for her body to mean and have value within and outside its contradictory representations.

In summary, this book traces the activities of *mulatas* and their use of hip(g)nosis. In the nineteenth century, they are lodge-keepers, artisans, laundresses, and servants of the sacred in Havana; participants in *plaçage* or concubinage in New Orleans and Havana; domestic servants in plantation economies; and dancers in domestic spaces and on stages in Havana. In the twentieth century, the *mulata* continues to populate cabaret spectacles and social-dance halls. She also wields hip(g)nosis globally: on the American and European stages featuring Cuban entertainers; in Mexican films featuring Cuban *vedettes*; in (inter)national spectacles containing Cuban dancers; in the *mulata* comics made popular in the 1970s; and ultimately at Havana's Marina Hemingway in the 1990s, where *mulata* dancers were used to lure foreign capital to Cuba after the fall of the Soviet Union. These examples are among the case studies and examples of *mulata* corporeality included in these pages. But first, what is hip(g)nosis and what can it do?

THEORIZING HIP(G)NOSIS

The development of the term *hip(g)nosis* and its corresponding theoretical framework mostly stem from my participant ethnographic work in Havana, Cuba. It is also informed by dance practice, analysis, and historical excavation. During my first research trip to Cuba, I was entranced by the reaction of European and North American men as they watched the *figurantes* and dancers at the famous Tropicana cabaret.[20] I noticed glassy-eyed expressions on these men's faces as they stared at the different movements of the hips, on and off the stage. This kind of hip-notism led me to examine literature, poetry, song, and historical information about the significance of the *mulata* in Cuba. The urgency I felt to find a way for the *mulata* to answer back to these problematic representations made this immediately into a feminist project.

As such, hip(g)nosis emerges as a feminist response to the mere objectification of the dancing *mulata*. It serves to contest the historical objectification while at the same time acknowledging the power and pleasure involved in wielding one's hips. If the body exists as a rich site of embodied knowledges determined and shaped by lived reality and socio-historical contexts, then hip(g)nosis is a theoretical method through which to understand it. In other words, hip(g)nosis makes the *mulata's* hips legible. Hip(g)nosis is a way to reconcile the problematic separation of mind and body by demonstrating how that body possesses and articulates knowledge through embodied activity.

Critical dance studies offer the capacity to illuminate the various and contested meanings within a particular hip undulation;[21] they make visible the body as a rich discursive site. The salient work of dance scholars with whom I have discussed this include Susan Foster, who turned the ballerina's *pointe* into a phallus in order to rescue her from mere objectification; Priya Srinivasan, who positions South Asian dance as transnational labor; Thomas DeFrantz, who examines the discursive power of black bodies dancing hip hop; Anna Beatrice Scott, who looks at the politics behind the Afro-bloco carnival performances in Bahia; Marta Savigliano, who set up a tango between politics and national history; Jane Desmond, who positions the body as always already cultural; and Anne Cooper Albright, who looks to historical bodies through her own.[22]

Critical dance studies articulate the reality of the embodied experience. As a result, the term *corporeality* functions as a way to read the body along the social, cultural, and historical processes that shape it. This is crucial to an understanding of what hip(g)nosis is and what it does. That is, dance studies allow the *mulata* to emerge as an active corporeality—a lived body with experiences in the material world—rather than as a static product of national discourses represented through visual art, literature, music, and religious iconography. Although the *mulata's* relationship to dance is significantly expressed in the Cuban cultural imaginary, the ways in which her body "duplicates, amplifies or exceeds norms of non dance bodily self expression within specific historical contexts" deserves examination.[23]

The word *gnosis* often becomes associated with knowledge, particularly spiritual knowledge. However, here I refer to a kinesthetic corporeal knowledge. I place the "g" in parentheses to highlight its usefulness in associating Òsun, the Yorùbà goddess, to certain hip movements that stem from Afro-Cuban praise dances for her, while at the same time allowing for hip movements or hip-nosis to be a theory of corporeal knowledge not specifically linked to Africanist cosmology. Not all hip movements in Cuba harken to a mythic-cosmological back story; however, within the Africanist worldview, the mind, body, and spirit are inseparable and interrelated. As such, it's almost impossible to *not* have the "g" in the rendering of hip(g)nosis in Cuba, as the majority of popular dance forms stem from Africanist dance or music practices.

I see the body as an intelligent materiality. As a dancer who continues to learn and practice hip rotations and mobilizations, I "know" that my body and stiff hips have "minds" of their own. As an observer of rotating hips, pulsing rumps, and swinging pelvises, I like to believe that I am a fair judge of when hips utter or stutter. These intelligent-hipped bodies are not rendered docile by the mind and human will. They operate through kinesthetic understanding and intelligence that are valuable and important for knowledge, as well as for cultural production. As a result, hip(g)nosis presents the *mulata* body as an intelligent, powerful materiality that can (re)write history, comment on socio-political situations, and question the construction of its identity and bodily inscriptions.

Hip(g)nosis further posits the idea of female sexuality through the body, specifically the hips, as a means for that very body to exhibit power, potentiality, and prowess. It follows, then, that the hipped enunciations of *mulatas* marked as tropes shift from being erotic suggestions for the patriarchal gaze to historicizing declarations about and for Othered women's labor and lives; she emerges as a deployment. Both a history and a lived experience, the *mulata* exists primarily as a narrative trope. The body is read as if it were separate from its inhabitant.

Further, this distance between the person who *is* a *mulata* and the trope that binds the *mulata* unleashes a series of tragic misencounters with the social, as the person who lives the reality is engaged as a living character in an extended melodrama, not a material witness to social processes and machinations of power. The violence of language here is the tragedy, not the body as evidence of miscegenation or racial mixing.

Hip(g)nosis relies on the epidermal reality, or skin color of the *mulata*. This dialectic between the *mulata's* body (skin color and movement) and its relationship to the world harkens to Frantz Fanon's discussions in *Black Skin, White Masks*, where he articulates the self-composition intrinsic in locating oneself in the world. This awareness of one's own "racial epidermal schema" informs how the subject chooses to choreograph herself into the social, all the while cognizant of the gradations and technologies of power within it.[24] In this way, the *mulata* has more possibilities to react to how her body already "speaks" for her. A *mulata* and her hips subsume language and its problematic assignment of meaning. As a theoretical intervention, hip(g)nosis establishes a place from where to witness the fissures, continuities, and complexities of a woman-centered history of and about black and brown women, not just in the Caribbean but throughout the Americas.[25]

Jutting to the left, a hip stands out beneath the waist and the small of the back, curvaceous and suggestive. Beneath and behind the curves lies discourse that complicates this signature piece of choreography of the hipped *mulata*. Until now, I have situated the *mulata* as a site of discourse. This body serves a larger purpose within hip(g)nosis, however. Here, the *mulata* operates as a gateway for asserting and revaluing the violated and devalued black bodies of the women who suffered under violent white male desire and who birthed those *mulatas* so venerated in Cuba and the Americas. In the witnessing of the *mulata* moving her hips, we see a complex history oozing from the blurry outlines of those hips.

Hip(g)nosis complicates the act of gazing, though. It problematizes the directionality of the patriarchy's lascivious stare. As a substitute, the *mulata* disguises the white male desire for the black woman; the fetish for blackness seems less of a vice when that same blackness pixilates around the *mulata* and her hips. Anna Scott succinctly theorizes blackness "as a type of space: portable, yet impermeable; contingent yet fixed through practice, valuable as a commodity but valueless as a state of being."[26] As an inheritor of that space, the *mulata* occupies it as a commodity for, or object of, the patriarchal gaze. She merely exists as flesh, waiting to be divided, diced, and consumed. Once that body is sensed or experienced, however, and not merely gazed upon, it operates as a referent to cultural and historical valences that those same hips appear to conceal through the spectacle.

Implicitly, said hip-notism establishes a space of aporia, where the hips communicate. Yet, where I read instances of resistance, pleasure, and history, hegemonic patriarchal ideologies do otherwise. Within these ideologies, said space becomes an innocuous, transcendentally hagiographic one—hence, the worship of the sensual/saintly *mulata* as quintessential symbol of a nation. It becomes impossible for the female body inhabiting it to be representable, let alone powerful or powerfully contestatory.

Through language and language's materializations (in ideology, culture, politics, history, and economic relations), the body becomes a tool, vehicle, site, and example that demonstrates its active position in culture, destabilizing popularly held notions of it as a passive receptacle of culture. On the contrary, the body materializes culture just as or even *more* effectively than language. Bodies make declarative statements regardless of what they are doing.[27] Language needs the exclamation point. Sometimes I find the term *habitus*, set up by Pierre Bourdieu, a useful one to help understand what I am trying to decipher as hip(g)nosis. Although his theorization assumes a body's cooperation and unreflective participation in the cultural codes from where habitus emerges, his positioning of social inscriptions onto bodies as signifiers of taste and class serves to situate the *mulata's* hips as signifiers. The *mulata* might even exist as a form of boutiqued habitus—something formulated for specific tastes—but more important, her hips choreograph a gendered history that travels through and across ideas of national and cultural imaginaries or territories. Such a history breaks with concepts of it as a linear, structured, forward progression and accumulation of times and events, turning to certain aspects of Africanist cosmology for its coherence. Just as the hips go around in a circle, so too does this history.

Cuba's fascination with the Ochún/LaVirgen de la Caridad del Cobre/ *mulata* triptych, who represent the national imaginary to itself, serves to elucidate my claims. While patriarchal monotheism attempted to fully annihilate Africanist/Amer-Indigenous everyday religious practices, some of those practicing bodies carried and concealed knowledges, rituals, customs. First, it was carried by the African and Amer-Indigenous copper slaves in Cuba in the sixteenth and seventeenth centuries, and then by the conflation of the imagined body of Ochún/La Virgen onto the miscegenated body set forth as a representative of the nation in the nineteenth century.[28] Given the paradoxical relationship between the idealized mis-cegenated body and the demonized *mulata* body, we see the *mulata* body respond as a material witness to the hegemonic histories that seek to still her hips. By wielding hip(g)nosis, though, this *mulata* continues to conceal the very practices and histories that led to its materialization in the first place.

Hip(g)nosis helps to explains why the official history of Cuba and its glamorization of the *mulata*/Ochún dyad works contrary to what the the-ory does in broad daylight. Put simply, hip(g)nosis is visible, yet hip(g)nosis purposely disrupts the gaze. Its witnessing requires a pause, a regrouping of the senses, a gathering up of the bodily senses and their contract with the visual. Hip(g)nosis requires a double take. It sets up a choice for the wit-ness: Do I want to be hypnotized and passive to the spectacle before me? Do I want to recreate and be complicit in the historical ways of looking and considering the *mulata*? Or, do I startle and interrupt the expected, per-haps even contractual, response as witness and become still—still enough to consider this embodied subject in a possibly new way?

Hip(g)nosis exposes the male patriarchal gaze. It addresses the politi-cal economy of pleasure and the consumption of certain bodies. It allows for the *mulata* to have pleasure as she wields it. Hip(g)nosis proclaims the strained histories and powerful exchanges and negotiations between race, gender, and Africanist religiosity in the Americas; it ultimately forces the viewer to acknowledge the "blackness" inherent in the history of the Americas, as it specifically relates to black female sexuality, its power, and its pleasure. When that *mulata's* hips move, it is holding the body perform-ing hip(g)nosis, and the bodies watching it (r)evolve, accountable for the long and significant history of blackness in the Americas. Such a history incorporates the violence inflicted on black, *mulato*, indigenous, female, and poor bodies. Ultimately, the history that the *mulata's* hips delineate acknowledges the importance of women of color, their history from the Middle Passage to the Americas, and the potentiality of a corporeal histori-ography choreographed for pleasure, beauty, sexuality, entertainment, and sometimes even resistance.

The deified energetic force of Òsun/Ochún, the Yorùbá /Afro-Cuban god-dess of fertility and love, figures into this discussion, for several reasons. Although she reifies gendered ideas of being, she (as she is understood and practiced among her devotees) nevertheless enables an understanding of women as knowledge bearers and producers. By tying the deified energetic force Òsun/Ochún into the *mulata* and hip(g)nosis, the person engaged in this amalgam results as a potent force. As deified energy and a product of pre-colonialist social orderings on the Western coast of Africa, Òsun, as a product of Yorùbà beliefs, deconstructs the divisions between masculine and feminine, acting as a democratizing agent where gender differences have no significance. For the Yorùbà, social organization was predicated on ideas of genderless living; value was assigned through age or seniority and kinship, not gender.[29] Amid this social reality, women were equally productive and vitally necessary in the production of knowledge and culture. Juxtapose this history with La Virgen de la Caridad del Cobre's role as a democratizing agent among the *cobreros*/copper-mine workers in seventeenth-century eastern Cuba. The Virgin's usefulness as an undeniable political tool for and by them shows the value that feminized labor (material, political, or spiritual) exerted on copper mining in a way that is analogous to Òsun's presence in the market. Later appropriated by Western patriarchal monotheism, La Virgen's political value shifted and converted into a national symbol of both an idealized and a miscegenated womanhood.

The power of women (real or imagined) and its containment through masculinist practices is not a new discourse. However, examining how technologies of power cloud the productivity of women and their ability to contravene the ruses of power through their own authoritative means can destabilize the behemoth of patriarchal power. It can then be seen as a construction built to serve its own purposes.

As chapter 1 attests, nineteenth-century Cuba trafficked in female potential. Many *mulatas* were quite economically self-sufficient. As powerful public women, they garnered considerable autonomy. Nevertheless, Cuban racial discourse about the threat of miscegenation turned these women's bodies into danger zones—femme fatales, if you will. In a similar vein, Òsun's multilayered archetypes and avatars of self-sufficiency—productive agent to mankind, healer, and social equalizer—became no match for the excessive beauty and flagrant bawdiness of Yeyé Móoro—the Ochún widely circulated in Cuba's national imaginary of who, what, and how Òsun "is."[30] To this day in Cuba, Ochún´s most popular avatar is that of a licentious, capricious coquette.

Òsun as a force tied to excess, wealth, beauty, and sensuality writhes and worms herself into hip(g)nosis. In her *oriki* (praise poetry), Òsun is venerated by hyperbole. There isn't always subtlety to her, as there cannot always be in the hips and its insinuations. One of her *oriki* has Òsun being called "the goddess who tucks her vagina inside to go fight another *orisa*."[31] That is, her biological gender does not interfere with her performative one, enabling her to become a warrior, a woman who battles like a man with other (usually male) *orishas*.

Òsun labors in "traditional," often under acknowledged female "tasks," primarily gathering: she carries baskets (Ibú Odonkí); as a vulture, she picks up the "mess" left by mankind (Ikolé); she sews, knits, crochets, weaves, and works in the cemetery with a hoe, shovel, or rake, making sure Olofi's (orisha of the palace, a major deity) punishments are carried out (Ibu Yémù); or, she engages in warfare, in iron making, and is a powerful warrior (Iyánlá). Collectively, Òsun represents "females in power, controlling not only law and economics but the ability to market their own natural resources."[32] These attributes figure prominently in how I read the mulata in the various examples presented in the ensuing chapters. Òsun, with her beauty, power, and ability to weave and cast spells, becomes a crucial component of hip(g)nosis and how I use it to read its operating in the dancing mulatas of these pages.

Òsun's beauty is demonstrative; it makes life materially and aesthetically richer, more sensual, erotic. Her beauty, or beauty (as a condition of Òsun), also exists as a commodity and as a method from which to produce or generate materiality and other conditions. The erotics of Òsun's beauty are such that what she desires and attains through merely being desirous will subsequently benefit others.[33] Beauty appears laborless, its affect magical. Part of deeming something beautiful is erasing the labor that went into its production; effortlessness adds to ideas of successful beauty. The object being witnessed and judged as beautiful merely emblematizes an indefectibility that has nothing to do with material reality or its processes of aesthetic hierarchies and/or taste. Òsun does the same. The hips do the same. The mulata does the same.

Beauty, whatever its culturally modulated definition, requires labor. I am not claiming that mulatas, Òsun, or the hips by nature are beautiful, yet these signs themselves erase the labor that goes into making them sites of culture, cultural production, and aesthetic pleasure. First, in Òsun's case, others must labor to appease her so that she doesn't incur her wrath or show her ghastly attributes.[34] Second, Euro-American patriarchy's vilification of (Othered) female sexuality removes the capacity for said sexuality to be considered generative, productive, or beautiful. Within this framework, hip movements and all that is related to that part of the female body (buttocks, vagina, sex, menstruation, childbirth) suggest a natural woman-ness with a tempting purpose.[35] And finally, the "mulata's" concatenation within discourses of gender and race set up the mulata as, among other things, a production of pleasure. As a concubine, a rumbera, or as a servant, she exists as an erotic amusement for capital, irrespective of how that same body has to work to literally "make" pleasure. Additionally, the mulata highlights notions that lighter skinned "black" bodies don't have to "labor," because the skin color automatically "labors" by reinstating value to the devalued Africanized body. Hip(g)nosis must contend with these laborious activities and it underscores how a body wielding it complicates its simple witnessing.

Hip(g)nosis speaks a boisterous, rambunctious language, especially for those who can follow it. Here, hip(g)nosis reveals its sleight of hand—or more accurately, sleight of hip. Although floating signifiers want to forcibly envelop the *mulata* and silence her, hip(g)nosis forces the focus to be the body wielding it. How said body choreographs *mulata*/herself into being *must* be dealt with. By choosing to perform whatever aspect of "*mulata* identity" necessary for some recognition, a *mulata* enacting hip(g)nosis has some agency in how she is perceived. Caught within the *mulata* trope, she has situational agency, not projected agency. She cannot completely decide for herself how she wants to be seen. Her body pertains to an economy of visibility that assigns it loaded signifiers: they supersede her. She can have aesthetic agency because of the different forms of value imposed on her skin, body, hair, or features, and then use this aesthetic agency to its advantage (or not).

Yet without hip(g)nosis, the *mulata* has no potentiality to be anything more than an amalgam of signifiers speaking for her across her skin on her behalf of and in the service of white patriarchal capital formations. Signifiers will always speak, owing to their culturally defined circulation, yet they do not speak a body into being, only into knowing. Although the signifiers labor for her, a *mulata* exerting hip(g)nosis allows the body to dialogue with, and perhaps overtake, the battery of signs overworking the body, even when it stays still. Hip(g)nosis provides a method for a body to actively organize how the *mulata* signifiers dance around its physiological facts. Thus, materializing as a *mulata*, she can contest the fixity of the *mulata* sign and mobilize it to chip away at the historical tragedy inherent in that sign.

As a theory, hip(g)nosis therefore encompasses several registers. Hip(g)nosis is a choreography coming from a repertoire of Africanist dances that train the hips to move in specific ways within the Cuban context. It is also a racialized and gendered choreography of identity particular to the historicization of the *mulata* in Cuba. Hip(g)nosis is also discursive; it produces ways to corporeally respond to the static discursive practices of Cuban colonial history that continue to mark the Cuban *mulata* body. It is an embodied theory emanating from the *mulata's* hips in motion (and sometimes stillness), it allows for her body to be something other than an object. She can learn how to mobilize it and set it forth in her choice of embodied subjectivity.

Lastly, and perhaps most important, hip(g)nosis is a brand. It is not an innate quality *mulatas* possess. They learn it. Some may adopt it as part of their embodied subjectivity; others may choose to forgo it altogether, while still others learn its tactical uses and engage with it only when neces-sary. Because it can be learned, like any corporeal technique, any *body* has potential to learn, practice, and traffic transnationally in it. Because I place it within a particular history of miscegenation in the Americas, the body engaging in it must contend with its positionality within or outside that particular history. In this way, hip(g)nosis does not fall into an essentialist space from which to identify the *mulata* as always possessing and wielding it. Instead, positionality allows for the body to negotiate how it wants to engage with, if at all, a theoretically engaged bodily practice. Put simply, the hips must know their history.

THE MADNESS OF METHODS, OR THE CALL
OF INTERDISCIPLINARITY

This book depends on interdisciplinarity. Dance and performance stud-ies, critical race studies, history/historiography, ethnography, and fiction/performative writing come together as I tell this story of the *mulata* and her fastidious hips. I am not a historian, although much of what I say is grounded in historical investigation. As such, this book does not purport to be a totalizing history, recovery or otherwise, of the *mulata*. Instead, it charts a way to understand the *mulata* through a genealogy of her body.

If anything, this type of history or genealogy that appears here remains incomplete. I leave it as a seductive invitation for others to add and compli-cate. It requires such an approach because of the messiness of history, pop-ular history, and embodied knowledge in general. I embrace the uncertainty of the project in the same way we embrace the spectacle of the *mulata's* hips. We can never fully know how she will move them, where to, or even if she will move them at all. She does engage in many improvised dances, after all. What I offer are some analyses, provocations, and stories woven together as the concept of hip(g)nosis. In this way, these stories when choreographed produce the *mulata* spectacle. I am particularly inspired by anthropologist Ann Laura Stoler's comment that "imagining what might be is as impor-tant as knowing what was,"[36] in that my own activity of imagining through the body might provide a productive methodology to enliven the stories in these pages. Part of this imagination comes from my family histories and my experiences in Cuba while I researched this project. I intersperse those as a way to intertwine lived, imagined, and recorded history.

I wonder how the connections between clasped fingers, masculine hands on feminine hips, whispers in ears, furtive glances, and conversa-tions absorbed in the heat of a moment of social dancing come to articulate narratives of subjectivity, racialized gender, pleasure, and the Cuban nation. It is these small, often inadvertent, and unnoticeable gestures that attract me—gestures that are traces of memory. I am drawn to Marta Savigliano's musings on tango and its requisite nocturnal ethnographies, where she states that "dancers can represent layers that move slowly and thus tell a history of looks, gestures and movements, situating these elements on the edge between truth and fiction, writing and living, acting and being."[37] What are those gestures, then, that assert *mulata* corporeality and its association with the hips? This book identifies some of them.

Here also, rumor, everyday stories, and oral history figure prominently as methodologies because, among Cubans, understandings of the *mulata* spectacle and her relationship to popular dance exist through stories and retellings. Much of the state-sanctioned histories of popular dance involve the Tropicana or other major entertainment venues. I am more interested in the everyday dancing in the lesser known cabarets, the *academias de bailes,* and people's homes.[38] Rumor and storytelling are important aspects of theoretical recovery for Afro-Latina corporealities because they present alternative forms of knowledge production that are crucial to understanding how these bodies make meaning for themselves and ultimately have value. However, what frames of analysis are discounted or left out by a reliance on rumor? And, what are the stakes? I address this epistemological problem by positioning the rumor alongside historical "evidence," all the while cognizant of my choice in this confabulation.

I take a cue from the political urgency of feminist methodologies that call into question the production of knowledge and power. I am interested in how *mulata* women—dancers in the *academias*, on the cabaret stages of Cuba or Europe, and my grandmothers and great-grandmothers—mapped out their embodied experiences. Much of that learning requires a labor of the imagination, something feminist philosopher Rosi Braidotti would encourage, as she believes that "the imagination is not utopian, but rather transformative and inspirational."[39]

There is something hopeful in the imagination. It envisions new possibilities and can even provide ways to understand or endure the past. Here, I am thinking of the many historical novels about *mulatas* and how they contribute to what will always be an incomplete archive.[40] Still, this imagining produces something I consider hopeful. This may help transform the tragedy of the *mulata* into something else—something that hip(g)nosis tries to materialize every time the *mulata* wields her hips.

During my various research trips to Cuba, stories were told to me; some were new, some repeated. I also began asking my relatives to share stories of our family and the *mulata* ancestors who began to seem similar (and had similar occupations) to the historical women I had encountered in my research. I considered how orality and history might create a method through which to retell Cuban dance history, with the *mulata* as the focal point. The idea of rumor seduced me, especially because I know we all like a good *chisme*, or rumor.[41] If written evidence is scarce, how can a rogue historian utilize oral evidence to piece together stories that can serve as historical record?[42] What kinds of truths will circulate in this fashion? Historian Luise White explains that

> people do not speak with truth, with a concept of the accurate description of what they saw, to say what they mean, but they construct and repeat stories that carry the values and meanings that most forcibly get their point across. People do not always speak from experience—even when that is considered the most accurate kind of information—but speak with stories that circulate to explain what happened.[43]

This book, therefore, takes White's premise and traces an embodied history of the Cuban *mulata* with words, memories, and imaginings of the dancing *mulata* bodies who populated the dance floors, then and now. It is not without its archival, literary, historiographic, and participant ethnographic methods, but rumor and its significance play a crucial role, particularly in chapters 2 and 4.

If the subject of this book is the *mulata*, her hip(g)nosis, and its significance within the Cuban cultural imaginary, then an analysis based on rumor and oral history stands to disrupt the (hi)stories on which the nation has constructed itself.[44] The *mulata* exists as a national legend. I turn briefly to what Gordon Allport and Leo Postman write in *The Psychology of Rumor* to set up the situation:

> a legend may be regarded as a solidified rumor. More exactly, it is an unusually persistent bit of hearsay which, after a prior history of distortion and transformation, ceases to change as it is transmitted from generation to generation. In order to become legendary, a rumor must treat issues that are of importance to successive generations. Topics pertaining to national origins and honor are such. . . . Other rumors are impetuous in nature. They spread like wildfire because they deal with an immediate threat or immediate promise.[45]

The legend or rumor of the *mulata* and those enticing hips bears investigation. It not only pertains to national origins (Cuba as a *mulata* nation where Europe and Africa come together), but it "spread like wildfire" because it dealt with the "immediate promise" of male heterosexual pleasure and *jouissance*. Here was a body, a seemingly domitable female body of color, that could be desired, possessed, and controlled through rumor and writings about the immediate threat she posed through miscegenation. De Céspedes's statement, which began this introduction, is a form of propaganda against the *mulata*. According to him, she has no value other than her limber, gaze-inducing hips. De Céspedes most likely repeated what was common discourse in late-nineteenth-century Cuba, when the country sought independence from Spain while at the same time it sought to establish a particularly whitened national identity.[46]

Despite the urgency with which I argue for a retelling of the history of the Cuban *mulata* through rumor and hip(g)nosis, I find myself caught between words and flesh. This seems to be a common predicament for those who write about the body within different historical moments—the here and now, or the past newly imagined. But, I am several steps ahead already. I take your hand and lead you into this retelling of the *mulata* as an aspect of Cuban-ness.[47] Similar to Anne Cooper Albright, I wonder what it means to "research historical bodies, dancing bodies, desiring bodies precisely through the intertext of an 'other' body—my own?"[48] How does one recapture the language of the dancing body through the written word? How have I told you this Cuban *mulata* story?

Chapter 1, "Historicizing Hip(g)nosis," introduces the factors that set up a market for *mulatas*. The nineteenth century particularly put into circulation a rich banquet of *mulata* signifiers that had come out of the libidinal economies existing in the plantations but not exclusive to them. For many *mulatas*, whether free or enslaved, concubinage was an alternative to a life of subjugation. In these relationships with white Creole Cubans (or other Europeans), *mulatas* gained an economic and social mobility, with many of them buying their own freedom and that of their offspring from these unions. During this time, prominent *mulatas* held *bailes de cuna*, or social-dance parties in their homes. Here, these types of relationships could begin and flourish. Furthermore, by the 1880s, when the *danzón* became the national dance and created anxiety among the Cuban elite and intelligentsia, based on a threat of Cuba's "Africanization," the *mulatas* were already dancing to a mix of European and African sounds. What types of negotiations did the *mulata* and her dancing hips make at these *bailes*?

The libinidal market of the *bailes* operated alongside a public sphere where *mulatas* were a visible female corporeal presence. Many of them worked as artisans, lodge-keepers, launderers, and seamstresses, and they enjoyed unprecedented economic freedom compared to white and black women. Additionally, as Cuba developed its exports of sugar and tobacco, European men began to travel frequently to the Caribbean, along with their money and influence. The *mulata's* body and a corresponding narrative of tragic availability were utilized as a way to attract additional foreign capital. The lithographed tobacco packaging series *Vida y Muerte de una Mulata* was perhaps the most efficient method through which Cuba circulated the trope of the sexually available, willing, yet tragic *mulata.*[49] Thus, this chapter highlights the different social, historical, and cultural factors that consolidated in the *mulata* iconography that continued into the twentieth century.

Chapter 2, "Hip(g)nosis at Work: Rumors, Social Dance, and Cuba's *Academias de Baile,*" provides an overview of Cuban popular dance in the 1930s, '40s, and '50s. Primarily focusing on the *academias de baile* (literally "dance academy," but more like taxi dance halls) where *mulatas* sold their dancing or sexual services, I make a case for how the *mulata's* dancing body became a national symbol and enabled a corporeal type of Cuban-ness to emerge. I highlight the choreographies of Cuban popular dance forms such as *son, danzón* and *cha-cha-chá* as means through which hip(g)nosis became interchangeable with *cubanía* and acted as a commodity in Cuba and beyond. I gather the voices of musicians who played at these *academias* because I was unsuccessful in finding a woman who used to work or dance in them. The absence of such a female voice nonetheless provides an opportunity to engage in various methodological strategies to materialize the dancing *academia mulatas.* Drawing from literature, oral histories, and interviews, this chapter explains how these nocturnal venues were crucial sites for reevaluating Cuban popular-dance history and historiography. Because the *academias* were rumored to be sites of prostitution, the Castro regime eradicated them (many of the buildings that housed them were torn down after the 1959 Revolution), not only physically but historically as well. Therefore, I piece together a possible history of these places, particularly focusing on the presence and various types of corporeal labor of the bodies within them.

Chapter 3, "Hip(g)nosis as Pleasure: The *Mulata* in Film," examines how Cuban popular dance traveled the world via the bodies of Cuban dancers such as Ninón Sevilla or Chela Castro. I examine a variety of films featuring a Cuban *mulata* character: *Tam Tam o El Origen de la Rumba* (1938), *Mulata* (1954), *Yambaó* or *Cry of the Bewitched* (1957), and *I Am Cuba* (1964). I conclude with two Cuban documentaries that feature social dance: *Los Del Baile* (1965) and *Son o no son* (1978).[50] Through this historical trajectory I demonstrate how the *mulata* and her relationship to pleasure, religiosity, and popular dance circulated through the power of the screen. I focus on the white *vedette* Sevilla, who plays a *mulata* in two of the films, including her performance of Afro-Cuban ritual dances for a transnational

(Latin American) audience. The reading of these films through the lens of hip(g)nosis demonstrates the complexities that bodies add to history, as well as their impact on cultural production and notions of territoriality, nationalism, and citizenship. The analysis also positions the performance of hip(g)nosis and *mulata*-ness as a national choreography that can be learned and circulated through film.

Chapter 4, "Hip(g)nosis as Brand *Despelote*, Tourism, and *Mulata* Citizenship," begins by examining the revolutionary *mulata* of Castro's Cuba, whose short-lived foray into civic duty is eclipsed by the fall of the Soviet Union and the collapse of the Cuban economy. After the triumph of the Revolution, national discourse aimed to deemphasize the allure of the dancing *mulata*. Instead, *mulatas* were now represented as working for the government's revolutionary goals. In the 1970s and '80s, cartoonist Wilson drew voluptuous, big-hipped *mulatas* engaging in work, education, and social welfare. Although his *mulata* bodies remained sexualized, his portrayal of their work embraced the new state goals. The drastic effects of the Soviet Union's collapse on the Cuban economy in the mid-1990s led to a resurfacing of the dancing *mulata* as Cuba's international commodity. The government began to reinvigorate its tourist and cultural industries, and the *mulata* again becomes its greatest commodity. Thus, this chapter examines the state's reappropriation of the *mulata* as a sex symbol. Of particular interest is an analysis of the contemporary social dance form known as *despelote* (loosely translated as an "unraveling") as a way to complicate the *mulata* as commodity once again. I argue that its frenetic hip movements corporeally represent the current socioeconomic climate in Cuba, as the country struggles to define itself in the global marketplace. This chapter draws some of its information from rumor, gossip, and oral history as I share exchanges with others about the role, significance, and allure of the *mulata* in contemporary Cuba. The hips get the last word in this book by taking over the conclusion.

In between these chapters, I have included three interludes. The idea for doing this comes from the structure of a cabaret spectacle, where a major act takes occasional breaks, which are then filled with shorter performances. Thus, these interludes partner with their preceding chapters, so as to have the performative writing provide an alternative way of engaging with the information that has just been presented. Viewed another way, the interludes enliven the scholarly discourse on the *mulata* body.

My inspiration for these interlude stories comes from my time spent with Cuban cabaret dancers from the 1950s and '60s, the photos they shared with me, ephemera from entertainment magazines, and even family photographs. In these interludes I ponder the perils and epistemological potentiality that performative writing affords when materializing subaltern subjects.

Interlude 1, "Telling Stories/*Echando Cuentos*," blends academic, performative, ethnographic, and confessional writing in an attempt to find diasporic connections between me, my family history in Cuba, and two Cuban *vedettes* I met. This idea emerged from a performance I did at the Black Performance Theory meeting in 2011. That year's theme, "Hemispheres and Souths," sought to link the translations, transmigrations, transnationalisms, and diasporisms implied by the notions of a Hemispheric South and a Global South to performance as practice and to nuances of race as performance. The goal was to create a group performance that would provocate unexpected routes of diaspora across "hemispheres" and "souths."[51] This is my reworked contribution to that event.

Interlude 2, "A Marriage Proposal," imagines a friendship between two women who work at an *academia de baile*. What happens when one of them finally gets that marriage proposal and the new life outside of their nocturnal libidinal economy that it promises? What types of intimacies occurred between these women outside of the *academias*?

Interlude 3, "Lost Baggage," reproduces a true event from a Cuban performer's travels and offers my imaginingss of how she endured the stress. To explain, I came across a fabulous photograph in a 1950s Cuban entertainment magazine, *Show,* of Chelo Alonso sitting on a camel, posing in front of the pyramids at Giza. The bawdy pose, along with the story of her lost luggage (which included loss of a mink coat worth $4,800), led me to wonder what happened before and after she posed for that picture. I took liberties in making her a practitioner of Santería, and I used some of the prayers for Ochún from chapter 1 to place them in a lived context.

Hip(g)nosis functions as a corporeal theory that enables a new understanding of what a body can do and how it can respond to historically oppressive discourses about it. For the *mulata*, hip(g)nosis opens up the possibility for power to be already existing in those hips that, through discourse, have been both vilified and venerated. It is not so much the case of the proverbial chicken-and-egg syndrome (were the hips innately bewitching or did the writing of the hips as bewitching make them so?) as it is an investigation of how embodied exchanges—bodies watching, looking, touching, and dancing with one another—offer considerations of how the dancing *mulata*, her representations and veneration, have participated and circulated, and continue to do so, in the volatile political and social economy of contemporary Cuba.

Sometimes I materialize a performative "I" in these pages, working through my implication as both insider and outsider. I locate this work within the methodology of embodied writing so as to illuminate how it provides ways to think about telling stories that feature everyday embodied histories. I welcome the errors and discomfort of trying to imagine and materialize Cuban bodies that (a) I never met, (b) pertain to my family genealogy, or (c) I met, interacted with, and have placed within these pages in an ethically responsible and courteous way. What does this work that uses dance as a critical paradigm for analysis do for the methods we utilize to write about others? What do these personal or recorded stories of travel and tours contribute to narratives of being and belonging? And lastly, how do these everyday exchanges of stories—about a performance, a dance, or a social gathering featuring *mulata* bodies; stories that are born in the viscera, muscle, and mind of the storytellers—perform what Della Pollock calls a "politics of possibility" for the subjectivity of the *mulata* with(out) hip(g)nosis, my own subjectivity, and the performative "I"?[52]

And, so, "I" begin.

CHAPTER 1

Historicizing Hip(g)nosis

I sit down to write and I cannot stop crying. I am hesitant to admit to these emotionally charged currents of tears, as it is not my intention to coyly perform a tragic *mulata*. But, in effect, the tears continue. I think about my maternal grandmother, Elba Inés, a Colombian *mulata*, hailing from the Caribbean coast of the country and working long, nervous hours at the mayor's office of Barranquilla, fearing for her job every city election. As a single mother of two daughters, she could not have risked unemployment. I imagine my paternal grandmother, Carmen, a Cuban *mulata*, walking down the narrow streets of Ranchuelo, Cuba, on her way to work at the Popular cigarette factory. She had worked for the founders of the cigarette brand, Los Hermanos Trinidad, since she was fourteen, and when they opened up their factory she remained there for another forty years. I try to piece together family narratives of my maternal great-grandmother also named Carmen (of black and indigenous descent) who died of a hemorrhage after a miscarriage, orphaning six children, one only six months old. To make a living, she worked as a seamstress and would also make candies and other sweets that her eldest daughter sold. I wonder what it must have felt like for my paternal great-grandmother, yes, another *mulata*, to have her eldest daughter, María, be recognized as the only legitimate child from her long relationship with a Spaniard from Asturias that produced seven other children. If he had recognized the other children as legitimate, my last name would be García, not Blanco. These are several of the *mulata* histories that make up my own—histories that time, my search for family legacy, and my scholarly research have only made more necessary to revisit. My tears suddenly lead me to recall the Afro-Cuban/Yorùbá anthropomorphic energy force, or deity Ochún/Òsun. What can "she" do? What does she represent? John Mason, a scholar and practitioner of Yorùbá spirituality, writes about Òsun's association with tears. He states, "tears are our first physicians; they carry away body poisons and signal that we are alive. They are a sign of deep feeling, pain, joy, sorrow, remorse, and remembrance. . . . Feelings . . . are the doorways to our ancestors."[1] My crying is not in vain.

This performative turn to the self-reflexive echoes what D. Soyini Madison writes when she explains, "how you, me, the self, or, more precisely, 'the self-reference' can actually be *employed*, can actually *labor*, even be productively exploited, for the benefit of larger numbers than just ourselves."[2] Thus, I bring in these personal histories into the larger historical framework of the *mulata* experience in the circum-Caribbean. I refuse to accept my family history as one solely fraught with characteristics associated with tragic *mulatas*: unable to completely inhabit one side of the racial dichotomy, riddled with socioeconomic problems, entering into heterosexual relationships out of economic necessity—to name a few. I reject carrying the burden of this loaded literary trope on my skin, my physicality, my corporeality. I would rather undermine the problematically constructed representations of the *mulata* that are unable to acknowledge her agency, potentiality, and prowess. As such, I struggle with the familiar moniker of the "tragic" *mulata* when I think about these corporealities' roles in the making of both everyday and "official" histories of the circum-Caribbean. I become baffled at the disjunction between the tragic narrative associated with the *mulata* and the visceral, vivacious corporeality moving through the rooms of a salon or ballroom, sitting at a desk and working long hours to support her family, using her hands to roll tobacco, or to make and sell confections, or even dancing today on the cabaret stages of the Havana Tropicana. Instead of admitting to the tragedy implied by discursive renderings of the *mulata's* inability to fully inhabit the either/or of constructed racial categorization, I propose to insert a radical shift in the thinking of the *mulata* as tragic.[3] By radical shift, I mean to corpo-realize this figure through her active mobilization of her own body. To "corpo-realize" means to make the body a real, living, meaning making entity; a focus on the material body in the social sphere enables an understanding of how subjects find and assert their agency. Drawing from histories, hagiographies, and hysteria about the transnational, circum-Atlantic body witnessed as *mulata,* particularly her choreographies of race and gender, I shall enable a reconsideration of her historical significance, her access to citizenship, and her body. A focus on the body adds a new dimension to an ongoing discourse about the *mulata's* role and significance within the greater African diaspora.

By comparing and contrasting several spaces where the mulaticized body prevailed, such as quadroon balls in New Orleans, or *bailes de cuna* in

Havana, the idea of a tragic *mulata* dissipates as the visceral, active body takes its place. The act of turning the noun *mulata* into a verb, mulaticize, reflects my theoretical postulation that bodies are interpellated as raced and gendered, not just by visible economies but also by the actual corporeal herself. As such, choreographies of *mulata* were in fact one of the few opportunities available to these corporealities where they could acquire some form of self-determination regarding their gendered, racial, and social status. Moving through different locales in the Caribbean allows me to draw certain examples of *mulata* economies to elucidate, first, how the European cultural imaginary's predilection for almost-other flesh established a libidinal economy where mulaticized bodies had particular spaces, labors, and value; and, second, how these bodies engaged in self-sufficient means of employment specific to the intersection of the political economy and libidinal economy where they circulated.

My analysis of the *mulata* depends heavily on her hips, as they become not just sexualized, deified, and vilified but, as I argue, emerge as the signifying characteristic of *mulata* bodies.[4] The *mulata's* hips serve as a rich site from where to consider her powerful potentiality. The use of those hips for acts of sex, labor, mobilization, pleasure, and dance provides a way to re-historicize the *mulata's* lived presence and significance in the circum-Atlantic, or as I prefer to call it, the hip-notic torrid zone.[5]

The *mulata* exists as a sentience that is always present and visible, staking out space, territory, and meaning with the same body as has been used against her. As a visceral body with embodied knowledge, manifesting, circulating, and remembering memories, and transmitting and producing knowledge, the *mulata* body inhabits a space outside, yet as valuable as logos. By positing the notion of voice outside the structuralist presupposition that voice and logos are concatenated, the idea of "voice" can insert itself onto the *mulata's* hips and turn them into a communication device and, more important, as a theoretical tool for dismantling the tragedy that discursive practices have constructed.

The *mulata* body is a form of performative labor, a racialized choreography. That is, her body develops and goes through the process of becoming and being read as *mulata* by and through the cultural work that precedes her. This is not to say that her body does not have the capacity to learn, manipulate, and mobilize itself in such ways that either encapsulate or resist preexisting constructions of said body. She has gestures, texts, and utterances that emanate from the hip, because what she says has already been discursively and socially prescribed. Thus, the power of the *mulata* comes from her ability to improvise and to choreograph her hip from undelineated texts. This then leads to the focus on the hips as tools for communication.

Although the hips have been racialized and gendered, the mobilization of this body part serves as a means to address the socio-historical situation where these mulaticized bodies came to be, multiplied, and were valorized for their mere phenotypical and epidermal realities: their *mulata*-ness. They populate the hip-notic torrid zone, making declarative statements with their bodies, both past and present.[6]

By focusing on the body of the *mulata* as a site and source of power and potentiality, her corporeality sets up a space betwixt and beyond mere locality. She in-sinew-ates a transnational body politic and epistemology through her body that speaks in tongues: not just English, French, Spanish, Portuguese, Creole, or other languages from the circum-Caribbean, but also a bodily rhetoric by and about women that sets to historicize a space, a place, and reconfigure and deconstruct notions of "race" as they correspond to gender.[7] In this chapter, I also draw from the genealogy of racialized religiosity in the Americas, specifically tying the *mulata* to the Yórùba cosmology and the energetic force deified as Ochún in Cuba. My use of Ochún as a trope, and "her" relationship/association with *mulata* bodies attempts to show alternative means for understanding how women who can inhabit this colonial sign of the unmoored, independent woman with the ever-moving hips of varying brown skin tones might negotiate an active socio-historical role. The practice of Ochún will manifest through the many corporeal activities of the *mulatas* moving herein. Occasionally, Ochún will "speak" through these pages offering insights of "her" own.

THE MARKET FOR *MULATAS*

Histories of colonialism in the circum-Caribbean have set up and maintained racialized exchanges of power and desire. To this day, Cuba continues to exist as a libidinous site for sex tourism, *mulata* and black female bodies often used as advertisements to lure foreign capital in the form of lustful men, yet ultimately becoming the targets of national discrimination against them.[8] Perhaps a genealogy of the *mulata*—namely the ways in which she moves through a changing yet still extant marketplace of desire coupled with race—might offer a way to think about its legacies, but more important, how history might engage with the bodies making, doing, or simply just making do. I introduce this *mulata* genealogy of the Americas by briefly contextualizing a history of concubinage beginning in the eighteenth century. Jenny Sharpe, a scholar of Anglo-Caribbean literature, has explained that for many black and/or mulatto women in the eighteenth century, concubinage existed as a means for them to extract certain favors from their white master (husband, lover, or patron). How did these women function within these constraints and utilize their mulaticized flesh and its value as capital in bargaining? Although these hypergamous affairs were indeed exploitative, the kinds of exploitations and power struggles within them were nuanced depending on the ideological system in place.[9] It is from these complex relationships and negotiations of power, a New World libidinal economy, if you will, that the role of the *mulata* as an exchangeable (but powerful) commodity solidified itself within the social spaces of the nineteenth-century quadroon balls in New Orleans and the *bailes de cuna* in Cuba.

By the nineteenth century, the market for mulaticized flesh that emerged from these competing narratives of desire—the *mulata*'s to have greater significance as a citizen, the white man's to be coupled—formulated certain economic opportunities for women of color working as shop-keepers, landlords, and servants of the sacred. In Cuba, for example, the nineteenth-century elite sought to replicate the social order so many of them had witnessed and admired in France and Spain, attempting to import the separate-sphere paradigm as a cult of domesticity. This cult of domesticity primarily assigned specific bodies to either private or public space. Despite the Cuban elite's desire to control and enforce the separate-spheres para-digm, it was difficult to adhere to, given the radical mobility of the *mulata*. "The strategies, maneuvers, or means [free women of color] deployed" and how these women were "motivated by a desire to place themselves beyond slavery" with "economic and occupational resourcefulness" stand out as remarkable given the various legal, political, and power struggles that filled their every day.[10]

A seeming disassociation from "blackness" occurs in how these women negotiated their spaces of identity, given the fact that blackness was syn-onymous with slave, and slave status did not offer any form of choice, mobility, or freedom. Because certain mulaticized bodies (depending on their phenotype and how closely it approximated whiteness) could move through varying spaces of (ambiguous) racial identity and domesticity, one might position the *mulata* as a woman with a certain degree of access. As a house servant or washerwoman carrying soiled clothes to wash by the river, she partook in and maintained the flow of domestic activities in the private sphere. As a concubine or *placée* (the term widely used in New Orleans to identify a *mulata* mistress), she was the public mistress of white masculine domesticity, a visibly sexualized and racialized female body used by the men who, in some cases, paid extraordinary amounts of money to conquer, buy, and keep her. Finally, as a public businesswoman (artisan, confectioner, seamstress, among others) one of her more notable roles was as a lodge-keeper, maintaining inns for European male travelers in cities like Havana, Kingston, and New Orleans.[11]

One of the more sensationalist spaces featuring moving *mulatas* were the quadroon balls of New Orleans, where concubinage, or *plaçage*, played a significant role in the everyday reality for many *mulatas*. These balls occupy the focus of several scholarly works that highlight the construction of the quadroon balls as nothing more than a dressed-up, fancy version of the auction block.[12] Caramel skinned, honey colored, tawny and/or tanned, the *mûlatresses* populated these social dance events set up as erotic entertainments for their display and exchange among imperial men with capital. The incentives and goals were the same: to parade mulaticized flesh for *plaçage* in a more relaxed and less socially constricted environment than the exclusively white balls. Ritualized codes, behaviors, and choreographies of exchange between *mûlatresses* and their would-be patrons cemented certain socioeconomic conveniences for these women, who sought to support and maintain their lifestyles and to secure the future of their offspring from such liaisons. Thus, the libidinal imperial economy created prescripted choreographies of racialized and gendered performances that *mûlatresses* adopted, learned, and exchanged as a way to gain greater access to citizenship and personhood.

Not surprisingly, legal measures and laws often attempted to control *mulata* "freedom" of access or expression. If as Lady Nugent, a British traveler to Jamaica from 1802 to1807 wrote in her journal that imperial men were "almost entirely under the dominion of their mulatto favourites," then something had to be done to contain the problem.[13] In 1786, the Spanish New Orleans governor, Esteban Miró, instituted the Tignon Law forbidding all women of color from wearing jewels, fine fabrics, elaborate headdresses, or feathers; it required "*negras, mulatas, y quarteronas*" to wear their hair flat or if styled, a modest scarf wrapped around their head, hair hidden, as a signifier of their lower status.[14] Sure enough, *tignons* began to be made out of expensive cloths, and many free women of color made fashion statements with their *tignons* as subtle defiance to the law.

This issue of *mulata* beauty bears mentioning for hair (color and type) represented part of the eroticism linked to the *mulata* body. Although they had to keep their hair "invisible," *mulatas* found other ways to demonstrate their allure (especially if their economic position depended on their allure), through the fabrics chosen for the *tignon* or simply by the playing up the face "unperturbed" by the hair. Jewelry made of "coral, gold or carnelian" further adorned and embellished them, with or without the *tignon*.[15] How their epidermal reality contrasted with the *tignon* and other accoutrements, and/or whether or not some of the ones with a lighter epidermal reality created a disconnect with the "race marker" of the *tignon*, surely added to the mystique and further eroticized the *mulata* and her "absent" hair.[16]

The nineteenth-century circum-Caribbean trafficked in women of color potential, yet female power and agency were constrained under a series of codified juridical and corporeal practices. The dynamic social participation of *mulatas* in the public sphere led to the contradictory development of the *mulata* as a social threat, a femme fatale and signifier of nation and religiosity, primarily in Cuba. Luz Mena's "Stretching the Limits of Gendered Spaces: Black and Mulatto Women in 1830's Havana" argues that because of the important social contributions made by free women of color in Havana, the white Cuban elite felt it necessary to denigrate the *mulata's* socially productive status to one of moral transgression and degeneration. In this way, her power and autonomy would be compromised. Although the mulata-as-sign (i.e., the culturally coded signifier of a racialized identity recognized/agreed upon as "mulata," a stereotype) operated as a public commodity, the visible corporeal examples in the public sphere challenged these stereotypical circulations, seeking "liberation" by whatever resources available to them. Writing in his travel journal of Cuba, which was published in 1871, Samuel Hazard describes a *mulata* confectioner as such:

> Now we meet a "dulce" [sweet] seller. As a general thing they are neat-looking mulatto women, rather better attired than most of the colored women one meets in the streets. They carry a basket on the arm, or perhaps on the head, while in their hands they have a waiter, with all sorts of sweetmeats,—mostly, however, the preserved fruits of the country, and which are very delicious, indeed,—much affected by ladies. We need not have any hesitation in buying from these women, as they usually are sent out by private families, the female members of which make these *dulces* for their living, the saleswoman often being the only property they own, and having no other way (or perhaps, too proud, if they have) of gaining a livelihood.[17]

It appears as if he assumes the *mulata* is "property" of another family, perhaps even a white one, as the use of the word "private" would indicate. Additionally, for Hazard the *mulata's* racialized body automatically renders her labor as "property," as work done for another's benefit. Fortunately, Mena's research enables a different interpretation, as many *mulatas* were their own employers, participating in a self-sufficient economy. Furthermore, they had a reasonable variety of occupations to choose from, given the woman-centered economy in which they operated; they were nurses, teachers, businesswomen, midwives, artisans, and peddlers, to name a few. Other than being astute businesswomen, *mulatas* were often moneylenders themselves, and given their daily activities involving money exchange, many were skilled in mathematics and business proceedings, often to the chagrin of the white patriarchal elite.

INTERVAL I

Singing begins to be heard in the distance . . .

Òsun se're kété mi, owó
Òsun se're kété mi, owó
Omi dára o dára oge o
Òsun Wére kété mi, owó

Ochún make blessings without delay for me, money.
Ochún make blessings without delay for me, money.
Beautiful water, you are beautiful and ostentatious.
Ochún quickly without delay for me, money.[18]

Òsun Speaks

Tears . . . crocodile tears that come as prayers of supplication awaken me . . . asking me for money. Yes, you will keep your possessions. No one can take what you earned away from you. It belongs to you and your sisters. My daughters, all of you, be firm, keep to your work. Strive, be tenacious. Use your charm if you must, enchant them on my behalf. Let them see your beauty that needs not eyes to be appreciated. Go, keep to your work.

Òsun/Ochún as Trope

Òsun/Ochún has arrived. She has responded to one of her praise songs.[19] Òsun is known as the "Occidental Venus" in the Yorùbà pantheon. Allotted love, luxury, beauty, and the sweet waters, Òsun represents those things that make life a sensual experience: money, love, sex, and family. Adorned in yellow vestments with wrists encircled by gold bracelets, her delicate hands carry a fan usually made of peacock feathers, her favorite bird because of its flagrant display of arrogance and beauty. In his canonical work on African and Afro-American art and spirituality, Robert Farris Thompson's *Flash of the Spirit* describes Òsun (or as he spells it, Oshun) this way:

[She has a] reputation for great beauty . . . she was romantically transmuted into the "love goddess" of many Yoruba-influenced blacks in the western hemisphere. But there are dark aspects to her love . . . her masculine prowess in war; her skill in the art of mixing deadly potions, of using knives as she flies through the night. . . . But Oshun's darker side is ultimately protective of her people.[20]

Additionally, Òsun "has a deep relationship with witchcraft, powders, charms, amulets, and malevolent forces."[21] Renowned for her beauty and charm, she is both sensual (hip) movement and an unmoored woman with a capacity to love, cure, enchant, punish, excel, and please as she sees fit. In the Yorúbà community, she is bestowed with the title of Ìyálóde, a title given to the most popular and powerful woman, in terms of women's affairs.[22]

The circum-Atlantic voyages of the slave and tobacco trade brought Òsun to Cuba, where her name slightly altered to Ochún and her myths, fables, and magic were interpolated by representations of miscegenated female bodies; by the nineteenth century, the concept of Ochún materialized as the beautiful *mulata* within the Cuban national imaginary.[23] Although Òsun has fifteen avatars or spiritual roads, each assigned a different aspect or personality associated with the deified energetic force, the avatar most widely accepted and circulated in Cuba is that of Ochún Yeyé Kari (Mother who is Sufficient) and/or Yeyé Móoro (Mother who Builds Wealth). This avatar is described as "the happiest, most extravagant, most flirtatious of all the Òsun. She is constantly on the stroll, wears make-up and perfume, and constantly gazes at herself in the mirror."[24] Some of her practitioners that I consulted claim that these avatars developed from praise names—that is, names pronounced during the rituals to invite her to manifest. They state that these names are not part of the original fifteen. The avatar Òsun Pasanga (the Stream that is a Prostitute) would then stand out as the avatar from where Yeyé Kari and Yeyé Móoro may have developed. This Ochún loves to dance, revels in coquetry, and represents salacious behavior. It was this Ochún that coalesced onto the (late) nineteenth-century *mulata*, further elaborated through textual, visual, and theatrical representations of this hybridized body as one that, despite its seductive appeal, was both a social and sexual threat.[25] These discursive practices served to cement the *mulata*-as-sign in the Cuban cultural imaginary, a palatable, corporeal representative of a colonized country searching for some form of national identity. The *mulata* sign reverberated as an apparently neat representation of not-so-neat and vastly different criteria. As a result, the *mulata* did not have to labor to become; rather, that body's meaning was fully inscribed and interpellated by the forces of colonial history, myths (both African and Creole/Cuban), and by widely circulated and widely held ideas about racial categorization. The *mulata*'s laborless body as mere sign enables a country to represent itself to itself, all the while denying/avoiding the subject status of the visceral body who occupies the space of *mulata*.

In contrast, Òsun/Ochún-as-practice becomes useful as a way to in-sinew-ate "her" onto the hip movements and somatic activity of the *mulata* and her explosive sign, and to mobilize her body through spiritual and corporeal labor. For example, devotion to Òsun, as reenacted in yearly festivals at Osogbo, Nigeria, celebrates her power, charm, wealth, beauty, and wisdom. Dierdre Badejo's *Òsun Sèègèsí* documents one of these festivals. While in Osogbo, Badejo witnessed how the festival drama and its production (in the Marxist sense) display the intricacies of these Nigerian women's daily activities—particularly how adroitly they conceive and materialize the festival. The renderings of Òsun's significations in the context of these Nigerian women laboring and producing a festival in her honor demonstrate how women's work not just materializes the principles of Òsun but also adds value to the social. Badejo explains, "The annual Òsun Festival and oral literature [of Òsun] attest that even within the patriarchal Yorùbá system, women are central to the proper function and survival of humanity."[26] Indeed, Badejo's concept of humanity erases the technologies of power and ideologies based on Enlightenment principles that separate human bodies based on their differences, yet it is the activities of these women—their labor, and their working, sweating bodies as they execute and demonstrate the multiplicity of factors involved in realizing an object of veneration—that best demonstrate how production of knowledge operates. Through this lens, the festival occurs not as a flawless, beautiful, or celebratory place where dancing, singing, and worshiping black bodies exist bucolically; rather, it is a site of social and political commentary, reverence, and female cultural production. Here, women negotiate in the market; they both acknowledge and challenge patriarchy and male authoritarianism; and they demonstrate why one of the praise names for Òsun, that of Ìyáloja (Mother of the Market) speaks to the social organization, business acumen, and skills of the marketplace that these "daughters" of Òsun demonstrate. Although Òsun/Ochún reifies gendered ideas of being, she (as she is understood and practiced among her devotees) nevertheless enables an understanding of women as knowledge bearers and producers.

Òsun/Ochún exists variously as the beautiful sensual dancer, the astute market woman, and the ornery "old woman spitting curses at the world because of the loss of her beauty."[27] Ornery and ornate, bedecked and bedazzling, the *mulata* as Ochún (re)appears as a re-membered, performed corporeal iteration of the complex histories in the circum-(Black) Atlantic, or more precisely, the hip-notic torrid zone. Named the "Black Atlantic" by Paul Gilroy and the "circum-Atlantic" by Joseph Roach, this particular territory is transformed into a hip-notic torrid zone by the bodies and histories of the figure of the *mulata* and her enunciating hips. It becomes a space for and about women of color—black, brown—of *mulatas* with their bodily labors, practices, histories, and defiances. The *mulata* as producer of Ochún becomes a participatory body in the socioeconomic networks of the colonies, unable to extricate herself from the political economy of desire. Thus, when *mulatas*, "in pursuit of their rights as women and free persons, [flaunt] gold jewelry, headdresses, and clothes that only whites were supposed to wear," and they continue to produce beauty with accoutrements that Ochún favors (gold, coral, feathers), it is a practice of Ochún, of Ochún having her way, ensuring not only the presence and vitality of these women but also their historicity.[28]

INTERVAL II

Singing heard in the distance . . .

Iya mi ilé odò. Ìyá mi ilé odò
Gbogbo àse
Obí ni sálà máā wò e
Ìyá mi ilé odò

My mother's house is the River.
My mother's house is the River.
All powerful
Women that flee for safety habitually visit her.
My mother's house is the River.[29]

Òsun Interrupts

I am the River. My sister is the sea. I dance with her. I lie next to her. I spill forth into her. I lead you from her to me aboard ships with mermaids on the prow. She leads the way. She rocks you. I undulate through and to a new place.

CHOREOGRAPHING *MULATA* BODIES

How, then, does a *mulata* choreograph her gender and her body, specifically through her hips, to make insertions into the visual, theatrical, and libidinal economies where her sign is most frequented? Might sexuality, acts of sex, be ways of choreographing gender? How might these women of color's choreographies become cultural productions produced, exchanged, and commodified as mulaticized bodies? Such cultural choreographies of identity manifested quite literally in *bailes de cuna* and in quadroon balls, social dance(d) spaces for representations and performances of *mulata*-ness, operating as local hip-notic torrid zones. Driving my analyses of the quadroon balls and *bailes de cuna* is my goal to intervene in the modernist opposition between the corporeal and the linguistic. By locating knowledge outside of its historically normative space of language and text, even disturbing pat assertions of "embodied textuality," the lived materiality of an acting body mobilizes the historical and cultural codes where it sits and, in this case, dances. At the quadroon balls and/or *bailes de cuna*, for example, the *mulata* made choices as to how to represent herself given her everyday surroundings, demonstrating how gender coupled with race operates as a seductive choreography—so seductive, in fact, that writers of articles, research, travel journals, novels, and films continue to submit to their allure.[30] These balls/dances, whether they took place in Havana or New Orleans—both burgeoning cities of the Spanish empire—provided the dancing *mulatas* a space to choreograph the complexities of race and gender that defined them to their male provocateurs and created codes of behavior for themselves to choreograph and (un)successfully perform.

A possible performance might be a woman who refuses to co-opt *mulata*, choosing to establish another form of corporeality with different sets of options. Henriette DeLille, for example, the founder of the Sisters of the Holy Family Catholic order in New Orleans, was in fact a quadroon with a family history of *plaçage*. She was expected to follow the "tradition," yet she, in effect, chose to still her hips and render her body inexchangeable. Her corporeality, through its religiosity, purposefully choreographed a *mulata* outside the libidinal economy.[31] Others may have specifically mastered the codes of *mulata*, for it provided them with a comfortable and recognizable space from which to act. Rosette Rochon, one such *placée*, made a considerable fortune in New Orleans real estate holdings and apparently left an estate valued at the equivalent of $1 million today.[32] It is important to note here how the *mulata* firmly situated herself in an economy of exchange and made an attempt at self-produced economic agency, essentially managing her body as (her) capital for some access and/or social mobility.

BAILES DE CUNA

A brief critical examination of Cuban cultural scholar Reynaldo González's analysis of the *mulatas* hosting and attending the *bailes de cuna,* in the nineteenth-century Cuban costumbrista novel *Cecilia Valdés* by Cirilo Villaverde, positions the *mulata* as a discursive site where ideas of race, gender, and class choreograph themselves. *Cecilia Valdés, o la Loma de Ángel* serves as one of the foundational texts in a trope of the tragic *mulata* in Cuba. Cecilia, the *mulata* of the title, falls in love with Leonardo Gamboa, a white, wealthy *criollo* (Cuban-born Spaniard) who, unknown to them both, is her half-brother. Their illicit affair—along with Cecilia's relentless desire for higher social and racial status—contributes to her tragic demise. A *baile de cuna* hosted by a *mulata* named Mercedes introduces the reader to their social interactions. Said reader, through Villaverde's exquisitely detailed accounts, experiences the *bailes* where wealthy *criollos* attended for the pleasure of being among the most beautiful *mulatas* in Havana.

These danced spaces served as spectacles of the pairings between race, class, and gender as performed by the *canela* (cinnamon) bodies of the *mulatas* and their white suitors. They danced *la contradanza cubana* or *danza* (Cuban *contredanse*, which eventually led to the development of the *danzón*), a syncopated version of European country dance described by Villaverde as follows:

> The feet moved incessantly as they were softly dragged to the rhythm of the music, the dancers mixed and pressed in the midst of a packed crowd of onlookers, as they moved up and down the dance floor without break or pause. Even above the deafening noise of the kettledrums, in perfect rhythm with the music, the monotonous and continuous swish sound made by the feet could be heard. Colored people believe this to be a requirement for keeping perfect rhythm to the danza criolla.[33]

Villaverde's focus on the feet fails to articulate other movements of the *danza* dancing body. For example, the syncopation led to "more lateral movement [of the] hips," these movements called either *escobilleo* or *sopimpa*.[34]

Villaverde's literary account differs from that of María de las Mercedes Santa Cruz y Montalvo, or the Countess of Merlin. In her journal from 1840, she wrote that the dancers moved "more with the body than the feet ... some seem to glide as if on wheels, [others use] quick turns and backsteps, now to the right or to the left [but] all keep up the same graceful movement of the body."[35] Considered transgressive to the elites because of the Africanist element in its rhythm, its close proximity required of the dancing couple, and its popularity, the *danza's* mystique only heightened if it could be danced in the arms of a *mulata* at a racially mixed danced event, such as a *baile de cuna*. The allure of the *mulata's* hips moving beneath cumbersome layers of fabric, and more specifically what lay between those hips, marked the *bailes de cuna* as spaces rife with meanings and negotiations in terms of courtship, arrangement for concubinage, pleasure, and economic stability for the *mulata*.

Cecilia Valdés features three incidents of danced drama, but it is the *baile de cuna* toward the beginning of the novel where the material for analysis is rich.[36] González summarizes:

> *Los bailes de cuna representaban el crisol del acriollamiento: el amulatamiento cultural. Los jóvenes blancos ricos que en ellos se sumergían, salían amulatados en su ánimo. Contribuían a este embrujo tanto la música que se escuchaba y bailaba como la seducción de las mujeres. Eran bailes dado por mujeres, por eso se les llamaba "la cuna de Fulana o de Mengana"; en ellos predominaba la regencia femenina, sus designios, sus juegos de tácticas y estrategias. Más que en el baile "de etiqueta o de corte," también dado por negros y mulatos, estas cunas, por su sencilla promiscuidad, propiciaban el entrecruzamiento cultural y racial.*[37]

The "cradle dances" represented the melting pot of creoleness: cultural mulaticization. The young white rich men who submerged themselves in them left mulaticized in their mood. The music that was danced [in these *bailes*] contributed to their bewitching as much as the seduction of the women. The dances were held by women, that is why they were called "the crib of so-and-so"; feminine regency dominated these places, their purposes, their games of tactics and strategies. More so than in the black tie dances or the court dances, also held by blacks and mulattos, these "cribs," for their simple promiscuity, propitiated the racial and cultural exchange.

In this rendering of the *baile de cuna*, González uses the positivist language of the nineteenth century to mark these *cunas* organized by women as feminized spaces of sin, seduction, and cultural intermixing. It is important to note that González writes from a privileged scholarly position in revolutionary Cuba, where part of its dogma asserts a specific, essentialized Cuban identity. In this way, many scholarly texts endorse a stable, universal idea of *cubanía, Cubanidad, mestizaje, mulato*-ness, transculturation: critically discursive neologisms used to describe the Cuban cultural condition and its cultural production.

At the same time, González's description of these *baile de cunas* highlights how the literary imagination adds to the complicated web of race, class, and gender negotiations critical to this study. For González, the mere act of integrating these nuanced terms led to simple promiscuity, thereby acknowledging the widely held nineteenth-century Cuban belief that intermixing led to moral and sexual degeneration. He also proclaims, using words usually associated with Michel De Certeau, that the *mulata*-actions within the *bailes de cuna* operated as "games of tactics and strategies."[38] (Un)knowingly, González affords some kind of power to these *mulatas*.

For my purposes, I want to transport strategies and tactics to the *bailes de cuna* and quadroon balls, where the mobilizers of strategies and tactics dispute simple categorization. Granted, these *bailes de cuna* and quadroon balls existed within the place of colonialism and its insidious ideological ramifications. Yet, the particular space of the *baile de cuna* as controlled by women and their negotiations for some kind of economic agency confirms how these *mulatas* shifted between what Gonzalez calls "games of tactics and strategies." I contend that *mulata* corporeality—specifically the hips of the *mulata*—existed as the primary tactic operating in these spaces. The desire for the *mulata* body (in the many ways that that might possibly manifest) set up the *mulata* as an active agent in situations that, given the complexities of power, might render her mute, passive, and merely objectified.

QUADROON BALLS

In contradistinction to the *bailes de cuna* of Havana, which were held at a woman's—usually a well-established or respected *mulata*'s—house and orchestrated by her alone, the New Orleans quadroon balls, or *bals en masque,* were white male capitalist productions conceived, controlled, and attended by them for their own material and sexual enjoyment. The prize or thing to be consumed, enjoyed, and exchanged, the capital, was the *mûlatresse* (quadroon). These balls "would emerge as the unique formula of Auguste Tessier, an actor and dancer with a local opera company."[39] His formula was quite simple: advertise it as a twice-weekly affair held exclusively for free colored women and white men. Offer some surplus value, or "perks," by way of carriages at the door and private-room rental at the end of the evening. Many other entrepreneurial men followed suit. They even respected each others' dates and avoided scheduling conflicting balls on the same night. "A man so inclined could still spend three days a week with his family," one man observed.[40] These balls were highly popular during the era of Spanish rule in New Orleans (1763–1803), tying these productions of gendered performance and power to those of Havana, another major Spanish colonial enclave.

Just as the *bailes de cuna* had (white) witnesses who waxed poetic in their journals or letters about the skill of the dancing bodies, the quadroon balls also enjoyed a fair share of discursive accounts. One such visitor, an Edward Sullivan, wrote about the quadroons' movements at these balls as "the most easy and graceful that I have ever seen. They danced one figure, somewhat resembling the Spanish fandango, without castanets, and I never saw more perfect dancing on any stage. I wonder some of the opera lessees in Europe do not import them for their corps de ballet."[41] His admiration of the *mulatas'* dancing skill suggests an association between their apparent talent and their race. Another observer, an H. Didimus, states the following about a particular quadroon who caught his eye: "She is above the ordinary height, and moves with a free, unrestrained air, distinguished for grace and dignity."[42] Again, movement renders her body noticeable and notable.

I realize most of these accounts stem from a white, patriarchal perspective, from desire mitigated by a supposed objectivity, and so rather than accept them as careful, factual accounts of what may have occurred, I read them as discourses that show how the corporeality of the *mulata* was something to witness and subsequently write about. These documents serve to memorialize the swaying, preening, turning, curtseying, *danza*-ing corporeality that so fascinated at these social events. There, the *mulata* could only rely on other *mulatas* and their acquired knowledge about their situation for the kind of protection necessary for optimum benefits. Therefore, when negotiations for *plaçage* took place, it was a mother, an aunt, or another close, trusted, older woman who took charge of the young *mulata* and made the arrangements with the white man. A matrilineal, matri-focal, or woman-centered production of knowledge circulated the *mulata*-product in these libidinal market economies. These women learned how to mulaticize themselves and then used the value that their bodies had to wield it as capital in marketing themselves.

Although the New Orleans quadroon balls lie in a mythological space somewhere among romanticism, nostalgia, and sexual exploitation, the lived presence of the *mulata* there serves to undo the myths and discursively rendered tragedy, offering a way to remake the space into one of negotiation and power exchanges. Herein lies the significance of the body or, more precisely, the hips.

AN EPISTOLARY BREAK

Two letters were discovered among the personal effects of a Mr.-----, whose ancestral home in New Orleans recently had to be demolished because of Hurricane Katrina damage. They found a worn leather folder inside a moldy wall. Miraculously, the papers inside were not damaged. There were two letters and some ripped pages from a book. Upon closer examination, the pages were from a book by Saint Teresa of Avila. The faint print of the poem *"En las manos de Dios"*/In The Hands of God could still be read. There was a faint trace of a circle around these lines:

Decid, dulce Amor decid:
¿qué mandáis hacer de mí?

Sweet love say
What do you want of me?

The letters tell of a correspondence between an unknown man and a Maria Garcia Granados. Mr. ----- claimed she is his five times great-grandmother. Upon further genealogical inquiry, we find that the man who received these letters was his five times great-grandfather. He never married Maria. It was not possible. He was destined for a successful career in the British Navy, but a long trip across the Atlantic killed him. The ship's log says sepsis. He never married anyone, so his only progeny were the three daughters he had with Maria. In his will, he left everything to them. His white family did not contest. Rumor has it they knew he loved Maria as a legitimate wife.

Although she speaks about becoming a nun, Maria never went into convent life. Instead, she became a seamstress and raised three daughters. Daughters of adulterous men within the Spanish empire were often sent to convents as a form of atonement for the sins of the father. Perhaps her refusal of the habit is tied to her father's sudden death (as recorded in church registers). With no financial support for her mother, Carlota (his mistress), Maria may have had to position herself within the tradition of *plaçage*.

The First Letter

The first letter appears quite formal and shows no evidence of any intimate relations. However, the second tells a different story. Like many of these histories, they remain incomplete.[43]

New Orleans, 29 June, 1801
Dear Sir:

I have been asked to compose this letter as tangible proof of the commendable work the convent has been doing in teaching and instructing many of the inhabitants of this great city of New Orleans. As a daughter of a Spanish nobleman who committed the grievous sin of adultery with a miscegenated Creole woman, my soul and name have been tainted therefore I have been placed inside this convent to not only atone for my father's sin, but also for my inherent sinfulness which I possess due to the illegitimacy of my birth. They tell me that I have the potential to be an erudite, dutiful and officious nun should I choose to become a bride of Christ once I reach my eighteenth birthday in December. Sister Marie Madeleine says I have an aptitude for the proper understanding of Scripture. I am especially drawn to the tales of the martyrs and saints, those noble, selfless souls who sacrificed their fleshly bodies for the love of God and eternal service in His name. I have a particular fondness for St. Agnes of Rome, patron saint of chastity. Sister M.M. is proud I have picked her above all others. Recently, we have begun discussing St. Augustine (or Augustine of Hippo for you Protestants). Sister says I must fully understand the concept of sin before we can really discuss other significant concepts such as guilt and shame. It is only after knowing the depths of my soul's depravity that I can truly submit to the Will of God and look to my Lord Jesus as the perfect example of submission and obedience to God. I do hope that this is true. I cannot think of how else to help atone for my father's adultery. They say my own mother's licentiousness was a factor, but if moral virtue comes from self restraint, why should she be blamed when it was my father who had already promised to love, honor and obey another?

Yesterday, Father Vega, a Jesuit who was visiting the convent, asked me to read from St Augustine's City of God. He says, other than the Bible, it is the foundation of teaching in the Catholic faith and that I should learn it well. We focused on the following that I most humbly share here with you: *City of God*, Book XIV, 13: "That in Adam's sin an evil will preceded the evil act."

Our first parents fell into open disobedience because already they were secretly corrupted; for the evil act had never been done had not an evil will preceded it. And what is the origin of our evil will but pride? For "pride is the beginning of sin" (Ecclesiastes 10:13). And what is pride but the craving for undue exaltation? And is is undue exaltation, when the soul abandons Him to whom it ought to cleave as its end, and becomes a kind of end to itself. This happens when it becomes its own satisfaction. And it does so when it falls away from that unchangeable good which ought to satisfy it more than itself. This falling away is spontaneous; for if the will had remained steadfast in the love of that higher and changeless good by which it was illumined to intelligence and kindled into love, it would not have turned away to find satisfaction in itself, and so become frigid and benighted; the woman would not have believed the serpent spoke the truth, nor would the man have preferred the request of his wife to the command of God, nor have supposed that it was a venial transgression to cleave to the partner of his life even in a partnership of sin. The wicked deed, then—that is to say, the transgression of eating the forbidden fruit—was committed by persons who were already wicked. That "evil fruit" (Matthew 7:18) could be brought forth only by "a corrupt tree."

The nuns tell us we are all corrupt and inherently sinful, and that this is the most important lesson to learn from Augustine's "well conceived passage." Surely if we maintain our focus and love on God and love one another, how can we possibly be sinful? I have asked Sister Marie Madeleine this numerous times, yet she quickly turns to Augustine again and makes me repeat the following phrase, "It was not the corruptible flesh that made the soul sinful, but the sinful soul that made the flesh corruptible."

Thank you for allowing me to write to you. Thank you also for your kind donation to the convent library. I have enjoyed *El Castillo Interior* by Saint Teresa of Avila the most.

May God bless and keep you safe in His Mercy, and may the peace of our Lord Jesus Christ be with you always.

Sincerely,

Maria de las Mercedes Garcia Granados[44]

The Second Letter

New Orleans, 5 May 1804
Dear Sir:

Thank you very much for the lovely fabrics you had delivered last week. I have several customers who will relish the opportunity to wear a dress made with them. The *plaçage* balls continue and the demand for beautiful clothes to wear at them continues as well.

I read and re-read your letters in your absence. They offer some comfort. I sometimes read them aloud to our daughters. Lila tore one apart the other day. I remember becoming quite upset, but she is just shy of two years. She could not have done it intentionally. Carlota Maria continues to grow. Yesterday she spent most of the afternoon on my hip. It was difficult to get any work done, but my mother spent some time here and watched both babies as I finished fitting a dress for Mademoiselle Renault. She can be quite demanding. She thinks because her benefactor is one of the wealthier men in New Orleans, she can treat the rest of us like her servants.

Thank you for asking my permission about the new addition to this humble house. I would gladly welcome a proper kitchen, and I am most grateful that you suggested it and asked my permission. Asking women like me for permission in this world seems quite unreal. My grandmother,

God rest her soul, always spoke about how she was always told what to do when she was my age.

May God keep you safe on your journey to Cuba, so that you can return in time to see Carlota Maria turn one this September.

Yours,
Maria

INTERVAL III

Yèyé yèyé mã wò'kun; mã yíyan yòrò

The Mother of mothers always visits the sea;
Always walking with a slow swagger to melt away.[45]

Ochún Interrupts

My daughters walk, they map out space. They take up space. They use their bodies, bodies I need to exist, bodies I bestow with grace, health, vibrancy . . . bodies that work for me, venerating me. Their eyes sometimes are filled with tears, and they cry. Their tears call me. Their tears connect many of us. They also work, they sweat, they breathe, they move, they dance. Theirs are bodies that both feel, and make you feel, make you sensate . . . experience . . . express, re-dress. Use your bodies, think with them, feel with them. That is me. Keep to your work, my daughters.

My Cuban grandmother, Carmen, did not like to dance. She preferred to watch my grandfather sway to the *danzón* in their kitchen on Sunday afternoons during the weekly *danzón* radio shows. She was demure in her appearance, wearing almost no make-up, faint perfumes, and a gold necklace with a round La Virgen de la Caridad del Cobre charm. Ochún (re)appears here as La Virgen as they operate coterminously in Cuba, syncretized versions of the same deified feminine force. Both are considered patron saints of Cuba, one Catholic, the other African. That both of my grandmothers did not dance strikes me as particularly ironic, given the intrinsic social role that dance played in their respective cultures (Cuban and Caribbean-Colombian). Nevertheless, I have laid out a genealogy of histories and situations that perhaps informed their understandings as to how their bodies could and should act. I often wonder what each would say if they saw me dancing for Ochún, dancing the *danzón*, or the *cumbia*—the heavy hip-laden dance of coastal Colombia.

As I sit, think, and write about ideas, (dance) histories, and racialized gendered bodies, I realize just how far removed I am from the kinds of labors my grandmothers and great-grandmothers had to engage in. Part of me wants my intellectual labor to serve as a form of honor and veneration for my female ancestors, yet somehow I believe that my body, dancing, thinking, moving, and perhaps even hip-notizing, acts as the real *ebo*, or offering, to them. I still think that my tears will get the best of me when I remember those that I knew and those that I (re)imagine. Yet, my act of crying is nothing compared to how *ellas seguirán*, how they will endure as I continue to sit and write, walk, and dance for them.

Telling Stories/*Echando Cuentos*

I want to tell you a story, *queridos lectores*/dear readers. Actually these will be several stories. But, I do not know where to begin. I do not know in what order to tell the story . . . I mean stories. Because a story is really stories, many of them, intertwined like gnarled tree roots. Often they begin and end in different ways. Sometimes they do not end. They become other stories. I am going to make mine circular because I dislike endings. I prefer shifts and continuations.

STORY ONE (1958/1972/2008/2011)

I think I will begin here: Ranchuelo, Cuba, circa 1958.

Before the 1959 Revolution, Cuba was divided into different social clubs/societies based on race or skin coloring.[1] There was the *Sociedad de Blancos, Sociedad de Negros*, and *Sociedad de Color*. Each "society" had its own meetings, social events, organizations. This is a picture from a *Sociedad de Color* event (Interlude 1, Figure 1). Here, they tell me, was the first time the Orquesta Aragón played in Ranchuelo, a small town about twenty minutes from Santa Clara, Cuba. Ranchuelo boasts the cigarette factory Trinidad y Hermano (Trinidad y Hno) as part of its historical legacy in that region of Cuba. I provide this information to give a sense of the type of industry that shaped the lives of many of Ranchuelo's inhabitants. How many hands from Ranchuelo helped roll the cigarettes that rest moistened in the mouths of smoking Cubans?

That evening, many people went to see this spectacular *danzón* orchestra perform; as at that time, it was one of the most famous Cuban music groups. *Danzón*: Cuba's first national dance and rhythm, or so the historical

Interlude 1, Figure 1. *Sociedad de Color*, Ranchuelo Cuba, 1958.

narrative insists. *Danzón*: a transculturated sound that blends African rhythms and syncopation with Spanish *danza* and French *contredanse*.[2] *Danzón*: the soundtrack to my paternal grandparents' home, especially on Sunday afternoons in 1958. In 1878, the sweaty conglomeration of (white) bodies touching other (browner) bodies, moving their hips gently to the music, potentially being "tainted" by black bodies created a scandal among the bourgeois and intelligentsia alike as they danced to *Las Alturas de Simpson*, or Simpson Heights, the first known *danzón*. Social dance history in the Americas emerges out of these entanglements between different classed and racialized bodies, yet I will not dwell here for now. Instead, I will ease back to 1958, eighty years after Simpson Heights premiered.

How do we tell stories about people dancing for pleasure, as a form of relaxation from a long day working at a cigarette factory, for example? How do these narratives become part of hemispheric histories that do not necessarily privilege these public and everyday spaces? Furthermore, what of these histories and their necessary insertion into an archive of Cuban cultural history?

Foucault posits the archive as the system that establishes statements as events and things, yet this particular archive of which I speak does not lay covered in dust; it does not contain pages with irregularly worn-out corners; nor does it have a site to house it. Bones, flesh, and memory house the archive of everyday enactments. Bodies walking home from the Trinidad y Hno factory, looking forward to animated conversations over a dinner table regardless of how much food may rest upon it. As such, the moment memorialized in the first photograph (Interlude 1, Figure 1) shifts the understanding of it from a simple family gathering to a moment where history, affective relationships, economic realities, and discourses of pleasure move through the room.

Women become repertoires and repositories of national history, their memories functioning as markers of time, space, and affect. Furthermore, their contributions—whether domestic (as mothers, wives, and homemakers), public (as workers), or performative (as dancers, artists), or even cigarette rollers—make history. Afro-Cuban poet and essayist Nancy Morejón explains the significance of formalist history, yet she immediately diverges from its potentially all-encompassing grasp, preferring to value the everyday histories of women and their labors. She comments that "history in capital letters has been important to me, and the history of small grandmothers was important, women prophets, the ones who embroidered the tablecloth where their own oppressors ate. A history of the lash, of migrations and stigmas that came by the sea and to the sea they return without apparent reason."[3] For Morejón, grandmothers play an important role because they signal a matrilineal register where women's labors and exchanges of everyday knowledges shape history. For me, my knowledge of self and family history rests on the memories and imaginings about both of my grandmothers and the times when and where they lived, their working-class jobs, their pleasures. One rolled cigarettes for a living, another loved to smoke them. Neither danced much, but both loved music. One loved *boleros*; the other, the *danzón*.

I come from a very matrifocal family, at least on the Colombian side. I met my maternal grandfather only once. My grandmother had taken me and my brother to a bakery. As he and I dawdled, we noticed she spoke with a white-haired man on the corner. He had a lot of white hair, and his hand was on my grandmother's shoulder. He seemed to be massaging it. "*Vengan a conocer a su abuelo*/Come meet your grandfather," my grandmother said.

I will never understand everything that happened that day. My grandmother never spoke about it again. She buried it. She tended to bury her past. (She eventually suffered from dementia. Her body buried her past for her.) The absent (perhaps even false) patriarch seemed like an important theme in my family history. It never made sense until I learned about the hemispheric histories of *mulata* women. Then I understood his absent presence. His name belonged to me—Borelli or Borelly—but never his presence.

Since I have brought up grandfathers I may as well honor the Cuban one as well. I never knew him, my paternal grandfather. He died while my mother was pregnant with me. My father was unable to return to Cuba to attend his funeral. He was unable to return to Cuba to attend his mother's funeral, as well. He never speaks about how he felt about either circumstance. This type of ceremonial closure that marks the end of a human life seems absent from my family histories. My mother chose to forgo her own mother's funeral services in Panama. She could not bear the pain of seeing her mother for the last time, she says. She has never been able to deal with emotional crisis. Seems like we all have our own aversions to endings.

STORY TWO (1953/2011)

In 1953, when Enrique Jorrín composed and later premiered the *cha-cha-chá*, La Engañadora "The Deceiver" Lalín Lafayette (or Agueda Alvarez, her given name) danced along to the infectious rhythm: pause, 2, 3, cha-cha-chá. She invented the *cha-cha-chá* dance style (Interlude 1, Figure 2). She told me this story briefly while I looked through a small collection of photos she brought out for me when I visited her. It was an unannounced visit. I had been in central Havana with my journalist friend Lam and quite spontaneously:

Interlude 1, Figure 2. *Granma International* article about Lalín Lafayette. This article is also available online.

"*Vamos a pasar por casa de Lalín*"/Let's go visit Lalín.
"*Quién?*"/Who?

He shared the short story about the *cha-cha-chá,* and I wanted to meet her immediately. It took us a while to find her apartment as he had forgotten where she lived exactly. Cuban neighbors proved helpful, and after knocking on many worn-out doors, we finally found hers and climbed the dark stairway to her apartment. For the majority of the visit, Lalín scolded Lam because we had arrived unannounced and she had had no time to get ready. Her hair was in curlers and, according to her, she wore a dirty old shirt because the water had not been turned on yet. She had been waiting all morning so that she could take a shower.

La Engañadora
A Prado y Neptuno
Iba una chiquita
Que todos los hombres la tenían que mirar.
Estaba gordita, muy bien formadita y en resumen colosal.
Pero todo en esta vida,
Se sabe, ni siquiera averiguar,
Se ha sabido que en sus formas,rellenos tan sólo hay.
Que bobas son las mujeres que nos quieren engañar.
Me dijiste.
Ya nadie las mira,ya nadie suspira,
Ya sus almohaditas,nadie las quiere apreciar.

Enrique Jorrín

There was a girl
Who walked along Prado and Neptuno
All the men had to look at her.
She was chubby. Well formed. To summarize, she was colossal.
But everything can be found out in this life.
They found out her body was just filled with padding.
How silly are women who want to deceive us.
Now no one looks at her, no one sighs
No one wants to appreciate her little pillows.

The lyrics of the song tell of a woman who possesses a spectacularly curvaceous body that turns out to be fraudulent because she wore strategic padding in all of her feminine places. Lalín used to act out the song and then dance along: 2, 3, *cha-cha-chá.*

Here, she shares briefly another encounter when she went to the Middle East (Interlude 1, Figure 3). This is from an interview she granted to Lam,

Interlude 1, Figure 3. Lalín Lafayette in Egypt. From Lafayette's personal collection.

which he subsequently had published in the Cuban newspaper, *Granma International*:

> I travelled throughout Europe and the Orient, I witnessed three wars. It was incredible how Cuban music and dance was so well liked, it was a sure success. I remember that on one occasion three of us [spectacular *mulatonas* from the *Mulatas del Fuego*, a dance/cabaret act from 1940s and 50s Cuba that had two incarnations: Lalín was part of the second incarnation, her two sisters were part of the first] went to the movies; we were wearing trousers and there was a riot, broken glass, rocks being thrown, the police had to come; women weren't allowed to wear trousers, but you know, we were atomic.

Atomic...bombastic...fantastic...elastic...haptic....hypnotic.Whatisit about the dancing *mulata* in/out/north/south/east/west of Cuba that causes such a fuss? (Interlude 1, Figure 4)

> *I'm the rumba dancing mulata*
> *Who dances to the sound of the bongo drum*
> *From Guira to Caimanera, no one dances like I do*
> *When I grind my hips*
> *The smell of raw sugar fills the air...* [4]

CABARET ALLOY. Las Mulatas de
Fuego, el dinámico Conjunto que se
hizo célebre en Centro y Sur América.
en la interpretación del mambo y el
cha-cha-chá, es uno de los números
que representan mayor erogación para
la empresa. Comenzarán en el "Alloy"
de un momento a otro.

Interlude 1, Figure 4. Mulatas del Fuego, as they appeared in *Show* magazine, June 1957. The Cuban Heritage Collection at the University of Miami contains an archive of *Show* magazine.

STORY THREE (1963/2011)

This is Mayda Limonta, the first cabaret star and first black Carnival queen in post-Revolutionary Cuba (Interlude 1, Figure 5). As a representative of *Cubanidad*, Mayda traveled to Japan, Poland, the former Czechoslovakia, among other places. She invited me over one morning. I had to wait for her to lower her apartment keys from her window. A cable with the keys tied at the end descended slowly. Her dark hair blew in the wind. I remember thinking she had a lot of it. When she opened the door she apologized for her appearance. She wore a white nightgown and said she had spent too much of the morning attending to her elderly mother so she was unable to get ready for my visit. Like Lalín, she disappeared into her room and emerged with a collection of photographs. She rescued many photographs from the fire at the Tropicana because the revolutionary government attempted to get rid of them after the "triumph of the Revolution."

This is my favorite picture in Mayda's personal collection (Figure 1, Figure 6). I think it tells many stories. Behind and above her head is an Abakuáfigure, a *ñañigo*. Abakuá is an all-male Afro-Cuban society based on fraternities from the southeastern Nigerian and southwestern Cameroon.

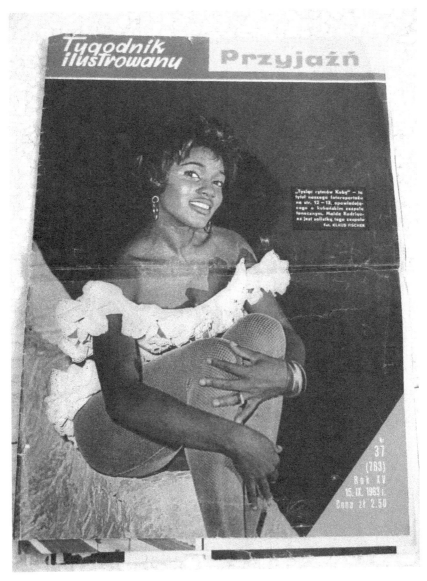

Interlude 1, Figure 5. Mayda Limonta, in a Polish entertainment magazine called "Friendship," 1963. From Limonta's personal collection.

In the nineteenth century, Three Kings Day celebrations were marked by Afro-Cuban dancing in the streets, as this was the only day they were allowed to parade, dress up, and take up social space with their dancing bodies. Cuba and its relationship to black spirituality, Creolization, the libidinal economy that contributed to the Cuban physiognomy, and the

Interlude 1, Figure 6. Mayda Limonta at a Carnival event, c. 1963. From Limonta's personal collection.

idea of the white patriarch all signify prominently in this photograph. Mayda in her white dress offers a stark contrast to the history of blackness she moves away from while led by her white escort. I did not ask who he was. I forgot. I thought too much about the multiple meanings in the photograph. I also did not want to take up too much of her time. I knew she had to take care of her mother. She asked me to photograph as many of her archived pictures as I wanted.

"*Hazme el favor y mandale algunas a mi hermana en los EEUU. Ella es profesora como tu . . . en California.*"/ Please send some to my sister living in the United States. She is a professor in California.

I emailed her many JPEGS from my office computer upon my return, but I wondered why Mayda did not ask me to take a recent photograph of her or her mother to send. I never insisted. What is it about remembering people and things as they were, not as they are? How does that help us sit in the stillness of our sometimes difficult now?

Her elderly mother appeared after about an hour. "*Ya ahorita es la hora de su almuerzo*"/It would be time for her lunch soon, said Mayda. Her mother looked at me intensely but did not speak. She sat on a rocking chair patiently waiting. Lalín also sat on a rocking chair during my visit. Mayda's mother sat in silence. Lalín kept admonishing Lam for bringing me over unannounced. That state of rocking, an almost mobile immobility. . . . Ochún has an avatar who manifests as an older woman on a rocking chair. She rocks and spits curses at the world, angry about the loss of her enchantments, aesthetic or otherwise. I cannot presume either woman sits in this similar contemplative space. Still, that insistent consistent back and forth, a movement between their respective now and then, this slight unwavering tenacity to still keep going . . . back and forth . . . back and forth. . . . I am stuck there. Not in the present, but not necessarily in the past; moving between the two as a way to find balance, negotiation, or even displacement. Their back has photos, performances, personal archives of their careers. I am unable to look back in my family's personal archives. . . . I wonder if they do the same? Is this part of the hip-notism between time and space that joins the bodies of these women: Lalín, Mayda's mother, Mayda, my grandmothers?

No puedo configurar el pasado completamente. Mis abuelas no me contaron mucho de sus historias. No sé si esto es un lamento porque yo sé que mucha gente ignora sus antepasados por razones de violencia, ruptura, o pleno olvido. Muchas veces, hay que inventar un pasado . . . inventarlo un poquito. Sólo un poquito. Sólo para aliviar las voces que no paran de susurrar.

I cant quite completely reconfigure the past. My grandmothers did not tell me much about their life stories. I don't know if this is a lamentation: I know most people ignore their ancestors due to violence, rupture or sometimes pure and simple neglect. A lot of times, to invent the past is in order. . . . invent it a little. Just a little bit. Just to soothe the voices that keep on whispering.

Do these stories seem incomplete? I think they are. I also think they need to remain that way. Does that honor these lives I am trying to highlight here? Perhaps they allow for the creation of other stories that could circulate as rumors? Rumors insist upon incompletion. Rumors also speak to some element of "a symbolic truth that stretches beyond the facticity of a specific event?"[5] Some stories are told over and over so many times that they become a type of truth which has real material affects in people's lives, in their embodied memories.

Because I dislike endings, I end this section with this next picture, just as I began (Interlude 1, Figure 7). The last part of the story I will share with you is that this photo shows some of my paternal family in Cuba: my grandfather, grandmother, aunt and cousins once or twice removed. I like to imagine my grandmother taking a rest from rolling cigarettes. She was just happy to keep her fingers still. Maybe she even enjoyed a cold beer. Apparently, my father was busy dancing so he did not get photographed. He was eighteen at the time . . . or at least that is how the story goes.

Interlude 1, Figure 7. My Cuban grandmother (seated center wearing a printed dress), aunt (behind her wearing a one-shoulder dress), and grandfather (back farthest right with glasses) at *Sociedad de Color* event, Ranchuelo Cuba, 1958.

CHAPTER 2

Hip(g)nosis at Work

Rumors, Social Dance, and Cuba's
Academias de Baile

The September 2011 issue of *Vanity Fair* featured an article entitled "All Havana Broke Loose: An Oral History of the Tropicana." The author Jean Stein, well known in literary circles for her oral history of Edie Sedgewick, amassed an oral history of people who remembered Havana, its nocturnal life, and the Tropicana before the 1959 Cuban Revolution. When I sat down to read it, I felt a peculiar feeling I will call "curious disdain." On the one hand, I was intrigued that an American magazine dedicated some space to a significant cultural history of a country with which the United States still has contentious relationship.[1] On the other hand, the article seemed like just another nostalgia-tinged account of a lost Havana, focusing mainly on the allure of the Tropicana's spectacle and its relationship with foreign celebrities, mob bosses, and visitors prior to 1959. I flipped through it haphazardly until I came across the "voice" of dancer Eddy Serra. She remembers:

> In those days, if you were really black, you had to be a headliner to perform. The dancers and showgirls were all white or very light *mulattas*. They mostly came from middle-class or low-income families, but many of them had studied dance and were very polished. I wanted to be a ballet dancer, but I got arthritis when I was 12, so I moved to modern dance. And that's how I came to fit into the chorus at the Tropicana.[2]

Serra articulates the racial prejudice involved in picking dancing female bodies at the Tropicana, but equally important, she makes specific assumptions about dance, technique, training, and physical capability. I wonder how she managed to get arthritis at the age of twelve? I also pause at the fact that she thought modern dance would be easier on her arthritis than ballet—both challenging and physically arduous techniques of the body, to be sure. She later shares stories about a transvestite performer's melodramatic "death" on a neighboring club's stage, and another dancer whom she admired by the name Sandra Taylor, who had "a tiny waist and large hips." Her last entry in the article provides information about what she was doing that New Year's Eve when Batista fled the country. That night, she had performed the "Rumba al Waldorf," which featured music from the film *The Bridge on the River Kwai* in a *cha-cha-chá* rhythm. How many others were moving to 2, 3, *cha-cha-chá* with agile footwork and compliant hips? What did it look like? Had they seen Lalín Lafayette ever perform the *cha-cha-chá*?

Questions and more questions arose as I read and reread these memories. Scholarly and personal desires to know more about the Cuban dancing bodies that populated the stage kept me reading. What did they do before the show? In what part of Havana did they live? How did they get to work? Did they like their jobs? Did they earn enough to make a living? Where did they go afterwards if they still felt like socializing? What did they eat? Did their feet or back hurt? As a scholar of the body, I burrow for clues about the physicality, corporeality, and social conditions of the dancers, musicians, and revelers. The body somehow eludes the fixity of written histories, but it maintains its presence through the words and actions of historical subjects.

Stein's article adds to the already rich corpus of popular discourse about the Tropicana, the "paradise under the stars" of a pre-Castro Cuba.[3] It further establishes Cuban social dance history as being primarily Havana-centric and, even more so, based on big, lavish entertainment venues catering to international audiences. Rumors about the collusion between the U.S. mob, the Cuban police, and the government figure dominantly in Stein's oral history, as this triumvirate worked together to ensure that these places of sanctioned yet "questionable" activities continued to exist until 1959. The constant stories about a Cuban heyday can produce a fascination with that history. Nostalgic longing of an imagined or lost past is a political-personal investment particularly for specific individuals of racial or economic privilege.[4] In these recorded reminiscences, an archive emerges of a *type* of nocturnal discourse about Cuba—one that hypnotizes and blinds the reader with the lights of the stage and the sequins of the moving, curvaceous bodies. Such submission to the spectacle of a sensuous Cuba renders peripheral other types of stories that occurred simultaneously— peripheral to the grand narrative of Cuban performance history, not peripheral in their inherent value to national history. It is these stories where the historiographic project of this chapter begins.

I particularly like the story or rumor about Marlon Brando in Havana. In one of the photographs featured in *Vanity Fair*, an earnest-looking Brando, photographed with Cuban writer Guillermo Cabrera-Infante, plays the *congas*. During my last research trip to Havana, I was told a story about Brando's visit to Cuba that illustrates the power of rumor, particularly in the social-dance history of Cuba. Rumor, as Ann Laura Stoler writes, is "a key form of cultural knowledge."[5] Well, rumor has it that when Brando arrived in Havana in 1956, he was taken to the glamorous, extravagant cabaret shows of the Montmartre and the Tropicana. Although he was impressed by the spectacle, he turned to his hosts and asked to be taken to the "real Havana." One gets the sense that he could see beyond the lavish display of sequins, flesh, lights, and sound and actually saw the Cuban bodies, those that worked every night as dancers, musicians, singers. *Where did they go after work?* perhaps he wondered. That is where he wanted to go.

Brando was taken to Playa de Marianao, a neighborhood in the northern part of Havana. A great number of stories and speculation exist as to what Brando did once in Playa de Marianao.[6] I am not so much interested in what he did as I am in his desire to go to these "peripheral" spaces of nocturnal Havana. I could quickly dismiss this desire as part of First World slum tourism, or in seeing how the marginalized and economically underprivileged live, yet his desire to see the "real Havana" suggests his understanding of the spectacle, both cultural and national, that the big cabaret shows created and how it differed from the activities in Playa de Marianao. In Playa, many nightclubs and cabarets lay interspersed amid working-class homes (Figure 2.1). They had modest names—Pennsylvania Club, Rumba Palace—where the orchestras debuted and played *son, rumba, mambo,* and *cha-cha-chá* to a crowd of night revelers—some of whom had come north directly after the end of the Tropicana or Montmartre shows, while others had been there since the start of the evening.

Unlike the audiences at the Montmartre and Tropicana, Playa cabarets featured a racially mixed crowd. Some of these clubs operated similar to the *academias de baile*, or taxi dance halls, where for 5 cents a dance men could dance with a particular female partner, usually *mulata*. It is those moments—the look between the client and the *mulata*, his approach, her ascension from her seat, or her walk away from the bar, her right hand clasping his left while his right hand lightly touches her waist pulling her close—where I argue that a popular history of mid-twentieth-century Havana nightlife, and by extension Cuba, develops. I aim to materialize

Figure 2.1. Events page from *Show* magazine, May 1958. In addition to the address and phone number of the club, the featured performers for that month were listed. Among them was Celeste Mendoza (Ali Bar Club), famous singer/*rumbera*. The Cuban Heritage Collection at University of Miami contains an archive of *Show* magazine.

this particular history in this chapter and its focus on social dancing at *academias de baile* and Playa de Marianao.

First, I have to come clean. Initially I wanted to find and interview a *mulata* who danced in an *academia de baile*. It did not happen. No actual *mulata* materialized. However, the *mulata* does not remain absent. Instead, she appears through the recollections of Cubans who remember those spaces, danced in them, and can still describe what some of them and the people looked like. I spoke with a woman who had a neighbor who worked at an *academia de baile*, but she did not share too much information. She merely said that some of these women wound up marrying their dance partners, and they proceeded to have a "good life" and become "respectable" citizens. Another friend set up an interview with a woman who had danced at an *academia*. I remember moving from feeling elated to that of deflated on the day of our scheduled interview. Her daughter called my friend and informed us that her mother's head was not well (*tenía la cabeza mala*) and could not really meet, let alone remember anything specific. I found out she was in her eighties, so I was not necessarily surprised, but days before she had expressed an interest in wanting to talk with me. The daughter's refusal to allow her mother to speak with me evokes Visweswaran's ethnographic refusal of the subject.[7] Here, the silence may perhaps speak to notions of shame, respectability, and bourgeois codes of conduct that situated the *academias* as sites for public women. Had she spoken to me she would have been admitting to being a public woman—and did her daughter feel uncomfortable with this label? I cannot know, but I began to consider how the idea of shame and ethics clouds the topic of social dancing prior to the Cuban Revolution. Because the military-dictatorial regime of the current Cuban state has had the objective of deemphasizing and, to some extent, extinguishing the historical relevance of social dancing pre-Castro, perhaps these spaces of social activity remain archived. As such, some Cubans may not feel completely comfortable in admitting their participation in the activities.

This chapter engages with the complexity of how to tell a history of nocturnal dance activities that have been archived in stories, rumors, metaphorical and real silences, and embodied memories. My stories come from oral histories shared by dancers, musicians, entertainment magazines of the era, and journalistic or fictionalized accounts of the *academias*. By focusing on oral history, dancing bodies, some gossip, and ephemera, I seek to challenge the historiography and national historical projects that have established prescribed ways to remember and materialize history through archives or other discursive practices. I make material the elusive *mulata* of the *academias* through these ephemera, voices, and recollections. Here, I take a cue from Luise White, as I am also interested in "expan[ding] historical epistemologies . . . to find the very stuff of history, the categories and constructs with which people make their worlds and articulate and debate their understandings of those worlds."[8] Rumor and oral history facilitate this function. Donna Haraway calls this "situated knowledges," and my interest lies in bringing this method of telling history to the foreground, similar to the way the *mulata* occupies the cabaret spaces center stage. The historical imperative here lies in rendering valuable everyday modes of exchange and communication.

In this Cuban world of the never-ending night, where the rhythmic echoes of the *bongo* drum and the swish of crinoline-heavy skirts accompany the bodies moving from club to club, from *academia* to *academia*, and from one body to the next, the *mulata* becomes the centerpiece of the story. From her body, narratives and discourses of race and nation emerge and partner with social-dance history to elucidate the project of Cuban nationhood. By aligning the *mulata* body with a social dance history of Cuba, not only am I demonstrating how bodies might serve as a primary site of inquiry but also I am providing another example of what Homi Bhabha would call the "narration of nation."[9] For me, the *mulata* is a Cuban archive, if not *the* Cuban archive. The Cuban cultural imaginary's investment in the myth of the *mulata* renders her an archive of the Cuban condition, the Cuban state, and thus further allows said archive to be pulled out, (re)written upon, circulated, and referenced during different moments in Cuban cultural history for different reasons. Thus, this genealogy of the Cuban *mulata* gestures toward a way to theorize the body as living history speaking with corporeal eloquence.

I piece together a (hi)story of the *academias* in three parts: through archival and literary information, through the memories of male musicians or dancers who were there, and through the experience of one dancer as recorded in a Cuban newspaper. A bit of hyp-notism will be necessary, as the story will seem tidy, structured, and orderly even though history is messy, problematic, and scattered.

Per dance historian Lena Hammegren's suggestions on the necessity of intertextuality to tell a dance history, I make use of interviews, literary texts, entertainment magazines from the time period, and photographs to approximate what it may have been like to dance and work at an *academia de baile*.[10] I also draw upon my research in Havana, where I attempted to locate the *academia* spaces by taking walks around the city and having conversations with journalists, historians, and musicians. Much of this relies on a shared narrative code of the *mulata* to function, in that her "absent presence" fueled my process of excavation. Outside of a scholarly desire to shed light on the significance of these dancing women's contribution to a Cuban national identity, I seek to demonstrate how women's bodies are intrinsically incorporated into discourses of nation and history, establishing a valuable embodied archive that sometimes slips through the cracks.

The "scenario" of the *academia de baile*, the "practiced-space" of Cuban social dance and identity, remains as detritus of pre-Revolutionary Cuba, fragments in memories, some neatly formed and remembered, others fading or broken apart—similar to the crumbled walls, worn paint, and rubble that characterize contemporary Havana.[11]

After the 1959 Revolution, the Fidel Castro regime was adamant about eradicating the bars, nightclubs, cabarets, and remaining *academias de baile,* both physically (many buildings that housed them were torn down or closed after his assumption to power) and historically.[12] Within Cuban revolutionary rhetoric, many of these spaces of entertainment are mentioned merely as aberrations from the corrupt Machado and Batista years, where excesses of capitalism tainted the potential for Cuba to be independent from foreign interests and desires. In Cuba, there hardly exist any published scholarly texts or written documentation of said *academias*.[13] I met with journalists, musicologists, and Cuban cultural workers who possessed personal archives of Cuban popular dance. Some had written essays that were never published (for example, José Galiño, archivist at Instituto Cubano de Radio y Televisión); others had collections of clippings or extracts from published books (such as Radames Giro, ethnomusicologist), while still others generously shared a rich supply of personal contacts and photographs (Rosa Marquetti, at the Sociedad General de Autores y Escritores [SGAE]).

When I noticed the repetition of rumors, stories, and names from different sources, I began to consider how crucial "rumor" can be to the historiographic project of nation. I also spoke with several musicians who played at *academias*, and a well-known professional dancer who would visit the *academias*. This conglomeration of voices, along with the scattered written archives about the *academias,* make up the body of this chapter.

In terms of methodology, I compiled the names and locations of the *academias* from the various sources I had consulted. One sunny January afternoon in Havana, I took my list and, with my Cuban entertainment-journalist friend Rafael "Chino" Lam, I walked to and photographed the sites or buildings (if they were still standing) where the *academias* had/might have been. I noticed that many were in close proximity to one another, a tactic surely meant to lure visitors and keep those nocturnal pastimes spatially contained and easy to access. *How many* academias *could one visit on a single night?* I pondered.

How, then, to proceed with a historiographic or even an ethnographic fiction?[14] Often, my corporeality became integrated in the investigation. Some of the Cubans with whom I spoke directed their fingers or their gazes at me when I asked them to describe what the women at the *academias* might have looked like. I know that, just because my corporeality approximates the Cuban visual economy of the *mulata*, it does not mean that I share the subject positions with those *mulatas*. However, a quick comment from a Cuban journalist—"*me imagino que eran mulatonas . . . así como tú*"/I imagine they were *mulatas* . . . like you[15]—elucidates how the visual and visceral of my body melds with a national discourse of a raced and gendered reality. His labor of imagining conjures and transforms my body into one of the women who might have danced in the *academias*. I doubt it is "me" whom he sees, but the ghosts of the *other* women—those who had to sustain long nights of dancing in hot rooms, wearing shoes that eventually became uncomfortable, smelling the sweat or alcoholic breath of their partners.

IMAGINING THE *ACADEMIAS DE BAILE*

Academias de baile began as *escuelitas* (little schools) in the nineteenth century. As stated in chapter 1, the *baile de cuna*, a possible precursor to the *academias de baile*, set up a situation where young Cuban Creole gentlemen would attend a dance held at a senior *mulata's* home in order to meet *mulatas de rumbo*, with whom they might later engage in cleverly orchestrated sexual liaisons. Cuban naturalist Felipe Poey attended one of these *bailes de cuna* and wrote, "[T]here, the girl gains something as she serves as the companion to the attendees which does not prevent her from maintaining her virtue."[16] Poey visited the *academia* inside the Escauriza Café located next to the Hotel Inglaterra. Today, the Café Louvre occupies that same space, and I often find myself sitting there, meeting friends or reading, when I am in Havana on a research trip (Figure 2.2).

By the 1920s, the *academias de baile* had become nocturnal spaces de rigeur in Havana. The following list provides the names of the *academias* that existed in a concentrated area of Havana, in addition to the cabarets, theatres, and other nightclubs. Not all of these *academias* existed at the same time, and many closed, reopened, switched owners, or suffered permanent damage due to fires. The photographs (Figures 2.3–2.15) provide a visual narrative of my afternoon searching for the locations of the *academias de baile*.

> Galatea (near Eden Concert cabaret)
> La Fantástica (for blacks only)
> Habana Sport (Galiano and San José streets)
> La Venecia
> El Polvorín
> Guirijay
> La Latina

Figure 2.2. Outside the Gran Café Louvre, Havana.

Marte y Belona (Amistad and Monte streets)
Rialto (Neptuno and Consulado streets, near a cinema of the same name)
Galeano y Barcelona (for blacks only)
Servelin o Encanto
La de Fernando Collazo
Sport Antillano (Zanja e/Gervasio and Belascoín streets)

Three *academias* figure significantly in Cuban popular music history: Marte y Belona, Habana Sport, and Sport Antillano. At these three *academias*,

Figure 2.3. The corner of Prado and Neptuno streets. The middle floor housed an *academia*.

Cuban groups such as Sexteto Boloña, Abelardo Barroso, La Orquesta Maravilla, and La Sonora Matencera played as part of the renaissance of Afro-*Cubanismo* and the development of *son* music.[17] Wages for the musicians averaged at about 1 peso 50 cents per musician at Marte y Belona (for La Sonora Matancera). The songs played had to be short. They did not contain a third or fourth verse, a long bridge, or even improvisational interludes. Brevity allowed for more music; more music allowed for more dancing. To dance with an *academia* dancer, a customer required a dance ticket. Since each song matched one dance ticket purchase, the shorter the song, the more songs could be played and the more dance tickets could be sold. For the owner of the *academia*, the financial objective rested on the quantity sold of dance tickets and the alcoholic beverages.

Often, *academias* remained purposely warm (even though there were ceiling fans, as one musician told me) so that the clientele would spend more money on drinks. One historian, Rosendo Rosell, claims that the *academias* increased the popularity of the *guayabera* with ribbons. Men no longer wore suit jackets, just a *guayabera* to fend off perspiration.[18]

Academias had similar spatial layouts: a large open space for dancing, floors of ceramic tile, and a stage to one side/corner for the musicians. Each *academia* sold tickets for 10 cents per dance. With each ticket, the

Figure 2.4. The building that used to house the Cine Rialto. Next door was an *academia* called Rialto.

ticketholder could dance one song with one of the women walking around vying for a dance partner. Some women would walk, others would sit, while others would remain by the bar. It was a choreography of variability, of chance. The location from where to begin varied, but once asked to dance, the aleatory game began. If her dance partner liked her enough to want to spend all of his tickets on her, then the woman avoided a night of repetitive back and forth: back to the bar, back to the seat, back against the wall. Some of the women at the *academias* had fifteen to twenty tickets from

Figure 2.5. The Eden Concert, one of the first cabaret spaces, used to be on this site but now, a hotel occupies this space. Farther down the street was Smokey Joe's Pub.

clients in a night.[19] At the end of the night, the women received remuneration according to how many tickets they possessed. They also received a percentage from the cost of the drinks their dance partners had consumed.

José Galiño explained how the wages were paid for every 10 cent ticket sold: the *academia* dancer would receive 1 cent, each musician received 2 cents per song, and the owner would keep 2 cents. In terms of wage equality, then, clearly the labor of the dancing female body was least valuable. Yet without her labor—waiting, smiling, dancing, seducing—the successful mode of production of the *academia* would

Figure 2.6. Galeano and San José streets, site of the Habana Sport *academia*.

have faced jeopardy. This does not negate the labor or talent of the musicians, nor the entrepreneurial prowess of the *academia* owner/manager. Yet, it's critical to note the importance of bodies here in materializing not only the production of the *academia* but also the *son* music—bodies playing the *clave*, the *bongo*, the *tres* guitar; bodies listening to those sounds; and bodies moving to the rhythms independently, or in partnership through the *son's* respective dance.

The *son* requires the conventional social-dance partnering of bodies, with the male's left hand clasping the female's right hand and his right hand around her waist. There's a slight weight shift at the knee to the syncopated beat of the *son*; you don't start on the 1 count, you begin on the 2. You step to the side and then alternate quickly between left and right feet, shifting weight ever so slightly and swaying the hips. The basic *son* step gets repeated: pause, left, right, left; pause, right, left, right. Movement analysis leads to other types of questions that may not have answers, given their corporeal nature: How close did she allow him to get? Did he have a pleasing smell, especially on hot evenings in August? Did she? Did the ceiling fans work properly? Where did the women go if they needed a break? What did they talk about? How much *meneo* (movement, from the word *menearse*—to move about, wriggle about) was necessary?

Figure 2.7. Habana Sport was on the second floor of this building, above a furniture store.

If the man found himself attracted to his dance partner, and if he wanted to have more intimate contact off the dance floor, he would have to request an arrangement called a "*sacarla particular.*"[20] This required paying an extra 2 pesos, either at the ticket desk, or to her mother or other chaperone, protector, or even a *chulo*/pimp. These intimate encounters after an evening of dancing invite the notion of prostitution to enter the history of the *academia*. Again, I consider all the different forms of labor these *academia* dancers did as within the same context. I am not interested in dismissing sexual labor as less valuable or moral than dancing. In this context, I would locate payment-for-sex

Figure 2.8. This building used house a *cabaretucho*, a second-rate cabaret called El Faraón. It is now a car repair shop. Above the entrances there are still details of the Pharaoh's profile.

Figure 2.9. Details of the exterior wall of where El Faraón used to be.

Figure 2.10. Advertisement for El Faraón, ca. 1935. Featured in Gold Levi and Heller's *Cuba Style: Graphics from the Golden Age of Design.*

as just another part of the *academia* dancer's job—something that not all the women participated in, but for some there were personal, economic, or other types of factors that determined this outcome.

Here, I echo Amalia Cabezas's work on sex tourism in Cuba and the Dominican Republic, where she elaborates on the term "tactical sex" as a way to understand the commodification of sexual relationships and how the women negotiated the murky terrain of desire, capital, and racialized eroticization.[21] Although she examines contemporary sex tourism, I suggest that given Cuba's history as a site of pleasure, the types of exchanges between racialized female bodies and heterosexual male ones have basic commonalities, regardless of the shift in historical moment. As this book argues, the

Figure 2.11. This is Zanja Street, between Gervasio and Belascoaìn streets. Sport Antillano may have been here. Across the street, the cafeteria Café Okey still exists. Arsenio Rodriguez (among other well-known musicians) went to eat there after his gigs.

Figure 2.12. The corner of Galeano and Barcelona streets. A "blacks only" *academia* was said to have existed here (either in the building on the left, or where there is now a park on the right).

Figure 2.13. Belascoaín and Tenerife streets (frente al Parque Albear, which is to the right of the photo).

desire for the *mulata* remains an economic constant in Cuba, and as such, it affects the different pleasurable modes of production that exist: *casas de cuna, academias de baile,* cabaret shows, brothels, and sex tourism. Because of this, I do not dismiss the *academias* as mere sites of debauchery. Instead, they were productive sites from which to examine how dance coupled with eroticized, racialized, and gendered labor enriches the national discourse of a country whose national myth is based on these specific bodies that danced. By the 1950s, the sheer quantity of nightclubs throughout Havana began to bring about the decline of the *academias* that remained in operation. Some oral history sources suggest that the nightclubs in Playa de Marianao did not have the same social stigma as the *academias,* thereby luring people away. Nevertheless, the Cuban Revolution ensured both the *academias* and Playa de Marianao's eventual demise.

FICTIONALIZING THE *ACADEMIAS DE BAILE*

Literary representations of the *academias* offer insight into the various forms of contacts and intimacies that occurred between the bodies. I engage in a symptomatic reading of these various texts in order to

Figure 2.14. The corner of Monte and Amistad streets, where Marte y Belona used to be. Now it is an outdoor snack area.

think of the *academia* as one rife with gendered, racialized, and sexualized exchanges. I begin with the following excerpt from Tomas Fernández Robaina's *Recuerdos Secretos de Dos Mujeres Públicas: Testimonio Literario* (Secret Memories of Two Public Women: A Literary Testimony), whose author spoke with some ex-*academia* dancers in order to write his tome. As he was a writer successfully working within the Cuban state apparatus, I wonder what type of fiction he created in his accounts and for what purpose. Does it fit into the circulating cultural imaginary that established a particular rhetoric of what these women and *academias* were like? Or, did he make a conscious choice to record his testimonies through the literary mode so as to protect Consuelo's reputation? Is his contribution a part of the nationalist agenda to revalidate the existing circulating discourses about these "fallen women?"[22]

Consuelo la Charmé (Charming Consolation, or Consuelo the Charming One) remembers working at an *academia de baile* and she shares some details of her life there:

> *Le hacían falta mujeres que supieran bailar bien, además de que se prestaran para otro menesteres. Pero yo le advertí que aunque puta, no entraba en ciertas componendas; lo que no hacía por placer, no lo podia hacer por dinero. Todavía estaba joven y era la*

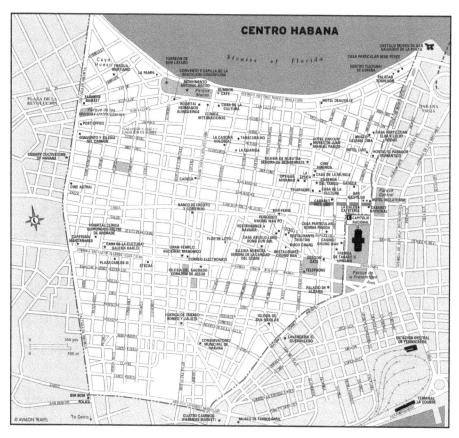

Figure 2.15. Map of central Havana. All the *academias* in central Havana were within walking distance of one another. Map from Avalon Travel.

Charmé en pleno; tal vez con el tiempo no me quedaría más remdio, pero ahora no. En la vida de la academia, las horas de trabajo eran muy movidas, no solo por el bailoteo. Una vez que entrábamos, no podíamos salir hasta determinada hora . . . aqui, cuando teníamos suerte para ganar más dinero teníamos que estar bailando y bebiendo durante toda la noche. Si conseguíamos algun cliente que prometía ser espléndido, no podíamos salir con él hasta que no termináramos el trabajo, o debíamos hablar con el dueño y tirarle algo, pues de lo contrario no podíamos hacerlo. Había mujeres que trabajaban allí solo bailado; no buscaban dinero extra por otra via, a pesar de que nos pagaban solo un medio [5 centavos] por pieza. Si uno era joven y bailaba bien, tenía asegurado, sin problemas, más de cinco pesos diarios; más de lo que podia ganarse en una colocación fregando o cocinando. No faltó alguna que no aguantara los asedios y cayera más tarde or más temprano en el negocio; otras, por el contrario, abandonaban la academia cuando comprendían lo que era en realidad aquello. Pero eran las menos.

Lo que más me molestaba, no era bailar, si no beber el trago preparado con menta y agua. . . . En las academias, cuando una comenzaba a perder sus encantos, tenía que largarse de allí. Muchas de las que engrosaban los balluses y de las que recorrían las calles, habían pasados largos años en las academias. Se habló mucho para que clausuraran la de Marte y Belona y la de Galiano [Habana Sport] que eran las mas famosas pero como estaban legalmente autorizadas y además, contribuían con cuantiosas sumas no legalizadas al buró, la secreta y la policia se mantuvieron por años. Una de ellas, la de Marte y Belona se tuvo que mudar cuando derrumbaron el edificio donde se encontraba; las otras siguieron hasta que el comandante mando a parar.[23]

They needed women who knew how to dance well in addition to being willing to engage in other occupations. I told him that just because I was a whore, I didn't just get involved in shady dealings; what I didn't do for pleasure, I couldn't do for money. I was still young and I was fully La Charmé; maybe later I wouldn't have a choice, but now, no. In the *academia*, working hours were very busy, and not just because of the dancing. Once we went into work, we couldn't leave until a designated time. Here, when we were lucky to make more money, we would have to dance and drink all night. If we met a client who promised to be generous, we couldn't leave with him until we finished our job, or we'd have to speak to the owner (of the *academia*) and promise him some extra cash; otherwise we couldn't leave. There were women who worked there just dancing; they didn't look for extra money doing other things, even though we received only 5 cents per dance. If you were young and danced well, you were assured, without any problems, more than 5 pesos a day—more than what you could make cooking or cleaning. Sooner or later, there wasn't a woman who could stand the pestering from the dance partners and would fall into "the business"; others would just abandon the *academia* when they understood what the reality was. But there weren't many of those. The thing that bothered me the most wasn't the dancing, it was having to drink this beverage made with mint and water. When you began to lose your enchantments (your looks), you had to leave. Many of the ones who were at whorehouses or worked the streets had spent many years at the *academias*. They talked about closing down Marte y Belona and the one on Galiano [Habana Sport], which were the most famous ones, but they were legally authorized and they contributed illegal sums of money to the police, *la secreta, el buró*, that they stayed around for years. One of them, Marte y Belona, had to move when they demolished the building; the other ones remained until the *Comandante* [Fidel Castro] arrived and ordered them to stop.

Consuelo admits she did not use the *academia* to gain additional income from sexual exchanges. For her, it was about the money she could earn dancing, although she admits to being a *"puta,"* or whore. She still maintained a certain level of autonomy as to with whom she chose to engage in transactional sexual relations. La Charmé makes clear the reliance on the aesthetic capital that these women had in order to procure clients, dances, dinners, evenings out, and most important, money. She articulates the power relations inherent in the *academia* with the owner of the *academia* possessing the authority to allow her to leave and/or make extra money (as long as he received some form of remuneration).

A type of hierarchy also existed in the kinds of jobs women could do and which ones were better paid. Jobs available to working-class women at that time revolved around domestic service, while dancing at an *academia* could generate more income. As a result, the *academia* became lucrative employment for working-class (*mulata*) women with a certain aesthetic appeal. *Academia* dancing promised income and, more important, the potential to move up the socioeconomic hierarchy if the woman met a man who was gainfully employed and that established the potential for long-term affective ties, ideally marriage.

In contrast to La Charmé's charming recollections, Enrique Serpa's unnamed narrator in his novel *Contrabando* provides a cynical, if not matter-of-a-fact, glimpse at Havana in the late 1920s and the height of the liquor trade between Cuba and the United States. Serpa's narrator suffers from bourgeois alienation (as it states in the introductory notes of the 1977 edition), and through his mostly interior monologues the reader experiences the activities of Havana nightlife. This novel takes place in 1927, a time in Havana's history when the city received the largest numbers of foreign visitors in the Caribbean, owing to the Prohibition laws in the United States.[24] In the following excerpts, Serpa's narrator visits a *cabaretucho* (second-rate cabaret) that receives a visit from a group of *academia* dancers.

> *Bruscamente irrumpieron en el salon, entre un escándalo de risa, diez o doce mujeres. Parecían albacoras regocijadas ante una indefensa mancha de sardinas. Todos los ojos se dirigieron a ellas, como la brújula hacía el Norte. Eran bailadoras de academias, que, al terminar su labor, acudían al cabaret en solicitud de compradores de placer. Vestían modestamente. En sus carnes marchitas, carnes de sufrimiento y de pecado, se reflejaban las malas noches, los días sin pan, las caricias a la fuerza, las entregas sin deseo, todas las miserias de la vida más sórdida y patética. Desgranaban mecánicamente sus carcajadas de alegría. Y entre sus labios de alquiler se emboscaba, perfumada y traidora, la avariosis. Ojearon el salon como cazadoras expertas. Luego se disgregaron, para situarse en lugares estratégicos. Una se dirigió a mi:*
>
> *"¿Me convidas, cielo?"...*

La muchacha pidió un ron con anis. La muchacha extrajo de su cartera una mota y un diminuto espejo. . . . Se volvió hacia mí, dándose toda en una sonrisa sucia de promesas. Luego, ladeándose, para que la luz cayese directamente en el espejo, se retocó la nariz y la frente. Por último, se humedeció los dedos en la lengua y se alisó las cejas.[25]

Ten or twelve women burst into the room with scandalous laughter. They were like happy albacores caught in a defenseless school of sardines. All eyes looked toward them, like a compass pointing north. They were *academia* dancers who, having finished their work, went to the cabaret looking for buyers of pleasure. They were dressed modestly. In their used-up flesh, flesh made up of sin and suffering, one could see bad nights, days without bread, forced caresses, acquiescence without desire, all of the most sordid and pathetic of life's miseries. They mechanically let out their guffaws of happiness. And in between their lips for hire, syphilis, perfumed and treacherous, waited in ambush. They looked around the room like expert hunters. Later they dispersed in order to situate themselves in strategic locations. One of them came toward me:

"Will you treat me to something, honey?"

The girl asked for rum with anise. From her purse she pulled out a stub of marihuana and a small mirror. She turned toward me, giving all of herself to me with a dirty smile of promises. Later, leaning over so that the light would fall directly into the mirror, she retouched her nose and forehead. Lastly, she moistened her fingers on her tongue and straightened out her eyebrows.

Serpa's narrator notices details about these women that align with Cuba's cultural imaginations about the public, available (*mulata*) woman. His is a discourse of contagion, hidden threats, and visceral distaste written in a descriptive prose that both sensualizes and sensationalizes the dichotomous allure and his rejection of these women. Not dissimilar from Céspedes accounts of prostitutes in Havana in the late nineteenth century, Serpa's descriptions become what Foucault might call "the making of the self through discourse."[26] Serpa's voluptuous prose evokes the look, sound, and movement of these women. Their modest dress does not belie the hips that he notices earlier on other women, similarly dressed, as they dance in the cabaret: *"las mujeres meneaban suavemente las caderas, subrayando con un movimiento de cintura ciertas excitaciones del bongo"*/the women wiggled their hips softly, underlining certain excitements of the *bongo* with a movement of the waist.[27]Their strategic placement around the salon space articulates how their bodies mapped out a stage for their femininized corporeality to attract attention, and by extension, money.

"Vamos a bailar, mi vida."

"Bueno" le respondí mientras me levantaba.

Unos estudiantes, de pelo reluciente y engomado, alborotaban alrededor de una mesa. Gozaban el placer que llevaban en si mismos como si lo hubiesen comprado en el cabaret. Debían ser muy jóvenes, y con su júbilo aspiraban a pescar la atención de las mujeres.

La muchacha se pegaba estrechamente a mi, entregándomelo todo. Sentía en mis muslos el fuerte contacto de los suyos. Para ofrecerse mejor inclinaba el busto hacia atrás, mirándome al través de sus párpados entornados y con un brillo lúbrico en el fondo de sus pupilas. Se brindaba en su actitud voluptuosa como en su valva una almeja. A veces se humedecía los labios con la punta de la lengua o hincaba en mis manos sus uñas afiladas. Un leve temblor le agitaba las aletas de la nariz. Y entonces arrimaba su cara a la mia, para excitarme con su aliento empapado de alcohol, cálido y sexual como la revuelta cama de una garçonnière.[28]

"Let's dance, darling."

"Alright," I responded as I arose.

Some students, with shiny and slicked-down hair, kicked up a racket around a table. Filled with pleasure, they enjoyed themselves, as if they had bought it at the cabaret. They had to have been very young, and in their joy they longed to attract the women's attention. The girl stuck closely to me, giving me everything. I felt the strong contact of her thighs on my own. In order to offer herself up better, she leaned her bosom backwards, looking at me through her half-closed eyelids and with a lewd shine in the back of her pupils. She offered herself through her voluptuous attitude, like a clam in her shell. Sometimes she would moisten her lips with the tip of her tongue, or she would sink her filed nails into my hands. A light tremor moved her nostrils. And then she moved her face closer to mine in order to excite me with her alcohol-drenched breath that was warm and sexual like the messy bed of a bachelor pad.

When one of the women makes the decision to move toward the narrator and "attract" him, I am drawn to her small gestures of femininity—quotidian movement phrases that serve different purposes, given the context and the audience. Here, the narrator is neither necessarily nor immediately attracted to the woman (he later admits to a specific type of disgust for her), but he is nevertheless focused enough on her body next to his to notice such gestural and aesthetic detail.

When she invites him to dance, Serpa's narrator provides further detail on her corporeality. Again, I realize these are literary imaginings, yet they offer insight into how Cuban female corporeality within these spaces was witnessed, imagined, and even constructed. It also reveals a world where libidinal exchange figured prominently in the social-dance interactions. Serpa's narrator later becomes annoyed with the music, the surroundings, and his dance partner. To her surprise, he stops in the middle of the song. He describes her looking at him with furrowed brows and a flash in her eyes: *"se colocó una mano en la cintura mientras sus ojos provocativos me recorrían de la cabeza a los pies y de los pies a la cabeza"*/she placed a hand on her waist while her provocative eyes looked at me from head to toe, from toe to head.[29]

Here, I want to highlight the gesture of the hand on the waist as another significant choreographic tactic. A slight weight shift into the hip where the hand lies is not impossible to more accurately demonstrate the surprise and affront she may have felt at his quick dismissal. I point this out to consider the possibility of how this variety of gestures suggests a gendered way of asserting agency in spaces where her body's value relied solely on her ability to attract clients and produce capital for the establishment.

At the *academia*, in a space where her body signified pleasure and the potential for sexual intimacy (at a price), this pause, this corporeal ellipsis, enables her to assert and exert her acceptance or refusal of a man. Admittedly, this is not a gesture specific to feminine *cubanía*.[30] However, within Cuban techniques of the body (that is, Cuban-ness as expressed through movement and gestural vocabularies exchanged and communicated from bodies to bodies), this gesture provides a glimpse into how bodies—marginalized, eroticized, racialized, and vilified—maintained dominion over themselves. Her pause and that askew stance allow her body to make tactical decisions. Should she wait for his mood to pass and see if he still wants to dance? Should she leave him and risk losing some money if no other man invites her to dance later that same evening? Is he trying to create trouble? Regardless of the speculative nature of these questions, her visible, active pose permits her body to respond to his sudden action.

Moments later, one *academia* dancer interrupts the couple on their way to sit down and shares the shocking gossip of another dancer's demise. I include it here to demonstrate how these spaces, even fictionalized, were sites of social intimacy among women. In between songs, during bathroom breaks, or while waiting for a client, they exchanged pleasantries, news, and warnings.[31] There always existed the danger of an abusive or jealous client. However, in the following exchange, it seems like the biggest threat was the disillusionment of a romance gone wrong, exposing the affective and economic desires of the *academia* dancers.

"Oye, tú, ¿te enteraste de lo de Anita?"

"Sí, me lo dijeron en la academia, ¡la pobre!" . . .

"Sí, tenía que ser, chica! Se lo buscó ella misma, porque yo bien que se lo advertí ¡como que no era ninguna ciencia saberlo! Cuando se quiso con ese hombre, se lo dije, pero no me quiso hacer caso y ahi tienes las consecuencias. Es un conductor de guagua, ¡dime tú!, ¿con qué iba a mantenerla?, y de contra, no quería vivir con la madre de Anita. La academia, con lo mala que está, no podia dar para dos cuartos, y él creo que no se ocupaba mucho de buscar dinero; es un chulito de esos que te cogen lo que pueden. Anita dejó de pagar el cuarto de su madre y acabaron por deshauciarla. Mañana creo que le ponían los trastes en la calle y Anita no pudo conseguir con qué mudarla. Y entonces parece que desesperada se tiró de la azotea a la calle. Dicen que cuando llegó a Emergencia ya estaba muerta. Si me hubiera hecho caso ahora estaría buena y sana. Pero lo que más lástima da es que nada más que tenía diecisiete años, una chiquilla, como quien dice. Cuando salga de aqui me voy al velorio; si quieres, te espero."

"No, no me esperes; no sé si pueda ir. Estoy con este amigo."[32]

"Hey, you, did you hear about Anita?"

"Yes, they told me at the *academia*, poor girl!"

"It had to happen, girl! She brought it upon herself because I told her it wasn't hard to figure out! When she wanted to be with that man, I told her, but she didn't pay attention to me and now there you have the consequences. He's a bus driver. You tell me how he was going to support her? And, he didn't even want to live with Anita's mother. The *academia* can't provide enough money for a two-room apartment, and I don't think he tried too hard to look for money; he's a freeloader, the ones that take from you what they can. Anita stopped paying her mother's rental room and they wound up evicting her. I think tomorrow they were going to put all of her belongings out on the street and Anita couldn't find anyone to help move her out. And then it seems like in her hopelessness she threw herself off the roof onto the street. They say that when she arrived at Emergency she was already dead. If she had listened to me she'd be fine and healthy now. The saddest part is that she was only seventeen, a little thing, like they say. When I get out of here, I am going to the wake, if you want, I can wait for you."

"No, don't wait for me; I don't know if I can go. I am with this friend."

Anita's suicide and its retelling situates the *academias* as more than just places of pleasure. Anita's desire to leave and have a man take care of her was not an uncommon desire *academia* dancers had, as this was expressed to me in numerous occasions during my conversations with Cubans. The importance of the mother and the responsibility to support her bears mentioning, as it connects this story to a larger one revolving around the matrifocal family. Like the relationship between mothers and daughters at the *bailes de cuna* or quadroon balls, where *mulata* daughters were expected to provide economic security for their families, Anita's employment at the *academia* operates within the same register. The underlying tragedy in Anita's story—a story that also may not have been that uncommon—is its hopelessness. As a result, Anita surfaces as a "tragic *mulata*," the fallen woman of the *academia*, although there are no specific references to her racialized body in this account.

Despite the gravity of the story, the *rubia oxigenada*/dyed blonde changes the subject and continues to gossip about other hearsay going on in the *academia*. Meanwhile, her friend stresses having to attend to the narrator alluding to the possibility of future financial remuneration. In this exchange, affective ties between the women become secondary to personal economic necessity. A silent understanding exists between them, one that only surfaces as a topic of conversation, or gossip, when success or tragedy befalls them. Their main objective remains financial.

These literary accounts contrast with the oral accounts of the male musicians whose voices are lodged inside scholarship about said *academias*.[33] Ethnomusicologists focus on the music inside the *academias*, glossing over the machinations and exchanges between the women and men who danced there. Those accounts tend to privilege the male musician's point of view. The mention of *academia* dancers leads to their interpellation as prostitutes; background, necessary, yet marginal labor as opposed to the real and "valuable" labor of the musicians inside the *academia*. If sexual relationships occurred as a result of dancing, it becomes crucial to investigate the negotiations involved.

By approximating the voices and experiences of these women who actually worked and danced in the *academias*, a more complex interpretation of these embodied pedagogical and sexual exchanges emerges. The following section provides separate accounts of *academias de baile*: from men who frequented them as working musicians or as social dancers. In doing so, I hope to provide a richer portrait of these disappeared sites by focusing on the memories, visual or embodied, of those who were actually there.

REMEMBERING THE *ACADEMIAS DE BAILE*: THE MUSICIANS

Alfonsín Quintana is a polite octogenarian with a bright smile. He seemed eager to speak with me, so we met in a private office at the Union Nacional de Escritores y Artistas de Cuba/National Union of Cuban Writers and Artists (UNEAC) in Havana one January morning. Quintana's career as a singer began in 1938, when he received an invitation to join Los Jóvenes del Cayo.[34] As I began my interview with him, he instead asked me the first question: *"¿Qué es lo que te han dicho de las academias de baile?"*/What have they told you about the *academias*? He seemed a bit cautious. I said that my intention in writing about the *academias* was to learn what it was like to be there, especially for the women. We chatted briefly about the social stigma attached to the women and the *academias,* and he made a point of explaining his presence at Marte y Belona by stating that he decided to perform there as a favor to his godmother (Figure 2.16).

As a white Cuban, perhaps claiming a familial duty justified his presence at a predominantly working-class black and *mulatto* club. His recollections shed some light on the types of exchanges that occurred inside the *academias,* in addition to reflecting his views on class, race, and gender relationships. I have chosen not to quote him verbatim; when I insert a transcription of our conversation in Spanish, it is to highlight strategically Quintana's feelings or thoughts, although I am attendant to the limits that language presents in this act of translation. In so doing, though, I am following Alessandro Portelli's claims when he clarifies that what makes oral

Figure 2.16. Poster from Marte y Belona.
Screen capture from Galiño and Prieto, *Daniel Santos,* documentary film.

history different is that it tells us less about *events* and more about their *meanings*. That is, what comes out of the oral history is the subjectivity of the speaker.[35] However, Quintana's subjectivity remains translated through my experience of sitting and watching him speak, of recording his words, and of thinking about what his words mean. (As an interviewer, I prefer listening to the silences and wondering why some words never come up for air. I am vigilant about the discursive formations and power relations I necessarily invoke as author, writer, and feminist dance scholar.)

In the mid-1940s, the owner of the *academia* (*le decían Pepé*/they called him Pepé) was the *compadre*/godfather/friend of Quintana's godmother. Marte y Belona was under threat of closure, so Pepé asked Quintana's godmother if she could persuade Quintana to perform there. It was not the most ideal financial situation, says Quintana, because the musicians would only receive 2.50 per person, but he agreed as a favor to his godmother.

Quintana informed me that *academias* usually hired two orchestras to play daily, and that the songs were between four to five minutes long—almost twice as long as the length Galiño had claimed. Although he was a featured performer with Los Jóvenes del Cayo for two years at Marte y Belona, Quintana remembered going there once a week because, at that time, he had seven live programs to record.[36] He even enlisted the help of well-known Puerto Rican crooner Daniel Santos, and brought him to sing several times at Marte y Belona. The women, he recalled, were in their thirties (*treintonas*, he said) and had difficult economic situations. The men who would buy tickets to dance with the *academia* dancers were in their forties or fifties. He said that men would pay 15 cents per ticket to dance with a woman of their choice. She focused her attention on getting her dance partner to buy drinks. "*Dame una gaseosa, un vermouth, o un anis*"/I'd like a soda, a vermouth, or an anise. Quintana stated that the *academia* dancers developed a tactic for ordering at the bar. Although she would ask for an anise or a vermouth in front of her dance partner, the bartender understood "vermouth" as code for soda and "anise" as signifying soda water. Her main objective was to get a percentage of the drinks tab from her dance partner and to acquire as many tickets as possible.

According to Quintana, 10 cents of a 15 cent ticket belonged to the *academia*, while 5 cents went to the *academia* dancer. He stressed that the bar offered the highest potential for income, not the dancing. By the way, *academias* did not serve food. The women did not want to dirty their mouths (mess up their lipstick). Neither did the men. If a man misbehaved and became drunk or aggressive, he was escorted out the door. Quintana remembered foreign men at the *academia* who eagerly paid the 20 cent entrance fee. If one of them sought the private company of an academia dancer, she couldn't leave before 12:30 A.M.

Yo no le puedo decir, ni siquiera me atrevo a cometer la indelicadeza de que ellas las invitaban a salir. Yo no las vigilaba, ni sabía que hacian ni con quien ni donde . . . pero sí me daba lástima. Madres que ya eran 50tonas que no tenían la facilidad y llevaban a sus hijas jovenes. Las muchachas lo que hacían era mejorar su situaciones económicas.

I cannot tell you, nor do I dare commit the indelicacy of saying that these women were asked out. I did not keep a close eye on them, and I did not know what they did or with whom . . . but I did feel sorry for them. Mothers in their fifties who no longer had the economic facility would bring their young daughters and the girls would just be trying to improve their financial situations.

Quintana adopted a measured approach in speaking about the *academia* dancers. He seems reluctant to make any type of moral judgment about the women. *"Yo quiero ser respetuoso con las damas"*/I want to be respectful with the ladies, he asserts, because this topic requires "delicate treatment" (*trátarlo con delicadeza*/treat with delicacy).

A man known as *el ponchador* would walk around the dance floor. This man approached the dancing couple, and punched the ticket the *academia* dancer held in one of her hands. At the end of the night, she returned these tickets (with holes punched in them) to the owner as evidence of her work. Her payment depended on the number of holes punched in the ticket. When Quintana spoke about the *ponchador*, he arose from his seat to show how the woman would stand to pass the ticket to the *ponchador.* It was usually handed over behind her partner's back, with a lazy wave of her hand that rested on his arm or behind his shoulder. Quintana saw me filming him as he demonstrated the ticket to *ponchador* exchange, and he became self-conscious. He teased me about being sneaky. He even asked that I eventually give him a copy of my book, because he wanted to read how I would portray him.

He reiterated that he helped "raise the profile" of the *academia* by bringing clients who wanted to hear and dance to the new songs by Los Jóvenes del Cayo or see one of their featured musicians. *Son, guaracha, pasodoble, danzón,* and *bolero* music permeated Marte y Belona, and as bodies danced to these Cuban national rhythms, they had to maintain a certain distance: *ahi no se permitía las parejas pegadas, besarlas, las caras pegadas*/close partnering, kissing, or face-to-face contact was not permitted. Drawn-out contact by the couples occurred in the act of agreeing to dance another song together. Because of the relative brevity of the songs (in order to sell more tickets), men had the opportunity to dance more than once with a specific *academia* dancer. If the dancing couples applauded, the orchestra would repeat the song. Quintana remembered that part as arduous and tiring.

Of the affective relationships possible at the *academia*, Quintana claimed that the musicians were not allowed to have any romantic interests in the *academia* dancers, though the women would immediately fall in love with the musicians: *"A los músicos nos prohibían tener un interés con ellas . . . porque ellas se enamoraban inmediatamente de nosotros."* He qualified such reasoning by claiming that it caused problems if a musician saw another man getting too close to his girlfriend/*academia* dancer. He did remember romantic relationships occurring there, though, because he saw men bringing gifts to a favorite *academia* dancer. I asked him if he could recall what any of these women looked like, or more specifically, to share some of the memories or impressions these women's appearances had on him.

"Eran muy pintorreateaba, muy ajustadita, vaya marcando sus cuerpos"/They were very made up, very cinched-in, you know, showing off their figures. He said that most of them were *mulaticas claritas* (very light *mulatas*) and that there were no black women: *"de color no."* Quintana made the Cuban gesture for "black" by rubbing a finger along his forearm. He looked around, as if to make sure no one saw. He also lowered his voice. Simón, a staff member at UNEAC, had let us into the office where we had been speaking; he happened to be *"de color,"* and perhaps Quintana wished to avoid a potential offense, should Simon have walked by or overheard our conversation.

Quintana proceeded to tell me about the different race societies that existed in pre-Revolutionary Cuba: *sociedades de color, sociedades de blancos,* and social dances in the countryside where a rope divided the dance floor, with whites and blacks dancing on their respective sides. He concluded that *"tan bueno un negro como un blanco . . . la calidad de la persona es lo que vale"*/a black person is as good as a white person. . . . It's the quality of the person that matters," as a way to perhaps change the tone of the conversation from pre-Revolutionary Cuban racism to consideration of inherent value regardless of race. Institutional critique did not figure into the conversation; instead, a universal assumption of equality in Cuba, regardless of the legacy of segregation and racism, collapsed the tensions and negotiations inherent in the libidinal economy of the *academia de bailes,* where class, gender, and race played significant roles.

Toward the end of our conversation, Quintana became reflective, concluding that he held the highest respect for Marte y Belona. Referring to the *academia* dancers, he said *"hoy en día esas muchachas hay que darles un premio porque son más recatadas que las de hoy . . . eran más respetuosas en el vestuario"*/today we should reward these women because they were more demure than the ones today. . . . They were more respectful in their dress. In other words, even if clandestine sexual activity occurred, discretion in one's appearance foregrounded a politics of bourgeois respectability. I read this comment as veiled criticism of contemporary Cuban women's preference for shape-displaying and body-baring clothing, particularly as part of the sex-tourism economy and aesthetic. A racialized component lies here as well, given that the *jinetera* culture features many darker skinned *cubanas* who make particular aesthetic choices in order to attract foreign capital or men. Quintana demonstrated how his taste lies within a particular historical and ideological moment in Cuba.

I close this section about Marte y Belona with a simple description of the *academia* that bore witness to the *mulatica clarita* bodies who danced, sweated, and stood inside its walls. To visit Marte y Belona, they had to climb a flight of stairs to the second floor. It was a big space, above a bar and sandwich shop that operated until late, but many of them couldn't take a break for food until their shift was over. They stood and danced all night on colorful ceramic tile floors. The ceiling fans helped them endure the moist sweat trickling down their backs and distracted them from their grumbling stomachs after a long night of dancing. *I will eat a ham sandwich later*, she thought.

REMEMBERING THE *ACADEMIAS*: THE MALE SOCIAL DANCER

Lázaro Montero Fragoso's perspective differs from Quintana's. Montero was a social dancer going from nightclub to nightclub in the 1940s and '50s. In his eighties, he still dances and performs, organizing a weekly jazz *peña* in central Havana. He belongs to the group Agrupación Los Bailadores de Jazz de Santa Amalia. Although I met with Quintana, Montero and I only spoke over the phone. He was unable to meet with me because his brother had been hospitalized and had no one else to care for him. Unlike Quintana, who seemed rather hesitant to begin sharing information, Montero immediately launched into his recollections. He confirmed the popularity of Marte y Belona as the most widely known *academia*. He kept referring to another *academia* on the corner of Galeano and Aguila streets, and then later he said it was on the corner of Reina and Aguila. His memory for location might not have been that specific, but as we spoke his sensorial memories provided other details that made the act of remembering for him (and for me, as the listener) a corporeal one set within a specific economy: transactional, libidinal, sensorial. He remembered the food stalls in the neighborhoods of the *academias*, and the varieties of food available: Chinese, pizza, sandwiches. He remembered the costs from *aquella época*/that time, and the affordability of a night out compared to the many cost-prohibitive options in a contemporary Cuba. I noted how he often repeated food items, and I wondered how much variety he experienced in his daily meals, given its limited access, and if his desire for variety informed what he remembered.

His visits to the *academias* began because of an American woman he accompanied there. He says they went more than three times, and each time they went, they (meaning she) would purchase a large quantity of tickets, but instead of dancing with other people, they would just dance with one another. When he did not go with this American woman, he admitted that he also went alone to the *academias* and/or Marianao after the dances at La Tropical or other clubs in el Vedado, a middle- to upper-class neighborhood in Havana. For Montero, the main motivation for frequenting the *academias* (and the nightclubs in Playa de Marianao) was dancing. As a professional social dancer, Montero followed the exceptional musicians and orchestras that played all over Havana. He could not enter certain clubs—specifically, the Sans Souci or the Montmartre—because he was black, but he gave me the impression that this institutional segregation had minimal effect on his ability to enjoy a satisfying nightlife.

Of the cabarets, nightclubs, and *academias* he visited, Montero named the following most frequently: El Pennsylvania, El Pompilio, and Marte y Belona. Generally, he addressed these spaces as ones on the periphery, geographically and socioeconomically: "*aquello era un cabaret marginal*." Pompilio emerged as the popular one owing to the notoriety of El Chori, the famous percussionist who often played there. Montero also made references to class and to the performance of a type of Cuban bourgeois respectability of which he and his friends engaged in:

> Nosotros formábamos parte de una falsa burgesía porque mis padrinos eran burgueses pero yo no, [aunque] yo me crié con ellos. Me enseñaron a estudiar, a vestirme, a ir a los buenos lugares, pero yo, yo nací en un solar y mi familia vivíamos en un solar que todavía existe (he was born en el barrio Colón, the neighbourhood known as the center of prostitution). Mi papá era sastre . . . en aquella época uno se vestía.

> We belonged to a false bourgeoisie because my godparents were bourgeois but I wasn't, even though I was raised by them. They taught me how to study, dress, and go to nice places, but I was born in a *solar* and my family lived in a *solar* that still exists. My father was a tailor . . . at that time, one dressed well.

Montero voices an understanding of a bourgeois respectability necessary for black Cubans at that time so that they could be allowed into certain cabarets—not the exclusive ones like Montmartre or Sans Souci, but to the *cabaretuchos* in Marianao that catered to a more racially and class-diverse crowd. His black working-class background provides a contrast to

Quintana's experience at the *academias*. Whereas Quintana seemed cautious about tying himself too much to these marginalized spaces, Montero spoke candidly, even stating that he had no reason to lie or hide anything. Perhaps his candor came from the fact that we spoke over the phone, which provided physical anonymity (yet I admit that this comes from my methodological preference to consider silences and absences on a par with statements and admissions). He mentioned twice that his wife was in the room with him as he spoke. At one point, when we discussed the transactional sexual economy occurring at the nightclubs and *academias,* he concluded with some generalized commentary: *"Yo no puedo decir más porque mi mujer me está oyendo lo que estoy diciendo. Yo no tengo nada que ocultar"* [and he laughs]/I can't say more because my wife is listening to what I am saying. . . . I have nothing to hide from her.

I want to situate this performance of respectability and silencing of a discussion about sexual exchange within the greater discourse of silence surrounding the *academias*. Silence permeates this chapter, or at least the remnants or hauntings of that silence and its ramifications on history. Still, bodies wriggle inside the silence: the *mulata* social dancers at the *academias* who were not singularly social dancers, but were sex workers who could dance; the social dancer who says he went to dance, but could have engaged in recreational sexual activity; the American tourists who went to listen to music and dance, but also did other things. Those same bodies wriggle in these spaces of pleasure, darkness, and desire; these spaces of late-night dancing and dalliances; these significant spaces that attest to embodied histories.

When I asked Montero to share his impressions of the *academias,* he focused on the different bodies present. His recollections consisted of character types not dissimilar from Cuban *teatro bufo* history: the *chulo*/pimp, *la camarera*/the waitress, *las que bailaban allí*/the women who danced there, *el protector*/the protector, *el turista*/the tourist, the American, *la negra*/the black woman, *la mulata*/the mulata. I asked about the women at the *academias,* particularly wondering if the rumor about the *mulata* and her "starring role" in nightlife culture had some truth to it.

> *Tengo que decirte sí, el por qué. No quiero decirte que no hubiera negras porque la negra ha tenido siempre tanta figura como la mulata. La mulata es la de la propaganda. Porque la mulata siempre por su color . . . y si tiene buena figura y es fundilluda . . . así habian negras— "negras de salir" con buen cuerpo . . . como pudiera decirle . . . tenían más experiencia. La mulata conseguia por su sandungeria, ella estaba graciosa, bonita pero sabia como conquistar al individuo. Todo el que iba ahi iba en función de mirar ese espectáculo como por la calle. . . . La mulata es un problema de fama pero es real que era así.*

I have to say yes, and tell you why. I don't mean to say that there weren't any black women there, because the black woman has always had a figure like the *mulata*. The *mulata* is the advertisement. The *mulata* because of her color, and if she had a nice figure with a big bottom [Spanish colloquial expression used], there were black women like that too, "presentable black women" with nice figures who had more experience. The *mulata* acquired [attention, men, money in the context of the *academia*] because of her allure; she was graceful, pretty, and knew how to conquer the individual. Everyone went [to the *academias*] to see that spectacle, just like in the street. The *mulata* problem is one of fame, but *it's true it was like that* [my emphasis].

Later, I asked about their dance experience. In other words, how did the women in the *academias* dance? Again, I understand the broad nature of this question, but my rationale stems from how witnesses perceived these bodies and what type of embodied description (if at all) they could provide. In this sense, I was searching for the way in which visual memory translates into an embodiment of the subject.

> *La persona que iba a trabajar en estos lugares tenía que bailar. Esas mujeres antes que supieran bailar, lo que hacían era **menearse** [vocal emphasis on this word and he said it very slowly]. Vaya, eso era su trabajo. . . . Eso era el elemento que ellas utilizaban para conquistar al individuo o bien para que aquél le pagara todo lo que ella quisiera. Era el meneo ese. Y ahí no se las cogían por la cintura si no por las nalgas. . . . Así era. Uno se restregaba con la muchacha.*

The person [woman] who went to work at these places had to dance. Those women before even knowing how to dance, what they did was wiggle. That was their job . . . that was the element they used to conquer the individual or for him to pay for what she wanted. It was that wiggle. And there, you didn't hold them [for dancing] by the waist, but by their buttocks. That's how it was. You rubbed up against the girl.

I want to point out three things in these statements by Montero: first, his assertion of a truth; second, the association of the black and *mulata* women with their bodies; and third, the use of the word *menearse*/to wiggle as the corporeal habitus of these women. As already established in this book, the relationship between the Cuban *mulata* and her body is a historically constructed one. Although Montero reinforced the circulating ideologies of the *mulata* and her body's ability to captivate as a spectacle, I consider his observations part of the ways in which the witnessing of the *mulata's* racialized and gendered choreographies sets up an embodied "truth" in the effects of the witnessing. In other words, the experience of that spectacle, regardless of its relationship to an overdetermined corporeality, provides some value to the corporeality in and of itself. Even if the *meneo*/the wiggle involved a poor, lazy, or half-hearted attempt in its execution, its partnership with the *mulata* body lends a kind of power in the libidinal economy, for her power remained limited elsewhere.

The problem here is the lack of individual recognition for these women as subjects, as working women, as women with nuanced daily lives. They merely occupy his memory as a racialized group who served as a spectacle in a given time and place. Indeed, the *mulata* problem is one of fame, as Montero commented, and part of that fame does emerge from her choreographed tactics of a racialized sensuality. But, if this hip(g)nosis is a tactic to attain value and a certain type of positionality within the landscape of the Cuban cultural imaginary, how might a *mulata* subvert or at least move through that landscape to find opportunities to maintain a certain sense of value as a woman, a citizen, a cultural worker? Who can ever take back the dances she has already danced?

REMEMBERING THE ACADEMIAS, OR *YA LO BAILA'O, ¿QUIÉN TE LO QUITA?*

(Who can take back what you've already danced?)

I conclude with the published and mediated memories of Carmen Curbelo, a *mulata rumbera* from the 1920s who worked at the *academias* in the 1930s and '40s (Figure 2.17). These memories come from an article that Leonardo Padura Fuentes wrote for *Juventud Rebelde*, a weekly newspaper published in Cuba. The piece reads like the transcript of an interview, but his voice as interviewer is not forcibly present. Instead, Carmen talks here considerably. However, as this is a publication within the ideological apparatus of the Cuban state, the construction of the narrative may adhere to the circulating notions of this type of *mulata* as *public* woman. But within this context, her memories still matter, and I will extract some meaning from what she does and does not say. Five subheadings structure the article: "The Artform," "Destiny," "La Playa," "The Trips," and "Nostalgia." In each section, Curbelo shares her memories from that particular period of her life. Her words feature here as much as possible.

A brief aside: Although oral history and its transcription misses the nuances of spoken language (its rhythm, elocution, speed), I foreground the life of this Cuban *mulata* who learned how to dance and engage in hip(g) nosis to make a living. I am attendant to the multiple layers of translation

Figure 2.17. Pictures of Curbelo in her eighties (left) at the time of the interview with Padura, and during her performer days (middle and right). Courtesy of *Juventud Rebelde*.

in my presentation of Curbelo's life, so I do not treat them as static memories, documents, and words. Instead, I emphasize the difficulty in retracing and recovering the everyday embodied histories of black and brown bodies. Thus, recording their words and memories through my use of language will always regrettably fall short. This wavering of confidence feels like a sickness, not unlike Derrida's archive fever, in that the archiving and recording process sets up the power and authority of the state.

By no means am I in the service of the Cuban state, but in my attempt to position these embodied histories as archives I find myself complicit in the ideological establishment of state archives. As historian Carolyn Steedman comments about the archive, "there is the feverish desire—a kind of sickness unto death—that Derrida indicated *for* the archive: the fever not so much to enter it and use it as to *have* it."[37] But, what does its possession set up? What is at stake in this process of setting up an archive based on memories, embodied and sensorial, incomplete yet temporal?

A proposition I put forward here involves the affective and intellectual labor of memory in the construction of a national history. It's not a new proposition, but within this context of a Cuban nightlife, I am interested in how this construction can help us understand how Cuban *mulata* subjects set up their relationship to the state and established its reliance on their choreographies of race, gender, and sexuality for meaning.

In Curbelo's interview, economic necessity and the financial possibilities that dance as a profession could offer emerge as the main themes. She speaks to the physical challenges that dancing presented, admitting that there were times when she would be done with work and would find herself "*hecha leña,*" a Cuban colloquialism that means to be exhausted.

> *El problema es que cuando son las cuatro de la mañana, o las cinco, y una está hecha leña después de haber bailado no sé cuantas congas, sones, danzones, pasodobles y rumbas y saca la cuenta y ve que no ganó ni pa'l chicle, entonces te entran ganas de llorar y tienes que tomarte un ronazo fuerte, reírte y mirarle la cara a la vida. Y decir: "Carmita, špa'lante!"*

> The problem is that when it's 4 or 5 A.M. and you are exhausted after having danced who knows how many *congas, sones, danzones, pasodobles*, and *rumbas*, and you take inventory and see that you haven't earned enough even for a stick of gum, you feel like crying and you have to drink a big strong rum, laugh and look at life in the face and say, "Carmita, keep on going!"

Although Carmen enjoyed dancing, she articulates the difficulty of dancing as a profession. Later in the interview, she admits that she did not learn how to dance until she arrived in Havana at the age of twenty. She was born in 1909 in Cienfuegos, the eighth of twenty children, and she left home in 1929, leaving behind two daughters: *"Yo ni siquiera soñaba que alguna vez iba a ser artista pero bien dice el refrán que la necesidad hace parir mulatos"/* I didn't even dream that one day I would be an artist but as the saying goes, necessity makes you give birth to *mulatos*.

Once in Havana, she discovered musicians from her hometown living at Amistad 17 (her memory is so good in this interview that she remembers addresses and streetcorners, even when the places no longer exist). They used to work at a cabaret called Mi Surco, which was by San José and Lealtad. She became a housekeeper for these musicians—cooking, cleaning, and laundering. One day, a woman from Pinar del Rio, La Piñareña, visited them. Curbelo couldn't remember her name, but this woman told her where she could go to earn more money. She took Carmen to the *academia de baile* located by Zanja and Galeano streets, where the owner immediately hired her. *"Pero había un solo problema: yo no sabía bailar"/*But there was only one problem: I did not know how to dance. The owner's choice to offer her a position evidences how the mythology of the *mulata* informed his decision. Here, her appearance labored for her and promised that she could not only dance but also attract attention that would translate into capital. As a *mulata*, Curbelo guaranteed a good business investment.

> *El caso es que como yo era joven y, sin vanagloriarme, linda de verdad—fíjate que me pusieron El Pollo—los hombres que iban a la academia sacaban tickets para bailar conmigo y me decían que no me preocupara, ellos me enseñaban a bailar. Así empecé a cogerle el golpe al danzón, el son, al pasodoble, y lo hice más rápido de lo que nadie se puede imaginar. Nada, tenía facilidad para el baile y al poco tiempo era yo la que daba lecciones.*

> The case was that because I was young, and without boasting, really pretty—they used to call me El Pollo (The Beautiful "Chick")—the men who went to the *academia* would buy tickets to dance with me and would tell me not to worry, that they would teach me how to dance. That is how I began to pick up the *danzón*, the *son*, the *pasodoble,* and I did it so fast that no one could even believe it. I had a facility for dance, and in a short time I was the one who was giving lessons.

In a history of the *son*, Adriana Orejuela Martínez writes that at the *academias*, "gentlemen indulged in the pleasure of dancing with true 'experts' in dancing material."[38] An interesting contradiction occurs here, as Carmen admitted to lacking dancing skill once she began working there. Her case may be an isolated one, but given the information gathered in this chapter,

I suspect that there were other women who—out of necessity, because of their aesthetic appeal, or through a social connection—procured work at *academias* without necessarily knowing *how* to dance. Their corporeality labored for them, even before they engaged in the labor of partner dancing every night. Orejuela Martínez's quotes around the word *expert* alludes to how the narrative of these *academias* was couched in bourgeois morality. Her statement could be read as ironic, with the real expertise of these women laying elsewhere, or if social dance could really produce experts at all.

Academias did not provide job security. Sometimes, the owner would have an altercation with the police or the government, and the *academia* would be forced to close. Musicians and dancers would then have to find another *academia* that would take them, hoping that this new one would not encounter the same fate. After working for about a year at the one by Zanja and Galeano streets, Curbelo had to look for a new job once it closed:

> *Yo tenía mis contactos en La Habana y me dijeron que en la valla de gallos de Marianao había otra academia que necesitaba muchachas. Allá me fui, me contraté y quiso la suerte que esa academia también la cerraran, después de una bronca que hubo en la que mataron a un hombre. Y otra vez yo en el aire y caminando y caminando fui a caer en la Playa de Marianao.... Eso fue en el año 30. Y estuve bailando allí hasta 1943. Una vida.*

> I already had my contacts in Havana and they told me that *(en la valla de gallos)* in Marianao there was another *academia* that needed girls. I went there, they hired me, and as luck would have it, that *academia* closed down as well after a fight in which a man was killed. Again, I was aimless, walking and walking, and I landed in Playa de Marianao. That was 1930. I danced there until 1943. A life.

Playa de Marianao became a hub for social music and dance activity. During the 1930s, Marianao began its rise in popularity, and many bars/clubs opened: El Pompilo, Los Tres Hermanos, El Paraíso, El Pennsylvania, El Rumba Palace. Curbelo mentions that many Americans visited these places, so full of multiple diversions. Curbelo, like Montero, states that the main attraction at Playa was El Chori (Silvano Shueg Hechevarría). He was a virtuosic musician and percussionist with legendary and unmatched skills.[39] Like Curbelo, he debuted at an *academia de baile* (his was the famous Marte y Belona), and it was El Chori who invited Curbelo to dance at Los Tres Hermanos (a club frequented often by Montero as well). By this time, Curbelo danced as a featured performer. With a Puerto Rican partner by the name of Luis Correa (who, according to her, was ugly, very short, had no teeth, but knew how to dance), they choreographed a *rumba* called *"el baile de la mula,*" during which she imitated a mountain mule while he attempted to grab her foot and place horseshoe on it. Audiences enjoyed the choreography because Curbelo remembers receiving copious applause. One can only wonder how she danced—what her body did and how she moved it—to receive the accolades she vividly remembers. Curbelo's skill as both dancer and choreographer directly links to her appearance and her engaging performance of hip(g)nosis. She admits to her lack of dance training, but as her dance career continued and the popularity of Cuban music and dance grew, Curbelo capitalized on how her appearance coupled with her developing dance training worked together to hip-notize audiences enough for the applause.

She stressed the importance of applause because without it, there were no tips. Her salary depended solely on tips and a percentage of the cost of drinks that she would entice the clientele into buying. A 1 peso tip would be split as follows: 25 cents for her, 25 cents for her partner, and 50 cents for the musicians. Furthermore, in order to have the right to dance, the union required a 1 peso contribution.

Occasionally, Curbelo and Correa danced at the Montmartre and the Sans Souci, where they were paid 5 pesos per show. While these places could feature black and *mulata* entertainers, black customers like Montero were not allowed. The salary disparities suggest the different economies operating in Cuban entertainment venues. Even though an evening of work for her would begin at 9 P.M. and not end until the last client left (often around 3 or 4 A.M.), she remembers enjoying herself immensely and taking small breaks when the night was slow: going out by the kiosks set up along the streets that sold different kinds of fried finger foods, dancing for pleasure, conversing, and waiting to hear the echo of El Chori's *timbales* to tell her she needed to get back to work.

Curbelo's career trajectory demonstrates the ability that (*mulata*) women who worked at the *academias* could have, especially if they became skilled dancers. Not only did she perform on the cabaret stages of the Montmartre, Sans Souci, and Teatro Nacional, but she also traveled to Chicago, Dallas, New York, and Hollywood. In Chicago, she was one of the dancers that accompanied the Septeto Nacional and the Septeto Montmartre when they performed at the 1933 Chicago World's Fair:

> Pero esa gira fue una pesadilla. Yo, casi acabada de llegar, resbalé, me caí y estuve ingresada una pila de días. Y de contra se sonó un frío en ese Chicago que para salir a bailar vestida de rumbera había que sonarse antes un par de tragos. Pero como todavía estaba el lío de la Ley Seca, lo único que se conseguía era un preparado que vendían los puertorriqueños y que nosotros le pusimos "arráncame la vida." Ya tú sabes cómo era eso: directo al pulmón. Entonces había que empezar a bailar: un son, una rumba y una

conga, diez minutos de descanso y empezar, otra vez el mismo repertorio, así durante seis horas seguidas. Yo creo que nunca en mi vida bailé tanto . . . en Dallas ganamos bastante dinero, aunque nos sentimos muy mal pues teníamos que ir de la feria para la casa, porque como éramos negros, no nos dejaban entrar en ningún lugar. . . . [M]i último viaje ya fue la consagración: A Hollywood, la Meca del Cine, para filmar con George Raft y Carole Lombard la película La Rumba. Este sí fue un buen viaje . . . nos pagaban 150 dólares semanales y estuvimos dos meses trabajando y las condiciones eran excelentes.

That tour was a nightmare. I had just arrived when I slipped and was hospitalized for many days. And what was worse is that it was so cold in Chicago then that to go out to dance dressed as a rumbera you had to down a couple of shots. But, it was during the Prohibition era so the only alcohol you could find was this concoction made by the Puerto Ricans that we called "Take my Life Away." . . . you can imagine what that was like, straight to the lungs. Then we had to start dancing: *son, rumba, conga.* Ten minutes of rest, then start the whole thing over again. It was like that for six hours straight. I don't think I have danced that much in my life. In Dallas we made a lot of money, but we felt bad because we had to leave the gig and go straight home since we were black and we weren't allowed to go anywhere. . . . [M]y last trip was the consecration: to Hollywood, the mecca of film to film *La Rumba* with George Raft and Carole Lombard. That was a good trip. They paid us $150 weekly, we worked for two months, and the working conditions were excellent.

Despite her opportunity to travel and earn more money than at Playa, in these recollections of her trips to Dallas, New York, Chicago, and Hollywood Curbelo tends to remember the hardships and the struggles: the cold, her accident, Luis Correa's disappearing and never hearing from him again, the length of time she had to dance, the little breaks she took, and the racism experience in the U.S. South. Her dancing, laboring body becomes secondary to other incidents during which her body experienced pain, cold, and discrimination. Dance was work for Curbelo. Arduous, challenging, and seemingly interminable work. She had to labor to learn how to dance, then she had to constantly do it; it was the mode of production that allowed her to gain capital.

In the section of her oral history entitled "Nostalgia," she states that she did not know how to do anything else but dance. When her second husband (whom she married in 1948) lost his job, she had to find another way to earn money because she no longer danced professionally. In fact, many working-class dancers who married usually stopped performing, out of an obligated respect for their husbands. They could no longer be public women. That was a patriarchal imposition, to be sure, yet some women willingly retired and preferred to become homemakers.[40] Curbelo explains that after 1948, nightlife in Havana grew increasingly difficult (she does not give reasons why), and because she married *un hombre bueno*/a good man, she retired. Padura concludes the article with Curbelo's longing for her youth. She wishes she could still dance, hear audiences applaud, and call out "Carmita! Carmita!":

> *Ahora lo que tengo que hacer es atender a mis nietos, mis biznietos y mi tataranieto, que dan una guerra tremenda. Porque de lo malo, ¿para qué acordarse? Por eso me gusta ver estas fotografías, verme cómo era antes, ver al Chori jovencito, a Luis y a mis otros compañeros y a veces hasta cerrar los ojos y sentir que otra vez soy el Pollo, Carmita la Rumbera, y entonces me siento rejuvenecer. Y qué ganas me dan de bailar.*

> Now what I have to do is take care of my grandchildren, my great-grandchildren, and my great-great-grandchild. They are a lot of work. Why should I remember the bad stuff? This is why I like to see these photographs, see how I was before, see El Chori looking so young, Luis and my other partners; and sometimes I even close my eyes and feel that I am El Pollo, Carmita the Rumbera again, and I feel myself rejuvenate. What a desire I get to dance.

Is Carmen Curbelo's story as common as the others—those are remain absent from these pages? Those that I never got a chance to hear? For every Carmen there may have been many Anitas. Although I staunchly argue against a narrative of tragedy for the Cuban *mulata*, it is difficult to ignore those that may not have overcome personal or economic obstacles. The life of an *academia* dancer emerges as precarious, but as Curbelo attests, it need not terminate in tragedy. Might not her nostalgic longing also be a kind of tragedy? Is not the desire for a body that can still move, dance, and receive applause a kind of tragedy? How might remembering that body's past labors and historicizing them "enact a particular kind of national imagining?"[41] Are not all projects of national imagining somehow tragic?

CONCLUSION, OR AN INCOMPLETE ARCHIVE

Throughout this chapter I have sought to reposition and remember the spaces of the *academia de baile* as volatile, vivacious, and visceral. I hope to illuminate the complexity of social relations, the coerced or performed subjectivities, and the power negotiations that occur on hot dance floors whose walls have shadows of lissome limbs clasping, gyrating, and swaying to the "exertions of the *bongo*." Knowledge and cultural production materialized in the dancing bodies of the *mulatas* and their partners, as well as in the performing bodies of the musicians who played the *danzón, guaracha,* and *son* music that got those *mulata* hips moving. These spaces haunt Cuban cultural history in various ways: through the romanticized nostalgia of the Cuban exile who remembers a country via particular lenses of race and social class; through the writings of music historians who describe the musical developments and performances that occurred there; and perhaps more importantly, through the bodies of the old and young *mulata* women walking through the streets of Havana today.

I feel haunted by these *mulata* voices bouncing off the dancing shadows on decrepit Havana walls. Not only am I seeking the ghosts of these historically silent women, but I long to hear their whispers alongside the voices and corporeality of the women who still live. It is this dance of flesh, memory, and murmurs that I want to conjure, watch, and attempt to describe here.

I am reminded of Avery Gordon's work on the ghost, and how the process of haunting, of listening to the ghosts of those once living beings, articulates the social conditions of a once lived reality—conditions that illuminate how the social might change for the better. For Gordon, the "ghost is not simply a dead or a missing person, but a social figure, and investigating it can lead to that dense site where history and subjectivity make social life."[42]

Sometimes, the promise of a recuperative history seems a flimsy attempt to give relevance of these women's lives and labors—not because they lack value, but because I am cautious about positioning their stories as merely part of a greater narrative of nostalgic pre-Revolutionary Cuban popular culture. Nevertheless, I remain wary of contributing to the nostalgic configuration, especially because economic conditions for some women in today's Cuba still involve transactional sex exchanges. They, too, must contend with the historical ghosts of women who danced for dollars.

Ghosts dance around Cuba, as do rumors. Rumors inform the listener where the best place to dance is on a given night, where the best-looking *mulatas* work in an *academia* or a *cabaretucho* in the fabled area of Marianao, what musicians will show up and entertain with impromptu sessions. The power and potency of rumors and ghosts attest to not just the repetitive nature of historical interactions but also the remnants of historical bodies dancing, laboring or desiring. Where can that untenable residue of corporeal history go? Where can it exist and be accounted for? What happens to those traces that never fully materialize but are still significant? How might we honor and speak for them?

In my attempt to carve out a space for a Cuban popular-dance history based *outside* the lavish productions of the big nightclubs, and to focus on the *academia* dancers, I do not aim to establish a totalizing narrative about the *academias*. I doubt this can ever exist. Instead, through this choreography (I like to think of it as a structured improvisation, much like popular Cuban dance) involving historiography, oral history, literary analysis, visual culture, and ethnography, I might make material something akin to what James Clifford speaks to when he states that ethnographic "experience can be seen as the building up of a common, meaningful world, drawing on intuitive styles of feeling, perception, and guesswork. This activity makes use of clues, traces, gestures, and scraps of sense prior to the development of stable interpretations."[43]

Just as the bodies in these *academias* could not always stand still, this chapter posits the instability inherent in telling stories and ultimately in writing a history in which the subaltern subjects never come fully into focus. Hip(g)nosis works hard here to give shape to some hazy outline of the *academia de baile* history. The haziness, similar to the aura of the ghost, enables conjuring possibilities—perhaps even the "phenomenological hauntings of black performance"—that complicate the consistent fuzziness of history.[44]

A Marriage Proposal

For S.V., with love and gratitude

Havana, October 1933

Two women dash out of Marte y Belona to catch the last cab on the corner. They are lucky. It will rain soon. Evelina looks over to her friend Ingrid and smiles. She slams the door shut and adjusts her skirts while Ingrid quickly opens her purse to pull out her last cigarette. The first drops of rain begin to tap on the roof of the taxi as Ingrid tells the driver her street address. Ingrid has always been so clever, Evelina thinks. No matter how many nights she has worked, Evelina has never been able to get a client to pay for a cab ride home. Ingrid usually procured cab rides for herself many times, but tonight Ingrid made enough on her own to treat them to a cab ride. *Gracias a Dios*, thought Evelina, because tonight, her ankle hurt. She reaches down to massage it.

"I told you not to wear those shoes again." Ingrid says as she inhales her cigarette. She stares out the window into the rainy Havana night. The air always smells cleaner when it rains. A temporary respite from that day's oppressive odors: car exhaust, alcoholic breath of dance partners, and burnt cooking grease. Evelina watches Ingrid as she inhales, exhales . . . inhales . . . exhales . . . the cigarette smoke disappearing quickly once she blows it out the car window into the wet night. After long nights, Ingrid always has more energy. She thrives on attention and the clandestine possibilities nighttime offers. She usually convinces Evelina and other girls to go with her to a *cafetería* after work. No matter how late, Ingrid orders a strong *cortado* with a cheese sándwich, then insists they stay up chatting and laughing until dawn. Evelina never says no to her, even when she cannot afford a sandwich. Tonight, though, Evelina senses something different in Ingrid. Her arms are crossed over her chest as she smokes. She keeps staring out of the window and has said very little.

"I thought you were going to give me your red ones . . . the ones *el gallego* bought you."

"Ay, Evelina, you have to remind me. You know how I am. . . ." She keeps staring out the window, but faintly smiles when she utters her friend's name. Evelina continues to look at Ingrid's face. She notices she still has no lines around her mouth. So many other girls did from the smoking. Ingrid's mouth remains plump and smooth. It looks especially pretty tonight with the faint fuschia stain of her lipstick. It looks even prettier when she smiles. Ingrid always smiles, except for tonight. Tonight she has been economical with her smiles. Inhales . . . exhales again. Her chest expands and Evelina notices a damp spot near her breast where her Virgen de la Caridad medallion clings to her moist skin. Evelina thinks she looks beautiful in the sulfur light of the street lamps streaming into the taxi. She always looks beautiful. Effortlessly so. Ingrid continues to stare out the window, unaware of her effect on Evelina. Always unaware.

"Do you know what I like best about working at the *academia*?" Ingrid asks matter of a factly. She still stares out the window.

"I know we complain all the time about being there, but I don't know . . . today, I was especially fond of Dolores. She can be so original with those accessories she puts on that nest of hair she has. I loved watching Pimienta insult that rude client who *still* comes back to dance with her, and I love the way you dance to *La Mora*. You are so cute when you lift your skirt during the *montuno* section. I love when you do that . . ." she smiles as she remembers. Evelina feels her heart beat faster as she watches Ingrid's face change as she smiles.

"You taught me how to dance the *danzón*, remember. I didn't know how to dance very much until you taught me."

"Yes, but now you're much better at it than me." She sighed again and touched her medallion.

Evelina remembers how embarrassed she felt the first time she danced with Ingrid. Ingrid possessed a nonchalant confidence and just kept reassuring her that, as long as she mastered the basic step, the rest would come easily. Many things did not come easily to Evelina, but she practiced diligently. She could not bear disappointing Ingrid. She worshiped Ingrid's smiles. Only they brought stability to her world.

"El *Gallego* asked me to marry him. Isn't that ridiculous? So ridiculous . . . he's ridiculous." Ingrid blurts out. Evelina feels the air leave her lungs and struggles to speak. She just keeps looking at Ingrid, desperately trying to find answers in her face. Ingrid sighs. She thought Evelina would want to know everything, but Evelina stares at her, somewhat catatonic. This moment is neither special nor exciting. All this time working at the *academia* since her brother died she imagined an offer of marriage would provide some relief. She imagined Evelina and the other girls throwing their arms around her, laughing, asking many questions. She imagined feeling happy. Instead, she feels nothing.

"I told him I would let him know tomorrow. He says if I say yes he can help plan the wedding. My mother must be dancing in her grave." She rolls her eyes and smiles half-heartedly. She prepares to inhale and finish her cigarette when Evelina grabs it from her hands and puts it quickly in her own mouth. She inhales, hoping that the moment between the inhale and exhale will calm her down.

"*¡Ay vieja, que felicidad!*"/How exciting. I'm so happy for you. I always knew he would ask you. He took too long, to be frank, but finally, finally. . . ." She quickly inhales to finish the cigarette and turns her face away. Ingrid must not see her eyes filling with tears. She throws the cigarette out and wipes the tear from her face before she turns to look over at Ingrid. She hugs her awkwardly. Ingrid feels stiff at first, but relaxes comfortably into Evelina's arms. Evelina inhales the faint aroma of Ingrid's jasmine perfume before she lets go for fear of more tears. Ingrid notices Evelina's nervous behavior. She smiles at her.

"Sometimes I wish we had other options." Ingrid reaches over to squeeze Evelina's hand. It feels moist and slightly jittery. "Loving him is not really an option . . . he's ridiculous." Her voice trails off. Suddenly, she begins to giggle. The giggle becomes a chuckle, the chuckle becomes a laugh and then suddenly, she folds over laughing heartily at her statement. She laughs, and laughs, and laughs. Evelina turns to the taxi driver and asks him to stop at the next corner.

"You live five more blocks that way! Why are you getting out here?" Ingrid asks amid waning laughter.

"I want to walk in the rain."

"But your ankle. . . ." As she reproaches her, Evelina exits the cab. She turns to lean in through the window and looks directly at Ingrid.

"*Ay, mi amor*, I'm really happy for you. I am. Thank you for everything." She hits the cab on the roof, signaling to the driver to start moving again. Ingrid turns around as the cab drives away. She watches Evelina grab a scarf from her purse to place on her head. She never likes getting her hair wet, thought Ingrid. Ingrid watches Evelina's slightly off-kilter walk and thinks this is one of the last times she will spend with her. When she officially accepts the marriage proposal, she will have to stop working.

El *gallego* never liked the idea of other men touching her every night, even if it was just for a song or two. Ingrid thinks of Evelina standing shyly waiting for someone to ask her to dance every night. *You have to smile more*, Ingrid would tell her. *Smile.* Who would get her to smile when she was no longer there?

The rain falls delicately now, unlike its earlier unforgiving insistence. Evelina could not breathe inside the cab anymore. Unable to make sense of what she feels, her only recourse lay in being alone. Perhaps by the time she arrives home, she will have an idea of what she can say to Ingrid tomorrow at work to excuse her behavior. Her ankle throbs the more steps she takes, so she decides to take off her shoes and walk barefoot. She spent most of her childhood waking barefoot around her grandmother's farm in Las Villas Province. Despite her need for stability and security, the hard wet concrete does not reassure her though. She misses the pliable damp dirt beneath her toes. She misses her grandmother. She will miss Ingrid.

As she turns the corner to her apartment block she sees a cab waiting in front of her *solar*. Suddenly, Ingrid emerges and rushes over to her, splashing through the puddles on the asphalt. She squeals as a large amount of water soaks her legs and the hem of the skirt. Evelina just watches Ingrid approach, unable to say anything.

"I can't believe you are barefoot. This isn't the country, Evelina. *Ay*, but your ankle must hurt a lot. *Pobrecita.*" Ingrid smiles while furrowing her eyebrows with concern.

Evelina realizes the rain has finally stopped. What can she say to Ingrid? How can she tell her how much she wants to hold her . . . to hold her forever?

"Well, why are we just standing here?" Ingrid grabs her arm and starts to pull her toward her door.

"What's wrong? Why are you not home?"

"I told the taxi to stop because there is something I forgot to tell you."

"Tell me inside, *vamos.*"

When they reach Evelina's door, it takes her longer than usual to open it. The humidity expanded the door and the lock feels more sluggish than usual. Even the *solar* wants to prevent Ingrid from being close to her. Once inside, the smell of stale cigarettes, rotting flowers, and bleach overpowers Evelina temporarily. Nothing about living in a *solar* was ever subtle. Not even the smell of her apartment. Evelina walks quickly over to her La Virgen de la Caridad del Cobre altar to remove the wilted sunflowers from the table. She drops her scarf quickly on the altar, and Evelina heads to the kitchen. Ingrid stands mesmerized by the flame of the candle on the altar. The liquified wax glows and casts golden hues on the wall. Ingrid goes to remove the scarf so it does not accidentally catch fire and notices a small picture frame to the right of the vase.

She remembers the day when they took that particular photograph. Her brother was still alive then, and he had invited her and Evelina to the beach. He had won the camera at a work raffle. Ingrid had to sell it when he died to help pay for his funeral. Evelina had never seen a camera until that day. While Evelina stared directly at the lens and smiled, Ingrid's eyes were closed. She had a grin on her face. Both of her hands were clasped around Evelina's arm, and her head rested on her shoulder. They wore similar swimsuits. Ingrid remembers being happy that day. Skin against skin, an excess of smiles. Photographs could not capture it all, but it was a happy day. Her eyes began to water. By the time Evelina returns, Ingrid sobs.

Evelina stands by her and gently touches her back.

"I'm ridiculous. . . . This night is ridiculous. . . ." Ingrid mumbles and giggles a bit as she turns to look at Evelina. Evelina wipes away at her tears.

"*Ay vieja*, you just need to sleep. Too much has happened." Evelina just looks at her.

Weeks later, when asked what else happened that night, she does not remember anymore. She only says that they walk over to her room. She hears Ingrid's shoes fall to the floor. They fall asleep side by side, still wearing their damp, sweat-stained dresses. They hold hands all night.

CHAPTER 3

Hip(g)nosis as Pleasure

The Mulata on Film

In Mikhail Kalatozov's stunningly photographed film *I am Cuba* (1964), the *mulata* functions as a metaphor for the plunder and exploitation of Cuba prior to the 1959 Revolution. In the famous nightclub scene, María (the *mulata*) enters the space with a noticeably large crucifix around her neck.[1] The American men vying for her attention make several references to it throughout the evening. It never leaves her neck, until one decisive moment later that night. Like the proverbial yoke around her neck, syncretic religiosity hangs from the *mulata* body and perhaps even imbues it with transcendental qualities.

Bearing in mind that hip(g)nosis stems from this dialectical relationship between corporeality and spirituality, this chapter focuses on how the *mulata* appears in films. It also examines the types of discourses that emerge when her body functions as a vehicle for religiosity and/or self-expression or pleasure.

My discussion will eventually turn to the film *I Am Cuba,* where the *mulata* undergoes a metaphorical crucifixion at the hands of signification, but first I will trace the appearance of the *mulata* in specific other films in which she dances in a cabaret/nightclub setting or at spiritual ceremonies. These two seemingly disparate sites for dancing continue to provide support for my argument that the *mulata* functions in a liminal space, a rigid binary that prevents her from achieving a subjectivity removed from linguistically derived dichotomies (e.g., virgin or whore). In many of these films, Afro-Cuban sacred dance (dance for the *orishas*, or spirits) positions the *mulata* in that liminal space where the tensions of *mulata*-ness pulsate in her body, specifically her hips. This tension between whiteness and blackness manifests in the jerky gestures that reverberate through her body; it is as if her body both craves and rejects the power of African rhythms while its ancestral ties belie the need to demur and negotiate acceptable (read: sanitized, whitened) ways of being. Put simply, the *mulata* featured in these films struggles with the overdetermined relationship her corporeality has with dance: the elasticity of her hips and her supposed natural sensuality. It is through hip(g)nosis, then, that the *mulata* facilitates our consumption of what has been historically rejected, namely blackness. My intention is not to grant automatic agency to the *mulata* based on her ability to move in contestation of the many signifiers assigned to her but, rather, to demonstrate how her body consistently negotiates the presence, impact, and power that discursive practices have on it.

Following the lead of earlier chapters, where I foreground instances of reclamation, I continue to focus on small moments (in these films) when the *mulata* body in question extracts pleasure from dancing, even when initially coerced. These acts of self-gratification through the pleasurable *meneo* (wiggle) of her hips continue this foray into hip(g)nosis as a strategy through which the *mulata* body can move away from mere victimization at the altar of signification. The capacity her presence has to enable pleasure and spirituality becomes the main thrust of this chapter, shown through the films it explores: *Tam Tam o el Origen de la Rumba* (1938), *Mulata* (1954), *Yambaó* or *Cry of the Bewitched* (1957), *I am Cuba* (1964), *Los del baile* (1965), and *Son y No Son* (1980).

How does the *mulata's* dancing body function in these narratives and what does her dancing enable, either for herself or for the narrative? Overall, each film inscribes a way of hip(g)nosis that I find fruitful, particularly when linked with religiosity, pleasure, and self-expression. My objective here is to highlight how the celluloid *mulata* as an always-already dancing body continues to communicate her struggles, identity, and desires through those "bewitched, bothered, and bewildered" hips of hers.[2]

TAM TAM O EL ORIGEN DE LA RUMBA (1938)

Tam Tam tells a short (22-minute) story of the *rumba* through a heterosexual romance plot that goes awry.[3] It begins with text informing the audience that the *rumba* emerged from the black population brought to Cuba. They brought "brute" rhythm while the melodic elements came later (the underlying assumption is that the Spanish imported melody):

> *Está película aspira a dar una síntesis de esa transformación basada en los amores de*
> *dos jóvenes mestizos, ella singularmente bella, otro esclavo desdeñado por la joven, la*

hace víctima de un maleficio conocido por "el santo" del que es liberada después en una ceremonia de impresionante solemnidad por su madrina y los sacerdotes de la tribú. La liberación de la jóven esclava culmina en un disolvente que muestra la rumba tal como es y como se baila actualmente en todo el mundo.

This movie hopes to provide a synopsis of the *rumba*'s transformation based on the romance between two young mestizo lovers, with the woman uniquely beautiful. Another slave, disdained by the young woman, makes her a victim of a curse known as *"el santo,"* from which she is freed after an impressive solemn ceremony performed by her godmother and the priests from the tribe. The liberation of the young slave culminates in a dissolve that shows the *rumba* and how it is actually danced around the world.

Chela de Castro plays the unnamed *mulata*. Not much biographical material exists about Castro, other than her real name (María Celia Ovejero Martínez) and her list of appearances in Cuban and Mexican films and on television. Perhaps she had some dance training, a statement I make judiciously given that her legs extend quite lengthily and her feet point to perfect arches when her suitor carries her gallantly off the boat. I admit I was pleasantly surprised when I saw how her body positioned itself in his arms: elegantly horizontal with a slow bend in her neck to allow for her head to cock sensually back. Such a pose, reminiscent of the reclining *mûlatresse* poses featured in many *Costumbrista* and Europeanist paintings of mixed-race women in the nineteenth century, pertains to a gestural taxonomy of the *mulata* that moves through these pages.

Castro's pose coincides with the constructed belief that *mulatas*, and by extension black Caribbean women, possess natural grace and allure. Benitez Rojo's *Repeating Island* attempts to theorize this idea of inherent grace. He calls it moving "in a certain kind of way."[4] While the attempt to establish a phenomenology of culturally choreographed ways of moving is ambitious, the idea of moving "in a certain kind of way" problematically sets up an ontological truth about blackness as it manifests in the hips, butts, and walk of Caribbean women. What interests me about this turn of phrase, however, is how this construction of slithery sensuality has currency, how it is an exchangeable symbolic capital that establishes a cultural imaginary—a way for the nation to understand itself without the perils of self-reflective critique. Hip(g)nosis allows both a distraction for the witness and a method of dialoguing (for the hip-notizing corporeality) with these disparate forces encircling her body: there is pleasure in both the watching and the doing.

Through a myth-of-origins narrative, *Tam Tam* uses the *mulata* as the metaphor for taming the primitive elements of blackness that can "seep into" and wreak havoc in the wider, whiter culture; such havoc is evidenced by the *mulata's* descent into a madness depicted as an evil possession that can only be cured through "ceremonial practices performed by her godmother and the priests of the tribe." Physically, her possession involves a jerky torso and a lack of equilibrium that contrasts with how she appears in the beginning of the film: languishing sensually on a boat rowed by her *mulato* suitor. The love triangle between the beautiful *mulata* slave, her *mulato* suitor, and the black slave reiterates the racial logic of Cuba, where a lighter skinned woman flouts the advances of a darker skinned man; this was often also the topic of many *mulata zarzuelas* in Cuban theatre of the early twentieth century. In return, the black man punishes her by invoking "black magic," or "*el santo*" (Santería), which requires appeasement by those knowledgeable in such rites. In its docilization, blackness does not necessarily disappear from the narrative. Instead, its threatening malediction shifts to the crucial component in the *rumba*—the rhythm that the whole world dances.

To the sound of beating drums, choreographed groups of women sitting with baskets, and a male figure dressed in raffia and carrying some gourds all perform a variety of gestures as the *mulata* dances around the fire, lifting her skirts, flailing her arms, moving her head from side to side. She moves her body recklessly and uncontrollably as it struggles to release the curse of blackness the resentful "*esclavo*" has placed upon her. Not until she drinks from a bowl given to her by her godmother, and she does one final dance around the fire, is the curse lifted. The camera frames her smiling face in a closeup, her head cocked backwards ever so slightly, perhaps to remind us of the first time she made this coy gesture earlier in the film. When the closeup on the *mulata's* face at the outdoor ceremony dissolves into a closeup of her face in a new indoor cabaret setting, the *rumba* in essence has become sanitized—and with it, the dancing *mulata*.

The first section's representations of blackness, the outdoors, and the unbridled physicality contrast with the contained cabaret-stage setting, where the bodies dance in structured choreographic patterns. The *mulata* appears on top of an oversized drum (functioning as a small stage), posing slowly with languorous controlled arm extensions. Her arms move downward, her hands land on her hips, and she concludes the movement phrase with a soft back-arched pose. She then spins in place, and the camera films her and her billowing, circling skirt from above, a shot that calls to mind the Busby Berkeley films featuring spectacular choreographies so popular at that time (or even Ruth St. Denis's *East Indian Nautch Dance* from 1932, which also features filming from above). She comes down from the drum-shaped platform and spins off the stage (screen) as the lavish choreography number continues.

Figure 3.1. A scene from *Tam Tam o El Origen de la Rumba* featuring dancers from the Edén Concert cabaret, and the music group *La Sonora Matancera*.

The *rumba*, now reborn as a mulaticized staged production, begins. The conflation between the *mulata* body and the *rumba*—or more aptly, the *mulata* as *rumba*—manifests not only in the transformation of the slave *mulata* from possessed body to *rumbera mulata* on stage but also in the lyrics of the song that introduces the second dancing *mulata* in the film. With Chela Castro's disappearance, a new *mulata* takes her place. Ever a commodity, a new *mulata* waits in the wings.

In this dance number, the *mulata rumbera*, dressed in the requisite ruffles, flounces, and big bow, dances solo surrounded by a cadre of mostly white *Cubanas* wearing contrasting costumes (Figure 3.1). Most notably their midriffs remain covered while the *mulata* wears a bra top to display her waist that, as the song touts, is poisoned (by an implied blackness and/or sensuality).

Buscamos una mulata, caballero
Que tiene una cintura envenenada
Que ella la reina de ese coro
Por ella nos reunimos a cumbanchear
Mira, ahí viene placentera

Ya viene la mulatona a vacunar

. . .

Ven, demuestra tu cintura
Ven, demuestra tu menear
Que baile la rumba . . .

We are looking for a *mulata*, gentleman
Who has a poisoned waist
She is the queen of this chorus
It's because of her that we get together to party
Look, see how she approaches so pleasingly
Here comes the *mulata* to vaccinate

. . .

Come, show us your waist
Come, show us your wiggling ways . . .

The *mulata* dances obligingly and with pleasure. She smiles, looks into the camera, moves around the space with the intention to *be* the spectacle, and enjoys it (or at least performs pleasure convincingly). She varies her steps from the *rumba* to some faint moves from Afro-Cuban *orisha* dance, particularly the *ñongó* step, a rhythmic, syncopated skip. She controls the choreographic syntax by first mixing the *rumba* with Afro-Cuban *orisha* steps to fit the rhythm, and then by how she chooses to move through the space.

The other bodies around her move in more prescribed, rehearsed, and structured ways. They remain in geometric formations and often stay in one place. A quick edit to a man in the audience shows his sudden glazed-over expression. He looks like he may faint. As with the *mulata* in the first half of the film, the *rumba* seems to be overpowering his consciousness and taking him to an altered state. His gestures resemble those of Chela Castro's *mulata* in the first half of the film: jerky, uncontrolled, and erratic. Sure enough, in a later moment of the film, he appears dancing center stage, possessed by both the *rumba* rhythm and the allure of the dancing *mulata*.

According to the logic of the narrative, *rumba* (and other Afro-Cuban rhythms) leads bodies to frenetic and frenzied corporeal outbursts. These unregulated movements require dissolution and temperance through the *mulata* body in order to make them palatable and acceptable for *sensuality* (non-threatening when slightly removed from blackness) to successfully materialize.

The film credits Henry Bell and Sergio Orta as the dance directors.[5] Sergio Orta went on to become choreographer and artistic director of the Tropicana cabaret in Havana, after having worked in Hollywood briefly.[6] Given the historical moment when *Tam Tam* appeared and the types of song and dance spectacles that emerged in Cuban and other Latin American films (particularly the cabaret genre in what is termed Mexico's "Golden Age of Cinema") afterwards, might *Tam Tam* function as an ur-text, a type of foundational film for the cabaret genre? Did *Tam Tam* and these types of racial, choreographic, and aesthetic representations inform later Cuban/Latin American cabaret spectacles in films and on stage? Furthermore, how does the genre of the filmic cabaret spectacle facilitate a way for *Cubanidad* to emerge?

The conflation of the *mulata* with *rumba* as portrayed in *Tam Tam* provides a cursory overview of the "history" of the *rumba*, which, for all intents and purposes, could be a "history" of Cuba as well. Yet, this depiction of Cuban history placates the extant racial, national, and gendered tensions that never properly dissolve from one time period into the next, in the way that the image of the possessed *mulata* dissolves into the image of the showgirl *mulata*, or *mulata de rumbo*, in perhaps *the* decisive moment in the film. I suggest that *Tam Tam's* choreography of *Cubanidad*—through the *rumba*-as-*mulata* as Cuban history—continues the trajectory set up by the *zarzuelas* and *teatro bufo* of the late nineteenth and early twentieth centuries. The signifiers of nation, race, and gender that successfully operated on the lyric stages merely shifted to film, where they could have a wider audience and broader appeal. Those signifiers did not disappear but, rather, they moved from one genre to another.

I focus on this dissolve for a moment here, as it synecdochically performs a rupture in time and narrative—or more precisely, the moment of hip(g)notism. The dissolve is a filmic representation of the *effect* of hip(g)nosis, a blurring of the past into the present through the spectacle of the dancing *mulata*. She does not erase the past. She does not have the powers to do so, despite being discursively imbued with an abundance of characteristics that could materialize a tabula rasa of sorts. Nevertheless, she makes the fraught colonial history of Cuba difficult to see if the witness maintains an exclusive focus on her spectacularity.[7] The *mulata*, in the case of *Tam Tam*, erases the colonial past, particularly its legacy of slavery. Instead, *Tam Tam* showcases the transformation of the *mulata de rumbo* as the quintessential representative of whitened *Cubanidad, rumba,* and rhythm.[8]

Cubanidad emerges in the figure of the sensual, rhythmic, and hipped *mulata*, and it renders hip(g)nosis as a defining characteristic in Cuban cultural production. In other words, *Tam Tam* cinematically sets up how hip(g)notism operates and informs the *rumba* myth-of-origins narrative that requires a *mulata* body to circulate it. Although hip(g)nosis as movements of the hips that involve articulate gyrations and occupation of space has the potential to be learned by *any* body, in the Cuban (and to a larger extent, the African diasporic) context, hip(g)nosis as performed by a *mulata* body draws attention to the historical absences and ruptures that cannot easily be made to disappear. In *Tam Tam's* utopian version of the *rumba*, the *mulata* remains at the center, while the other bodies come together and perform synchronized movements in deference to her featured acrobatics and aesthetic uniqueness. The cinematic apparatus provides the opportunity for the *"mulatona"* to successfully remove blackness, and to replace it with her *"cintura envenenada,"* or poisoned waist. Blackness, like the spell, becomes exorcised.

While *Tam Tam* succeeds in removing any uncontrollable aspect of blackness that could color the sanitized vision of the *rumba* it seeks to disseminate, the next film to be discussed, *Mulata*, looks to blackness as a way for its main protagonist, the *mulata* Caridad, to forcibly declare her identity. For Caridad, her desire to reconnect to blackness offers a sense of place, identity, and comfort that her material reality fails to provide. Despite the limited and stereotypical qualities assigned to the *mulata* protagonist, Caridad (this particular name tying her to La Virgen de la Caridad del Cobre, the mixed-race patron saint of Cuba who is syncretized with the Santería goddess Ochún) offers a nuanced rendition of the "tragic *mulata*" trope. Although Caridad does die at the end, her death signifies a return to her matrilineal heritage, or more precisely, a return to blackness. Her death serves as the culmination of her life's journey to be in a "place" where her color and black inheritance do not matter. This *mulata* must leave the material world, as it has no place for her. Her path to this "transcendence" includes several hip-shaking moments when she asserts her *mulata* corporeality using hip(g)nosis. Let's take a closer look at the film.

MULATA (1954)

The film *Mulata* depicts various stereotypes of the *mulata* figure: fatherless, poor, virtuosic dancer, sexualized yet infantilized, and of course, tragic.[9] Many other characters in the film are reminiscent of Cuban *teatro bufo*: a *gallego* man who lusts after the *mulata*, the *gallego's* wife/counterpart who dislikes the *mulata*, a *mulato* suitor, and a white suitor. Although the film is marred by the trope of the tragic, displaced, desired, yet unloved *mulata*, it demonstrates how *mulata* corporeality allows the use of its interpellated status as a means for survival. The *mulata's* demise caused by the excesses associated with the cabaret and her *mulata*-ness neatly package the widely circulated and well-known *mulata* trope in Spanish-speaking America (safely assuming that audiences in Latin America other than Mexico and Cuba saw the film). Despite the notoriety and circulation of the trope, I am offering a counterintuitive means of watching the film, the choreography, and Caridad's body through the theory of hip(g)nosis. That is, there are contestatory moments in Caridad's gestural vocabulary or cabaret dance performances when she refuses to allow the moniker of tragedy to stick to her gyrating hips.

Ninón Sevilla, who portrays Caridad, was born in Cuba and is famous for her performances of *cubanía* in Mexican films of the 1940s and '50s. She capitalized on Mexico's Golden Age of Cinema as a *rumbera-cabaretera* archetype, moving her hips beneath ostentatious outfits in films like *Aventurera* (1950), *Perdida* (1950), and *Sensualidad* (1951), and by playing a Cuban *mulata* in *Mulata* (1954) and *Yambaó* (1957). She choreographed some of her own dance numbers and was instrumental in introducing Santería/Afro-Cuban ritual dances into her choreography.

Ninón serves as an example of someone who traffics in hip(g)nosis. In the film *Mulata*, she inhabits a corporeality that does not belong to her—that of the *rumba*-dancing *mulata*—but because of territoriality (her white Cuban dancing body), she's able to use hip(g)nosis and perform *mulata* to gain both economic and cultural capital. Although she plays a "tragic *mulata*," in the films *Mulata* and *Yambaó,* Ninón was quite the contrary. In both films, two versions of hip(g)nosis appear: the fictional *mulata's* quasi-liberation through her dancing, and Ninón's use of it as a brand signifying Cuba so as to achieve fame in Mexico and Latin America in *cabaretera* films.[10]

The sailor Martín (played by Pedro Armendáriz, a famous Mexican actor from their Golden Age) narrates the tragic tale of Caridad (Figure 3.2). He portrays an errant sailor who arrives in Cuba looking for new opportunities. The opening scene invites the audience onto his boat, where he watches over Caridad, who lies feverish in bed, mumbling to herself. His narration pairs Caridad with a loaded term, "poor," setting her up as tragic from the beginning. He tells his tale of Caridad through flashback; the story situates her in a masculine linear history, a history antithetical to the motion of her hips.

We gain access to Caridad only through Martín's memory. When she dances and expresses her history and inheritance from her mother (her Africanness), or more precisely, when she wields hip(g)nosis, does she liberate herself from the rigidity of the term "*mulata*" and its non-film-subject status? Except for three instances, she is not referred to by her name, Caridad; she is simply "*mulata*." Thus, Caridad's subjectivity not only remains unrecognized but she also becomes an interchangeable, expendable, and commodified object, her body plagued by the interpellations assigned to it by circulating ideologies.

Caridad continually refers to her strong relationship with "blackness," her inheritance of the legacy of Santería from her mother, and the limited

Figure 3.2. Martín (Pedro Armendáriz) looks out at *bembé,* where Caridad dances, in a scene from *Mulata.*

opportunities she has as a *mulata*. When she shares her history with Martin, he dismisses her "inheritance of old stories" as worthless. For him (as representative of patriarchy and "proper" history), these *orisha* texts (deified forces of nature in Yorùbà /Santería cosmology), her legacy of "blackness," and her consistent contextualization of her racialized identity are of no value because they are not visible. For Martin, things can have importance only if they operate within the realm of the senses. He says that it is better to focus on the tangible or material—things that one can touch:"*tocar [cosas] como tú . . . ven, descansa y olvídate de todo*"/touch things like you . . . come, rest, and forget about everything. Martin's insistence that she forget and acquiesce to his desires instantiates how her corporeally situated history comes secondary to him; it takes no precedence over the power contained within patriarchal desires. She is just an object for him and will be situated in history as a thing in his ledger books.

Caridad's dancing ability in the film is constructed as "natural" and instinctive. Even she claims ignorance about where her affinity for dance comes from; somehow, it is part of her bodily composition. Alluding to Caridad's inheritance of "blackness," these danced iterations of her identity outside the confines of the *mulata* trope are where I witness Caridad's hip(g)nosis in the film. In these moments, unmarred by others' descriptions of who she is or what her body does, her hips forcibly speak all those things that Martín insists she forget. What follows are three moments in the film when Caridad displays hip(g)nosis, contesting the rest of the film's tragic premise of the "poor *mulata.*"

The *Bembé*

The opening titles of the film *Mulata* offer this information:

> *Por primera vez se presentan en una película escenas de un bembé auténtico. Su terrible audacia no tiene nada de inmoral. Los que ejecutan sus ritmos están haciendo una ofrenda de orden religioso, y ajenos al mundo, ofrecen todo lo que tienen, el alma y el cuerpo, al llamado mágico de las antiguas divinidades africanas. Cualquier sugestión de impureza, en consecuencia, estará en nuestros ojos demasiado civilizados, jamás en la embriaguez purísima de su frenesí . . .*

> For the first time, scenes of an authentic *bembé* [dance or celebration for *orishas*] are presented in a movie. Its terrible audacity has nothing immoral about it. Those who execute the rhythms are making a religious offering, as they are alienated from the world. They offer everything they have, soul and body, to the magic call of the ancient African deities. As a consequence, whatever suggestion of impurity is [because of] our too civilized eyes, never in the pure drunkenness of its [the *bembé*] frenzy . . .

While working at the tavern owned by the *gallego* couple, Caridad hears *batá* drums (drums used for Lukumí/Santería worship). A *bembé* (celebration for the *orishas*) takes place at the nearby beach, and she feels drawn to these ancient rhythms. In response to the *gallego's* orders to continue working, she says, "I can't hear anyone, they're calling me"—*they* being her ancestors. When she finally joins the group of worshipers on the beach, they are singing, dancing, and praying to Ogún, the energetic force deified as the god of iron. The *bembé* proceeds through various *orisha* songs and dances: Ochosí, Yemayá, Ochún, and Changó. The *bembé* scene alternates between shots of the *bembé* with Ninón/Caridad photographed mid-thigh up, waist up, but never close up, surrounded by Lukumí/Santería practitioners dancing alongside her. Wide shots from above the circle of worshipers and moves to mid-frame focus of Ninón flanked by other (darker) women are interspersed with shots of the observers from the *gallego's* tavern. Until Caridad begins to dance Ochún, the observers at the tavern are never really watching. They

Figure 3.3. Caridad dances Ochún at the *bembé,* in a scene from *.Mulata.*

hear the drumming and make comments, and then the camera cuts away from their tête-a-tête and back to the *bembé.* However, once the *bembé* for Ochún begins and Ninón/Caridad breaks away from the group and begins to dance—at first with two women on either side of her, and then alone—the camera returns to the tavern, where it focuses on a medium shot of Martín for the first time. A solo shot of Ninón/Caridad from her mid-thigh upward is followed by one of Martín staring at her (Figure 3.2). Martín watches, enraptured, ignoring the advances of another woman: *"Confiesa, la esperas, verdad? . . . Olvídate de esa mujer, te puede embrujar. Es hija de santera"*/Confess, you're waiting for her, right? . . . Forget about that woman, she can bewitch you. She's a *santera*'s daughter." His hypnotized gaze metonymically represents the heterosexual male gaze that sexualizes Caridad's worshiping body, and hence Ochún as a godforce as well.

Ninón/Caridad's hips subtly sway from side to side as she alternately places one foot in front of the other in place, dancing the basic Ochún step (Figures 3.3–3.5). Her arms are usually held away from her torso, from shoulder joint to elbow perpendicular to her torso, from the elbow joint to her hands parallel to her torso. Sometimes, when she becomes invigo- rated by the music (or the singing and dancing), the intensity through which she executes the movements increases. Her dancing strength is

Figure 3.4. Close-up of Caridad dancing Ochún at the *bembé,* in scene from *Mulata.*

Figure 3.5. Caridad's dancing to Ochún becomes livelier and she begins to use her skirt, in a scene from *Mulata.*

much more evident compared to the two women on either side of her. They barely move their arms and just keep the rhythm with their feet. Ninón/Caridad picks up her skirts, and we catch glimpses of her thighs, then she dips and spins around and moves away, out of the imaginary horizontal line created by her and the other two women. Here, Martín's narration contributes to the mounting energy of the *bembé* and Ninón/Caridad's dancing.

Ochún's dance is followed by Ochosí, the deity associated with hunting. Martín as narrator erroneously attributes the hands coming together with two fingers forming a cross—a gesture representing the bow and arrow that Ochosí as the hunter carries with him—as calls to the virgins (saints) and ancestors (Caridad's mother) they venerate. The music changes again. Martín continues to explain that now they are praising Changó, the deified force of male virility. Although Martín speaks about Changó, the drumming and song belong to Ochún: "*Kole wa ye o*"—this chant corresponds to the *apataki*, or tale, where Ochún becomes a vulture to take a message from earth to Olodumare.

The choreo-story loses its meaning and gets misinterpreted as a masculine deity's tale, removing its significance in this instance. However, during the "*Kole wa ye o*," Caridad falls to the ground, overcome. She shakes furiously and uncontrollably. In *bembés*, falling signifies the appearance of *egún* (ancestor spirits), not the arrival of the deity.[11] However, in the film, her fall is misinterpreted as a possession. But a more alarming moment follows. When the drumming and singing changes to Elegua, orisha of the crossroads, suddenly (primarily due to the film's image and sound editing), other women begin to fall down and strip from the waist up, revealing their breasts while writhing sexually on the sand. According to one of my Ifa/Lukumí consultants, nakedness at a *bembé* implies disrespect. Cuban cultural scholar Reynaldo González corroborates this claim:

> *Los aspectos "rituales" que muestra el filme están lejos de reflejar actos verdaderos de la Regla de Ocha o Santería, donde el nudismo de los oficiantes se consideraría profanación de las deidades que adoran.*

The "ritual" aspects that the film depicts are far from the true acts of la Regla de Ocha or Santería, where the nudity of its practitioners would be considered the profanation of the deities they worship.[12]

Chants for Ochún: "*Ala Om' Ashe 'M Ashe*" "*Ala Omo Ashe/ Omo Ashe*" (loosely translated as The Child that is covered with Godforce) echo throughout the film. Later, this chant "calls" Caridad "home" right before she dies on

Martín's boat. She is finally free, Martín tells us, her death symbolizing her freedom from the lexical constraints of the material world. Although floating signifiers want to forcibly envelop Caridad and silence her, the hip(g)nosis forces the focus onto the body wielding it. In these danced moments of religiosity, Caridad enacting hip(g)nosis has some agency over how she is perceived. Such hip(g)nosis also occurs on the cabaret stage where she becomes a star.

El Cabaret Las Vegas

A violent showdown between the *gallega* and Caridad leaves Caridad injured when the *gallega* hits Caridad in the head with the heel of her *white* shoe. In savior mode, Martín takes Caridad to Havana, where he brings her to a cabaret. While she sits and watches him surrounded by, and flirting with, other women, a *cha-cha-chá* begins to play. She approaches him, wanting to dance. He asks her, *"¿Quieres bailar para mi, mulata?"*/Do you want to dance for me, *mulata*?, and then proceeds to lift her onto the bar, which doubles as a stage. She starts to *cha-cha-chá*, not only for him but also for the entire cabaret (Figure 3.6). I read her dance as a corporeal affront to

Figure 3.6. Caridad improvises her *cha-cha-chá,* garnering an attentive audience.

Martín's having ignored her. Initially, it appears as if she dances to please him; however, with each flip (dip, sway, pulse, pump) of her hips, she carves out a hip(ped) response to not just having been ignored by him and what he expects or wants from her, but also by what he represents: *machista* notions of being. The cabaret audience adds to Caridad's affront, showing how her dancing body can attract more than one pair of eyes.

The pleasure involved in her "hip poetics" represents the pleasure Caridad insisted she has not had up until she left her hometown and went to Havana with Martín: *"Nunca me imaginé que existiera tanta felicidad"*/I never imagined that there could exist such happiness, she says to him, while she lays on a bed inside a hotel room in Havana. Subtly couched within a language of phallic virility's ability to give pleasure, almost no allowance remains for Caridad's pleasure to be anything but based on a man. Only when she dances, improvising through a *cha-cha-chá*, pummeling her audience ever so gently with the enunciating curves of her hips and buttocks, does she seize pleasure ever so briefly through her deployment of hip(g)nosis.

The beginning of her dance number has her filmed from the waist up, leaving the film audience to infer the hip sway occurring beneath. The neighboring bystanders' gazes shift to her dancing body, and eventually the camera pulls away and the film audience gets the opportunity to experience her enunciating hips and buttocks.

When dancing the *cha-cha-chá*—2,3 . . . *cha cha-chá* . . . and so on—the feet alternate stepping to this rhythm while the arms, torso, and more important, the hip/butt complex can play with the rhythm by improvising how to move in the space to the rhythm. Because of the alternating foot action and slight weight transfer between them, the hips must sway to the corresponding side of the weighted foot/leg. Ultimately, the hips become the focal point demonstrating the dancing body's finesse. Caridad's *cha-cha-chá* has her tapping her feet and pumping her pelvis back and forth, like a piston (Figure 3.7). Between swaying, pulsing, and circulating motions, Caridad's hips mesmerize her audience. The bartender gazes wide-eyed up at her, and even when she moves out of the frame, the camera lingers on his transfixed state, showing the effectiveness of those moving hips to indeed hip-notize (Figures 3.8 and 3.9).

Guevara, the cabaret owner, arrives during her "show." Several point-of-view shots from his perspective situate Caridad as the spectacle of the cabaret. Martin goes over to speak with him, and we find out he has unsettled debts. Guevara offers Martin money only if Martin can persuade *"la mulata"* to work for him. For them, she exists as an exchangeable commodity going from one man to another: *"Convéncela que se quede aquí y firme un contrato conmigo y yo te consigo el dinero para rescatar tu barco"*/ Convince the *mulata*

Figure 3.7. Caridad swings her hips as her audience watches her intently.

Figure 3.8. A transfixed bartender stares wide-eyed.

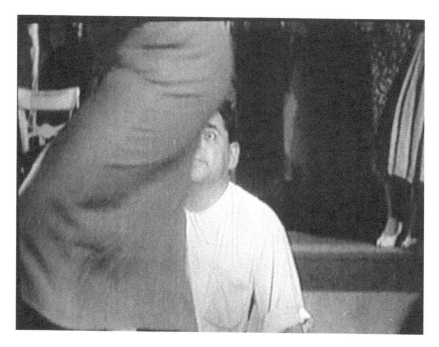

Figure 3.9. He can't take his eyes off her dancing body.

to stay here and sign a contract with me, and I'll help you find the money to get your boat back, Guevara enticingly offers Martín. Quick to demonstrate which "item" he prefers, Martín abandons Caridad to the life of the cabaret.

After Martín leaves, Guevara conveys the news to her in his office. She has been "sold" for a boat: "*¿Ahora qué vas a hacer, mulata?*"/Now what are you going to do, *mulata*? She throws a shot glass, walks over to the door, and opens it to look out onto the cabaret. She turns, looks straight at Guevara and says:

> *Siempre nos han vendido. Nos han tenido como esclavos. Pero ahora yo, la esclava mulata va a vengarse. Martín y tú, mi nuevo dueño, quieren que yo me queme en el infierno del baile. ¡Jmf! ¡Pero muchos van a arder conmigo!*
>
> They've always sold us. They've kept us as slaves. But now, I, the *mulata* slave will avenge herself. Martin and you, my new owner, want me to burn in the hell of the cabaret. Hmph! A lot of people will burn with me!

Caridad's having been abandoned and "sold" to the cabaret, a quick edit cuts to her triumphant entrance onto the cabaret stage after she pronounces her revenge. What follows is a rich description of Caridad's choreography so as to render the complexity and variety involved in hip(g)nosis.

Caridad enters stage left with arms diagonally stretched outward from her body, presenting that very same body to an audience (Figure 3.10). As she enters facing front, she continues with elevated arms to move sideways across the elevated stage. Her hips snap to the left and then to the right, like a rhythmic pendulum. She executes a small, syncopated jump—almost a double jump—and then the hip that corresponds to the foot where her weight has shifted to punctuates the downbeat. These "jumps" are abrupt, quick knee-flexion bounces with alternating hip pumps from side to side (Figure 3.11). Whereas *Tam Tam* erases the spectres of blackness through the cinematic device of the dissolve, *Mulata* positions Caridad, particularly in her big dance number, as a necessary inheritor of blackness while simultaneously distancing her from it.

As she moves across the stage, black figures painted on the wall function as visual reminders of the legacy of blackness that Caridad proudly asserts throughout the film. They stand there, totemic, offering their surplus value as fetishistic objects in a cabaret that relies on Afro-Cuban rhythms to attract clientele. Yet, in 1950s Cuba, the social reality outside the cabaret exposed the constrictions Afro-Cuban bodies experienced—constrictions

Figure 3.10. Caridad makes her grand entrance at the Cabaret Las Vegas.

Figure 3.11. Caridad shakes her hips briefly.

that seemed ludicrous given the creative labors they performed in cabarets both in and beyond Cuba. In other words, the Afro-Cuban body could be contained as long as it was in the service of *Cubanidad*, within the confines of a cabaret.

To contrast, the *mulata* had the potential to move within and outside these socio-culturally restricted spaces, and in this particular choreographed number, Caridad demonstrates the multiple ways her hips allowed this mobility, both metaphorically and corporeally. While the black figures remain on the wall, Caridad moves all over the cabaret space. While they wear raffia skirts and gold hoops, which make reference to a primitivist imagination of blackness, Caridad wears contemporary cabaret accouterments in white.

When she arrives stage right, hips swinging from side to side and arms still above, she starts descending stairs that will take her by tables filled with cabaret onlookers. As she walks down those steps, she shimmies her shoulders and brings her arms down to be level with her shoulders—and suddenly she pauses. She does basic *rumba* steps with corresponding hip swirls, takes the last two steps, and when she arrives at the cabaret main floor, she straightens her legs, bends her torso forward, and salutes an

Figure 3.12. Caridad stops suddenly and pushes her hips and buttocks back into a riveted and hip-notized spectator.

onlooker with her bottom (Figure 3.12). A declarative pronouncement of her hip(g)notic appeal.

Her bottom hides beneath a huge multilayered white tulle bow and train that bob according to her pelvic enunciations. She continues along the cabaret floor, flutters her shoulders, and traces a full circle around the floor to wind up in the center facing forward. She has been shot wide angle up until now, allowing the film's audience to both see all her moves and the cabaret audience's reactions.

A series of improvised *rumba* steps continues: legs bend, weight shifts, her hips sway, swirl, and circle. After several counts of the *rumba* step facing her audience, she turns around and the big white tulle bow makes figure-eights, illustrating the shapes her hips trace in space (Figure 3.13). Perhaps she thinks we may not have had enough of her big white bow, so she does a quick jump, leans forward with her back still to us, and on the balls of her feet she runs in place, tracing little circles with her hips/ butt/bow. The circles become semicircles become ovals become half-circles swinging side to side like a swing set, all at the discretion of the rhythm and this *mulata-cum-rumbera's* improvisational technique. She kicks one leg toward the drummers (who play in front of her when her back is to the

Figure 3.13. Caridad makes figure-eights and circles with her hips, accented by the tulle bow.

audience) and turns around to face her adoring public once again. Camera shots are generally wide ones, encapsulating her entire dancing body, permitting ample witnessing of not only how that body moves through the cabaret space but how other corporeals react to its moving and performing presence. All eyes rest on this dancing *mulata*. She is the main attraction, the cocktail special of the evening: the new infamous *Mulata*, served at Cabaret Las Vegas.

By performing hip rotations, undulations, and pelvic movements associated with her presupposed intemperate sexuality and brazen nature, and through an acute awareness of the material value of those kinesthetic iterations, Caridad is a *mulata* wielding hip(g)nosis, who appropriates the very body that has been used against her. This is hip(g)nosis at work. In so doing, she removes her body's status as fetish, as violence and iconographic subjugation, while at the same time highlighting the socio-politically constructed nature of race. It is through this racialized performativity that she asserts her historically denied subjectivity. Thus, her body serves as both cultural construct and site of redress, further complicating notions of race, gender, and subjectivity.

Caridad dances pleasurably, frenetically, almost deliriously. Her hip(g)notizing *mulata* performance sits entrenched in a historical struggle between the

Figure 3.14. Mid-frame close-up of her hip circles with the bow moving with her.

state, consumerism and consumption, and Cuban *machismo*. This danced act of revenge thus attests to the fact that, as Foucault claims, "power is everywhere; not because it embraces everything, but because it comes from everywhere."[13] If this is the case, then there lies power in hip(g)nosis. It is not simply the power to dazzle, enliven, enthrall, swindle, or entice, but also to contest the multiplicity of force relations acting upon that body. She can thus enact a contestatory resistance through the seemingly "natural" revolution of her hips, even if only for the length of a *rumba* performance.

At the refrain of the "bow dance," the camera moves in for a tighter shot (Figure 3.14). This time, she inhabits the frame from mid-thigh to the top of her headdress, and we see the bow move closer. In interchanges between wide and medium close shot, she continues to hip-notize her public.

Another barrage of *rumba* steps follow as the buttocks lead the way back toward the drummers, all combined with fancy footwork: jump, cross right in front, across left, jump cross left in front, across right. During a drum solo she imitates the male version of the *rumba*, the *columbia*, in that she lifts her knees alternating them while her torso quickly rotates from left to right, the movement initiated by the waist, hips stable. With her back to the audience yet again, she jumps and lands on the floor, knees bent, back arching until she touches the floor with her back, neck craned to look

Figure 3.15. She finishes her performance and raises her arms to the thunder of applause.

at audience. Meanwhile her arms are outstretched, perpendicular to her torso, and she shimmies her shoulders to another percussive drum solo, while lying half supine on the floor.

When she gets up, her energy and pace slow down, she does several *rumba* steps facing the audience, stops as the music flourishes to an end, lifts her arms triumphantly, and smiles (Figure 3.15). A *mulata's* vengeance, achieved through hip(g)nosis.

These examples of hip(g)nosis within the confining narrative of Caridad's life acknowledge hip(g)nosis's ability to assert a corporeality's lived presence. What is more, hip(g)nosis forges a real or, quite specifically, a material response to the impositions of the limiting signifiers used to categorize the *mulata* (*mulata cochina*, *mulata asquerosa*) in the film. If an articulate *mulata* body wielding her hips for pleasure, vengeance, or defiance can be considered an assertion of identity, a veritable choreography of the self, then it becomes crucial to consider bodies—racialized, gendered, sexualized, and sensual—as sites of knowledge, history, and power.

YAMBAÓ, OR CRY OF THE BEWITCHED (1957)

While *Mulata's* portrayal looks to the *mulata's* inheritances of blackness as liberation, in *Yambaó*, the *mulata* Yambaó moves defiantly within the tropes of blackness and its ties to Lukumí/Santería traditions.[14] *Yambaó* relies on superficial and sensationalist signifiers of Santería to situate its *mulata* as different from the other slaves on the plantation. Her difference reads as dangerous, particularly since she shirks authority and wanders in and out of the plantation home uninvited and unannounced.

Yambaó remains consistently unmoored. The film appropriates Santería to promulgate the primitivist fantasy of a bewitching *mulata* who engages in trickery, sorcery, and seduction in order to assert her identity. Like Caridad, Yambaó also ends up a "tragic *mulata*" figure. Unlike Caridad, Yambaó sacrifices herself in an act of self-castigation for allowing her black grandmother, also named Caridad, to turn her against the master of the plantation, Jorge, her paramour.

I read Yambaó's choreographed actions against this tragic end and highlight those moments in the film when she enacts hip(g)nosis and displays pleasure, religiosity, indignation, and disdain. What interests me is how dance functions as Yambaó's means of communication for her presumed uncontainable and uncontained physicality. Again, the conflation between the *mulata* body, rhythm, seduction, and dance unfolds in four particular instances in the film. While the film offers robust imagery for critical engagement and analysis about Cuban cultural imaginings of their plantation economy, I focus on Yambaó's body and how it materializes further imaginings of the sensual, hipped, and hip(g)notizing *mulata*.

Dancing hips speak loudly in this film; theirs is not the shy whisper of the master's white wife or the subjugated murmur of the black enslaved bodies who attend to her needs. Attached to Yambaó's *mulata* body, her hips enact defiance and resist containment, particularly when dancing to Afro-Cuban sacred drumming. Yambaó's dances belong within the framework of diasporic black dance, which "may be likened to verbal language most in the dance's conspicuous employment of 'call and response' with the body responding to and provoking the voice of the drum."[15]

The film credits Roderico "Rodney" Neyra as the choreographer. Rodney, as he is affectionately remembered among Cuban popular-culture aficionados, had already been choreographing lavish spectacles at the Tropicana since 1951. Here, I highlight the ways in which stage choreographers from the Cuban cabarets chose (and to some extent still choose) to highlight in their narratives a myth of Cuban origins in which the African and the Spanish neatly amalgamate. This narrative moves to films that continue to circulate such potent, yet problematic tropes. Nationalist themes function as the vehicle for hip(g)nosis to become a type of Cuban brand.

All of Yambaó's dance numbers in the film involve her body in relationship with the drum, within the context of Afro-Cuban sacred music. It is this relationship that allows her dancing body to audaciously occupy space and claim a quasi-liberation through her ability to hip(g)notize. Her hip(g)nosis does come at a price, when she battles between her grandmother's desire for revenge through the possession of her body and her own desire to be coupled—in the arms of Jorge, the master of the plantation with whom she has had an illicit affair. Fulfilling the requisite "tragic *mulata*" trope, Yambaó plunges to her death after a frenzied dance number. Death becomes the only way for her to stop her black grandmother's evil intentions of harming Jorge. Through her sacrifice, the *mulata* Yambaó saves the plantation from the perceived threat of blackness. Her liminal appearance and her ability to move between her grandmother's dark cave—the sugarcane field where the slaves toil—and the plantation, where Jorge and his expectant wife live, disrupt the social and racial order of that plantation. Like every femme fatale, she must die, even if it is by her own hands.

Yambaó's Arrival

Here is the Internet Movie Database (IMDb) summary for the version of the film that is available on YouTube :

> Cuba, 1850. On a sugar-cane plantation, the master and his wife are happy: they're expecting a child, their slaves are quiet. But tonight, as the full moon rises, the sound of the drums are in the air. Yambaó, the grand-daughter of a sorceress killed 15 years ago, has come back . . . with her grand-mother's spirit.[16]

And here are the words of the narrator in the English-language version of the film.[17]

> Only a century ago, a hundred and fifty years after the witch burnings in Salem, the peaceful atmosphere of our tropical island was shattered by a strange terror unleashing excesses of hatred and love from the deepest wells of primitive feeling.[18]

The film summary and the opening narrator remarks demonstrate how mythologies of plantation life, threatening women, and primitiveness provide a logic for the film's narrative. The evocative power of words such as *full moon, sorceress, primitive feeling* and *drums* renders Yambaó's character as desirable, mysterious, threatening, and more important, excessive. Such excess in both feeling and physicality becomes the driving forces of the narrative. The film begins with wide shots of enslaved bodies in colorful clothes walking leisurely through the sugarcane fields, singing. That is a bucolic rendering of a violent reality, as sugarcane plantations were notoriously dangerous and life threatening for those who worked in them.[19] That evening, the full moon rises. *Batá* drums—sacred drums that normally call out to *orishas* and ancestors in Santería ceremonies—operate as non-diegetic heralds. Jorge, the master of the plantation, has just returned home; his wife struggles with the terrible heat, and the slaves recognize the drumming sounds.[20]

One slave, Damián, tells Jorge that those sounds have not been heard for over fifteen years on the plantation. Their incessant pulsing calls Jorge and a group of slaves to a clearing in the woods. In the clearing, a woman stands playing the *okonkolo*, the smallest of the two-headed *batá* drums used in Afro-Cuban sacred drumming (see Figure 3.16). *"Yambaó! Yambaó!"/ She's back.* Damian and Jorge pronounce her name as they stare at her. They are framed in a closeup, so the audience can appreciate their looks of surprise, shock, admiration, and disbelief when they hail her as the subject of the film, agent of threat, and for Jorge, object of desire.

When her gaze meets that of one of the male slaves, Lázaro (who has been in love with her since they were children and is played by the same actor who plays the *mulato* suitor in *Mulata*), she makes a quick nod with her head, beckoning him. He understands the gesture as an invitation to approach, and he does so—eagerly. She gives him the drum. While he pulls the strap over his head, she stands with her hand on her hip, leaning to one

Figure 3.16. Yambaó's arrival in a scene from *Yambaó*.

side and waiting for the drumming to start, waiting for the song of prayer to begin. The camera cuts quickly to a man who sings the opening antiphon of a praise song for Obatalá, the Santería *orisha* who represents the Elder archetype.

A curious coupling occurs with the song for Obatalá and Yambaó's sensual dance. Clearly, the Africanist rhythms allow for her body to become more eroticized, sexualized, and black while at the same time highlighting her difference from the rest of the black and brown population on the plantation, as one of the slave characters states that this type of drumming/music has not been heard on the plantation since Yambaó's grandmother died. (They are not aware that their attempt at killing her failed and she is hiding in a cave.)

With both hands on her hips, she pulses her shoulders to the rhythm and shifts her weight from side to side. She begins to walk over to where several male onlookers sit watching her. Hers is a languorous walk, with wide, slow steps and long arm extensions. Once she reaches her first potential partner, she violently grasps him by the hair, raises him up toward her, and then brusquely and abruptly pushes him back down. As he is unsuitable as a partner, she moves on to a second man. She chooses. She picks. She dismisses. She has power.

Her hips invite her second partner toward her. They lure his manhood. She moves toward him, leading with her circling, swaying hips. He responds and both dance in synchronization to the rhythm and to one another. Suddenly, he attempts contact. He grabs her, turns her quickly around, and presses up against her, her bottom against his pelvis. She rotates her hips slowly and enticingly, taking some pleasure from the slow, sensual mimetic gesture of copulation. He starts to touch her waist, and she dismisses his advances with a symbolic act of *coitus interruptus*: she juts her buttocks back and pushes him away with it so forcibly that he loses his balance and falls to the ground. A striking metaphor for the power of hip(g)nosis?

She continues on to her next conquest. Her third partner, like the others, finds himself drawn to her hip call as she sways over to dance with him. He succumbs to her sensual power by getting close and trying to dance even more closely with her. They do a couple of hip rotations together, until she grabs his head and abruptly pushes him down and away from her. This particular corporeal conversation concludes with two hip sways before she falls and lies prostrate in front of the sacred *batá* drums.

She immediately rises and moves to the center of the space opened up for her. Three men have risen and dance in their respective areas, waiting for her to approach. Her first partner in the circle receives the same dismissive pelvic thrust backwards from her as she moves on to dance quickly with the other two.

She eventually moves to the center again, and this time the combination of the drums, chanting, and her own moving body begin to have an effect on her state of consciousness. Her head moves in frenzied circles, she appears about to lose her balance, her eyes close, and she begins to jerk her torso. Here, the choreography of possession physically represents the apparent dichotomy between body and spirit, blackness and non-blackness, and Yambaó's will versus that of her grandmother's.

Slowly she gains control over her body once more. Has her grandmother possessed her successfully? Or, has she managed to ward off her grandmother's intentions for now? As she sways lazily from side to side, she notices the master of the plantation looking down at her. She begins to walk rhythmically over to him and stands defiantly in front of him. In what becomes her signature gesture in the film, Yambaó stands with her hands on her hips, jutting out her chin: a corporeal declarative statement, an assertive occupation of space.

He stands above her, but her raised chin and insolent stare attempts to dismantle his authority. The camera films him from below, thereby granting his downwards glance an air of authority. It cuts to a wide shot, and she suddenly spits at him, a clear sign of her disdain. After she spits, she dashes away. Yambaó is definitely back.

The First Enchantment: The Love Spell

Yambaó casts two spells in the film: a love spell and a curative spell. Both utilize different Afro-Cuban or Afro-Haitian rhythms as soundtracks to the sorcery. Again, blackness and its associations with primitivism and animism are not critically articulated, let alone respectfully represented; instead, what ensues is a theatricalization of animal sacrifice and a spectacularized version of the Cuban cultural imaginary's interpretation of the power of the *mulata* to entice and bewitch.

Because Jorge rescued her from potential harm at the hands of some of the male slaves, Yambaó develops feelings for him. She sneaks into the plantation— demonstrating her ability to have access to both public and private spaces—and steals some of his discarded clothes, intent on making him love her back. This narrative device insists that Jorge *cannot* be drawn to her out of his own volition or out of mere concupiscence; she must engage in some form of trickery to fuel his desire.

Figure 3.17. Yambaó and her dance with the daggers.

Yambaó casts her love spell against a tree in the woods. In its hollow rest an Africanized idol, coconuts, candles, fruits, and other items that would be on an *orisha* altar. She carries his clothes and sets them before the altar. The non-diegetic music features chants to the *orishas* with the voice of Cuban soprano Xiomara Alfaro, perhaps functioning as the "voice" of Yambaó as she dances and casts the spell. From beneath the altar, Yambaó retrieves two daggers. She begins to use them in her solo dance, a dance that mixes the *columbia*, the solo male version of *rumba*, with some lyrical slow extensions of her legs and arms, perhaps to highlight her body's sensuality. Her hands move vigorously, the daggers slicing through the air as her lower half performs the intricate frenetic footwork of the *columbia* (Figure 3.17).

The use of the *columbia* dance to accompany Afro-Cuban sacred drumming reflects choreographer Rodney's repertoire. Already established as the artistic director of the Tropicana by the time of Yambaó's release, Rodney had experience making choreographic numbers that utilized many of Cuba's well-established tropes of *rumba, mulatas,* and blackness. Before his tenure at the Tropicana, Rodney had started a group called Las Mulatas del Fuego (they had first been known as The Mulatas de Rodney, until a trip to Mexico in 1948) with the original intention of finding dancers to work on a film called *Zamba Rumba.*[21] These "fiery *mulatas*" performed throughout Latin America, Europe, and the Middle East in the 1940s and '50s.

In 1948, Las Mulatas were awarded a contract to perform at the Teatro Follies, in Mexico City, by its then owner, Chato Guerra. Another "fiery *mulata*" by the name of Esther "La Reina Karula" Lafayette (sister of Lalín

Lafayette) had her own performance alongside Cuban bandleader Beny Moré. His real name was Bartolomé, and Karula admits to having found the nickname Beny for him.[21] As a featured dancer in Moré's shows, La Karula enthralled audiences with her solo *columbia* dancing. She created a sensation because this dance form was normally performed by men. In her hands she also wielded daggers. It may be likely that Rodney's interactions with Las Mulatas and La Reina Karula included seeing one of La Karula's performances. If so, then her influence appears in Yambaó's dance of enchantment. I am aware of the speculative nature of this claim, yet I take into account how embodied acts and memories move through performing bodies. Dance scholar Priya Srinivasan stresses how Ruth St. Denis failed to completely acknowledge the Indian Nachwali dancers in the development of her modern dance movement vocabulary.[22] In similar vein, I pry open the possibility that Rodney, in perhaps watching La Karula more than once, conceived and then re-choreographed her dagger dance onto Ninón Sevilla.

Bodies learn from others bodies. They learn, translate, and re-choreograph. The failed acknowledgments create empty spaces in dance history that can take shape when the attention shifts to the subaltern body. As such, La Karula haunts Ninón's dagger dance . . . and perhaps even messes up her steps on purpose.

Rodney, then, becomes instrumental within the genealogy of the *mulata*. His productions on stage and screen circulated hip(g)nosis as a national brand. Although the bodies of both Lafayette and Sevilla function in different racialized registers (Lafayette as a "real" *mulata*, Ninón as a performative one), it is their hips and the narratives they materialize that become commodities for Rodney to then organize as a Cuban type of choreography. Certainly both Lafayette and Sevilla could perform culturally conditioned versions of "*mulata*" regardless of their actual racial affinity to *mulata*-ness. Yet, in service and deference to the vectors of historicity and embodied experience, I make a benign critique of the mode of production that Rodney utilized in bringing La Karula's dagger dance to the screen. This is not because I want to leave the issue of cultural and choreographic appropriation in dance unfettered, but because of the assumption that nationalistic affinities allow for these kinds of appropriations and enactments to happen.

In the circulation of Cuban signifiers, what matters in this case is not *what* gets circulated (as problematic as that is) so much as it is *who* does the circulating, how, and for what purposes. At issue here is the fulsome use of *mulata* signifiers as representatives of a fiery sensual *Cubanidad*. Furthermore, while the contexts of La Karula and Sevilla's dagger dances differ, ultimately the performance of a dagger dance by a *mulata* alerts the witness to a "certain kind of way" *mulatas* act, even if that "act" is indeed just that—an act. Thus, while the bewitching and enchanting *mulata* proves to be a powerful trope on stage and screen, the question remains why only *that* trope—and why keep circulating it? How does its repetition engender a certain kind of hip(g)nosis—the kind that leaves lacunae about history and the *mulata's* experience in the memories of the *mulata's* audience?

My interest here lies in unsettling the ways in which this small act of appropriation by Rodney from La Karula to Sevilla points to the larger ramifications of hip(g)nosis. If Yambaó's dance of enchantment functions as a surrogation of La Karula's famous Mexican dagger dance, then where does the pleasurable and rehearsed performance of the dagger dance for La Karula get its value?[23]

No longer a pleasurable performance per se, it is now a circulated commodity branded as commodified hip(g)nosis—the dagger dance in *Yambaó* shifts in significance. As a choreographic tactic that carries the narrative of the trickster *mulata* forward, Yambaó's dagger dance erases the impact the dance may have had initially when performed by La Karula—especially if, as sources indicate, she was the only woman to dance the *columbia* with daggers in her hands. La Karula's daggers cut through the pretention of Cuba's mythic nationalist origins (or even the origins of a choreographic instance) and reveal the bodies that work and materialize the Cuban nation—one that in its circulations of limited and limiting nationalist iconographies removes the historical nature of these bodies. Foucault writes that, "the origin lies at a place of inevitable loss, the point where the truth of things corresponded to a truthful discourse, the site of a fleeting articulation that discourse has obscured and finally lost."[24]

Origin denotes loss, erasure, obscurity. In its stead, the project of genealogy moves history and its messiness forward while not dwelling on the past. Here I assert how a small choreographic moment—the dagger dance—exists as a robust site for genealogical excavation of the dancing *mulata's* significance and signification in the Cuban cultural imaginary. While La Karula's dagger dance illustrates the way hip(g)nosis travels and hip-notizes, Yambaó's dagger dance also hip-notizes both the film audience and Jorge. He appears at the forest clearing once she has finished casting her spell.

When Jorge renounces her advances, Yambaó threatens him: *No te dejaré dormir. Mi voz se te meterá en los oídos hasta hacerte gritar . . . Te quiero pa' mi sola*/I won't let you sleep. My voice will enter your ears until you scream . . . I want you just for me. Jorge had succumbed to her mouth previously, kissing her right after he had rescued her from the plantation's perpetrators. Nevertheless, he returns to his reason (his sense of duty as patriarch, master, and husband) and scorns her advances. This return to reason will appear once more in the film (as well as later in this chapter, when I point out a particular dance scene in a Cuban documentary that best demonstrates the dichotomy between mind/reason and the hip/emotion). In the meantime, Yambaó's spell takes effect after an explosion summons Jorge to her. He appears somnambulant and shirtless while she rolls on the floor with his stolen clothes.

As she cast the spell, she violently stabs his clothes, penetrating them with the angry weight of her desire. Not only do I read these stabs as narrative devices to show her determination to make him hers by any means necessary, but more significantly, they function as fits of revenge for the historical wounds and afflictions caused by men like him on women like her. Clearly, her violence pales in comparison to the gendered and epistemic violence inherent in the master/woman-of-color dialectic, yet herein lies the multi-valent potential of hip(g)nosis to offer such a reading.

When he arrives to stand above her, subservient and bewitched, Yambaó rises from the ground, wide-eyed. She seems genuinely surprised her spell has worked and then goes on to perform a longer version of the dagger dance she began by the altar. Full-body shots show how she circles around him: small leaps, fast footwork, daggers flailing in her hands. Suddenly he succumbs and faints. The spell cast, he falls ill with a serious fever ("the plague," as the film calls it) and must return home. His desire for her has literally inflamed his body to a state of feverish oblivion. He lies in bed, unable to speak. Yambaó has ensured that his desire supercedes any access to language he might possibly have.

The Second Enchantment: The Curative Spell

Yambaó arrives at the plantation house unannounced once more, and tells Beatriz, Jorge's wife, that she will cure him. Yeya, Beatriz's maid, distrusts Yambaó's "witchcraft," but Beatriz allows Yambaó to remain because the town doctor has taken ill as well. As Jorge lies in bed, Yambaó sneaks into his room and lies next to him.

> Soy yo mi amor. Yambaó. Oye mi voz. Escucha mi nombre. Yambaó. Yambaó. Quiero que mi nombre entre en ti y aunque yo esté lejos vendrás a mi. Vendrás porque ya no querrás a nada menos que a Yambaó. Tu Yambaó, tu amor/ It is me, my love. Yambaó. Listen to my voice. Hear my name: Yambaó, Yambaó. I want my name to get inside you and, though I may be far, you will come to me. though You'll come to me because you will want nothing but Yambaó. Your Yambaó, your love.

To save him from imminent death, Yambaó begs her grandmother to help her. At first, Caridad becomes intransigent, citing the revenge they both must exact on Jorge because of his father's ill treatment of Caridad. Yambaó's disobedience and scorn force Caridad to help her, and she provides Yambaó with some instruction on how to perform a spell that may save Jorge: *Go to the woods and sacrifice a pure animal according to the rites.* These rites she mentions stem from the Santería tradition (as well as other African ancestor-worship belief systems) whereby animal sacrifice functions as a way to send messages to the ancestors or deities.[25]

The choreographed number begins with Yambaó carrying a white goat into a forest clearing. Four bare-chested men (presumably plantation slaves) join her, each appearing from a different side of the clearing. They undulate their torsos and move into a straight line behind her as she lifts up the goat to the heavens. The men hinge backward, arms extended, and plant their knees on the ground. Torso undulations alternate with slow hinges backwards.

In the background, groups of women slaves sit unobtrusively functioning as decorative bodies. When the non-diegetic drumming rhythm changes to *palo* (*petwo,* in Haiti), Yambaó and the four male dancers rise. Their torsos continue to undulate. In their hands the men carry straw hats, from which they draw out a yellow powder and hurl it at Yambaó. Meanwhile, Yambaó stands in a wide-legged stance and moves her arms in gestures that mimic the riding of a horse (Figure 3.18).

Figure 3.18. Yambaó casting a spell; notice the background dancers preparing to get into hinge position.

In the Haitian spiritual tradition of Voudou, when the *loas*, or spirits, want to commune with their worshipers, they mount or ride (literally possess) the worshiper's body.[26] This action appears removed from its spiritual context in this instance, yet the movement vocabulary of hinges, leg extensions, and wide bent-leg stances connotes the Haitian dance form Cuban *palo* has strong correlation to Haitian *petwo*, particularly in the eastern region of the Cuba. The male dancers also lean to one side and lift a leg up horizontally, parallel to their hips. Yambaó performs this movement phrase in addition to other ones: slow self-touch, standing in place while undulating laterally.

After a quick edit, the scene shifts from their dancing to Jorge's bedroom, and Yambaó now appears dancing with a rope tied around her hips held by two of the men, a ripe metaphor for the way in which hip(g)nosis has been historically contained. Power lies in those hips. By tying them and continuing to throw the magic powder on her, the men ensure that the intensity of casting the spell ensues. A long tracking shot from the door of Jorge's bedroom toward the bed where he lies infirm demonstrates the power of the spell as it draws nearer to the object of its purpose. Yambaó breaks free from the ropes, clasps her hands, and looks upward in an appeal to a higher power. She offers herself up as a sacrifice, should Jorge not survive the plague: *Save him. Give him back the life you have taken away from him . . . or take my own!*

He calls out her name, and immediately she knows her spell has worked. She runs to the house, enters uninvited and unannounced once more, and goes directly to his room. There, his wife waits with Yeya. Yeya and Yambaó exchange a glance, with Yambaó jutting out her chin in similar fashion to the first gesture she made in the film, that time to Lázaro. Beatriz and Yambaó stare at one another until Yambaó turns her eyes downwards, a quiet acquiescence of Beatriz's claim over Jorge as his wife. She turns and walks away.

A Song by the River

Life seems to have returned to normal on the plantation, and all the enslaved bodies continue with their work. Meanwhile, Yambaó goes to the river to wash her clothes (Figure 3.19). The river functions as a force of nature in the *orisha* Ochún, as well. It is also a dominant site for historical *mulata* labor, given that in the nineteenth century many *mulatas* in Cuba (and the Caribbean) worked as laundresses.

The scene, which seems a bit out of place in the film (probably to showcase famous Cuban singer Olga Guillot), begins with a representation of

Figure 3.19. Yambaó singing across the river in a scene rich with Ochún symbolism.

gendered divisions of labor by enslaved bodies. The men cut cane, the women walk to the river to wash. Their everyday movements of coerced labor (as enslaved subjects they do not have ownership of their own bodies) establish a rhythm that corresponds with the extra-diegetic sound that eventually becomes diegetic, or part of the film. The sharpening of the machete adds to the pulse of the soundtrack.

Hands on hips, Olga Guillot walks to the rhythm, adding her voice singing, "*O le le . . . .*" It is a bucolic, colorful representation of slave labor, with Yambaó on the opposite side of the river (Figure 3.20). In contrast to the enslaved labor of washing clothes for the plantation home, Yambaó's washes clothes for herself. The river acts as the border between alienated labor and pleasurable tasks. This exchange between Yambaó and the slave character played by Guillot offers a new register through which to read Yambaó's (and by extension, the *mulata*) extractions of pleasure in the film (Figure 3.21). Unlike other song or dance sequences in the film where men are involved, this exchange occurs between her and another woman. They sing to one another in the Africanist aesthetic form of call and response; and in the context of the choreography, film editing, and the lyrics, it could be seen to contain sexual innuendo: "*O le le, O le le, Ay pruébalo u(s)ted, qué rico se ve*"/Why don't you try it? It looks so good. What should she try? And what exactly looks so good? [27]

Ostensibly, this insinuation opens a queer space for these two *mulatas* on screen, especially since until now I have cited moments of pleasure usually framed around masculinist impositions, male bodies, or patriarchal

Figure 3.20. Olga Guillot singing across the river to Yambaó.

Figure 3.21. A wide shot of the exchangeover the river.

control. However, in this scene the *mulata*, normally a historically explicit heterosexual object of desire, ruptures the expectation and emerges as a possible non-normative subject in relationship to the other *mulata* (Olga Guillot). Is this a siren call of desire or mutual *mulata* recognition? In their musical exchange, do they communicate only something that they can understand?

As their call and response continues, Olga remains standing, hands on hip, shifting from side to side, maintaining the rhythm. Yambaó responds by humming the tune, not articulating its consonant sounds of *O-le-le* but, rather, the *mmmmmmm* of (self) pleasure. Yambaó's hip swaying is not about a shift in weight. Her knees are bent, her body seems more grounded, and she punctuates the downbeat with an upswing of her hips. Additionally, her upper torso and shoulders move while Guillot's torso and hips stay parallel to the horizontal plane. The camera closes in on both faces singing to one another. This exchange creates a moment of sensual intimacy and racialized gendered affinity. *Ay pruebalo u(s)ted, Qué rico se ve!/ Try it! It looks so good!*

Even the labors of both women remain quite distinct from the rest of the female group: Guillot arrives and distributes pieces of sugarcane from her basket and remains standing, swaying her hips and singing, displaying the actionable assertions of personal pleasure and enjoyment. Yambaó appears to have only one item of clothing to wash and as she is free, she need not be in any hurry to finish. Theirs is a languorous exchange, one that Ochún would approve as the goddess of pleasure.

Later that day, the enslaved Afro-Cubans dance, sing, and pray to Ochún. The mistress of the plantation sits nearby but looks unwell. The rhythms and prayers to Ochún, goddess of pleasure and fertility, affect her pregnancy. She swoons and must be brought inside. Meanwhile, Jorge languishes alongside Yambaó in her thatched hut. Yambaó urges him to leave with her. She wants to get away from the plantation and start a new life elsewhere with him. Jorge tells Yambaó that he would like to see his child born and thereafter he will leave with her. She promises to give him many children. Lázaro interrupts their idyll to announce that Jorge's child will shortly arrive. He rushes out, leaving Yambaó alone; a close-up of her face shows a worried expression.

With his wife still lying in bed after giving birth, Jorge apologizes to her, claiming madness as the reason for his indiscretions with Yambaó. She gently places her hand on his head as a gesture of forgiveness. The film cuts to an image of Yambaó standing outside her hut in an attempt to call out to Jorge as she has done before. The wind carries her name to him, but he does not hear. Now, as a father with a legitimate heir from a legitimate wife, he can no longer hear it. Patriarchy, paternity, and lineage silence Yambaó's call for good.

Caridad, Yambaó's grandmother, convinces Yambaó that she must kill both the mother and the child if she is to have power over Jorge again. Upon her orders, Yambaó runs to the plantation and sneaks in unnoticed. Beatriz appears frightened as Yambaó lifts a knife over her head, ready to kill her and the baby. Outside, Caridad orders her to *"mátalos, mátalos"*/kill them, kill them. The faithful Damián sees her and promptly stabs her. When Caridad falls dead, a quick cut takes us to Yambaó, who appears to come out of a hypnotic trance. She registers her surroundings and her intended act of violence by apologizing and insisting on her benevolence: *"Yo no soy mala, no quiero ser mala. Él no me quiere a mi. Él quiere a Uds. dos"*/I'm not bad. I do not want to be bad. He doesn't desire (want, love) me. He wants both of you.

As the apologetic and remorseful *mulata*, Yambaó transfers the threat and evil of blackness back to Caridad. Caridad's desire to end the family lineage of the master, perhaps the greatest threat to white Cuban patriarchy in the nineteenth century, disappears once she dies at the hand of the dutiful Damián. Thus, the *mulata* emerges as the docilizing agent of blackness. When Caridad dies and can no longer wield her influence over Yambaó, the social order of the plantation can return to normal.

Caridad's Funeral and Yambaó's Sacrificial Dance

The next scene features a celebration that shifts to a funeral once Caridad learns of her grandmother's death. Signifiers of Afro-Cuban Lukumí/ Santería ritual meld in the final scene/musical number of the film: cigars, *batá* drums, the prostration on the floor, beads. It begins benignly as an outdoors celebration in the woods in honor of the peaceful social order the plantation can now enjoy. As in the other instances, Yambaó dances alone, occupying the center cipher position. Surrounding her, the bodies dance in unison with simple *rumba* steps to the side with the occasional solo (black) dancer stepping out of the group and joining Yambaó for brief moments. Yambaó's legs are in a wide second position most of the time, knees bent. She appears much more grounded than in earlier dance performances. Additionally, her arms reach up and outward, her limbs stretching widely above and below. When her movements become more contained, she resorts to simple *rumba* steps to maneuver around the space and acknowledge the other black bodies around her. This gesture of acknowledgment resembles the Santería greeting in which the initiates lean diagonally into one another, touching shoulders. Many ceremonial gestures from Afro-Cuban Santería appear in this final choreography, but they are quite decontextualized. Although they lose their spiritual efficacy, they still emerge as movement acts of worship and/or pleasure.

At one point, Yambaó invites a young boy to dance with her. She beckons him with a deep grounded wide-legged position and outstretched arms. By this time, the music crescendos to a more insistent and faster rhythm that has everybody dancing. Yambaó and the young boy dance an innocuous *rumba* until she sees the body of her grandmother brought into the dance circle. She screams in horror, the celebration stops, and everyone falls to the ground.

An enslaved woman rushes over and leans over the body of Caridad, calling out the chant for Oya, the *orisha* goddess of the dead. Yambaó kneels over her grandmother's body in mourning. The chant shifts from Oya to that of Changó, god of thunder and the drum. Here, Yambaó rises to dance, accompanied by two black women. As in the film *Mulata,* where she dances to *orishas* flanked by two black women, Ninón Sevilla's white Cuban body gains currency through the labor of these women. Although the choreographies of Changó are not the exact gestures and steps I am familiar with and have learned, the verticality of the body and forceful leg thrusts downward are visible.

As one of the black dancers seems to fall into a trance and executes gestures of possession, Jorge appears. Suddenly, Yambaó begins to lose control over her body. She sways and touches her head. Damián mentions to Jorge that Caridad's spirit tries to possess Yambaó. Yambaó notices Jorge, rushes over to one of the men, and grabs a dagger. She runs to Jorge in a fierce attempt to kill him. He looks at her and says her name, "Yambaó." He says it gently, confidently, acknowledging her presence and her subjectivity. He has spoken her into being (so to speak), and he has brought her back to consciousness, to herself.

When Yambaó goes to kill the master (possessed by her grandmother's vengeful spirit), an enslaved woman (played by the famous Cuban singer Xiomara Alfaro) sings to Ochún, the sweetness of Ochún's chant presumably calms Yambaó, and she begins to dance the *iyesa* rhythm of Ochún with detached abandon. She moves slowly and sensually, giving into the pleasure of the communion between song, dance, and rhythm and her body's ability to respond to all three.

Groups of women walk into the clearing, swinging branches above their heads with their arms—choreographic gestures stemming from the Abakua/Carabali dance for women called *Brikamo.* Normally, the arms need to be bent more with vigorous brushing or sweeping movements.[28] Male bodies carry chickens and make wide expansive steps, almost arabesquelike as they enter the clearing. This movement syntax demonstrates how choreographer Rodney may have been thinking about how to shift Afro-Cuban dance vocabulary from ritual to stage presentational setting. Although the film presents these dances in their supposed rural "authentic" settings, the combination of cinematic apparatus and Rodney's modernist choreographic intentions alter the dances' presentations.

Yambaó dances as if possessed. She succumbs to the pleasure of her body moving to the *iyesa* drum rhythms. She produces Ochún (Ochún as pleasure) through her pleasurable kinetic response. Her outspread arms and legs, coupled with her grounded stance and swaying hips, not only asserts her pleasure, her body being open to anything and everything, but it also symbolizes her body's refusal to be contained. The crowd gathers around her, with baskets of fruit, chickens, pulsing torsos, swaying limbs. The corporeal freneticism starts to overcome Yambaó and she drops to her knees, her head moving in quick circles. The camera cuts between Yambaó's dance mostly in full-body shots and Jorge's face in close-up watching her. The male gaze never leaves the dancing *mulata* body. The filmic apparatus makes this evident.

Once the music switches from Ochún, goddess of love and pleasure, to Elegua, trickster god and owner of the crossroads, Yambaó's body becomes unstable. She no longer moves comfortably to the rhythm. Instead, her hands go to her head and she struggles to find a balance. Is her grandmother's spirit trying to possess her again? Is she unsure of what her life will be without her grandmother? She encounters the unknown, a figurative crossroads (edged on by Elegua's—the owner of the crossroads—music). Does this liminal space remove the pleasure of her embodied present moment that only Ochún can provide? The music continues to swell as she runs away from the crowds. They follow her and Jorge calls out her name. It appears as if it is too much for Yambaó. She succumbs to the tragedy embedded in her corporeality and hurls herself from a cliff.

In *Yambaó*, the *mulata's* relationship to blackness operates as a threat. Furthermore, her corporeality asserts her ability to be unmoored. She moves around the plantation as she pleases, she swims naked in its rivers, and she goes into the master's house uninvited and unannounced. The *mulata* body refuses containment within the logic of the plantation social order. As a result, it must be made docile or disappear. Yambaó's last dance becomes a struggle for control over her own body. It moves between Caridad's ancestral control of her body and the plantation's social order. Neither provides comfort or stability, so Yambaó sacrifices her body instead—allowing no*body* to control her body, once and for all. If she cannot dance pleasurably for and in control of herself, she will not dance at all.

Yambaó joins *Tam Tam's mulata* and *Mulata's* Caridad in these dances of self-possession, where an apparent uncontrollable physical response to rhythm functions as a liberatory tactic. It is through this apparent loss of control that they maintain control of their bodies. While Yambaó contends with her grandmother's desire to possess her body in order to plot her revenge, Yambaó's choreography of possession is a corporeal refusal of her grandmother and the blackness she represents. Yambaó's rejection of her grandmother is really a rejection of blackness, played out in her choreography. Yambaó renounces Caridad's ancestral call for exacting revenge on "the son of the man who did me so much harm," in favor of her own amorous feelings and desires. Here lies the power of hip(g)nosis once more: its ability for the enacting body to seek pleasure from it regardless of the historical weight attributed to its pleasurable components.

In these films, blackness serves insofar as its attributed benevolent qualities provide something quantifiable or commodifiable: the *rumba*, a family legacy, loyalty, curative properties, or a momentary escape from the impositions of the material world. Yambaó's liberation comes from not only her affective desire for the master—a problematic method of liberation, to be sure—but also her own refusal to be controlled by either her grandmother or the plantation economy. However, in accordance with the logic of the "tragic *mulata*" trope, the master's well-being *must* be preserved, regardless of the cost to the *mulata's* own.[29] Thus, Yambaó sits neatly within the Caribbean narratives of the *mulata* concubine and her white male patron, as explained in chapter 1.

Through her act of self-sacrifice, Yambaó reengages with codes of containable femininity within the plantation economy, thereby removing her status as threat. Once dead, she can be mourned as the self-sacrificing woman who saved the master and his beloved plantation. Essentially, the erasure of her corporeality removes all overdetermined characteristics of *mulata*-ness from the narrative. In her place, the "tragic *mulata*" emerges, an easier trope to manage, contain, and recirculate. Even though Yambaó's dance of liberation, self-possession, and pleasure allows a new way to consider the *mulata* body, the trope of tragedy scampers several steps behind.

I AM CUBA (1964)

In the film *I Am Cuba*,[30] María/Betty serves as an example of how Cuba became imagined as a *mulata* by a Soviet propaganda machine after the Cuban Revolution.[31] María's economic condition forces her to go to a nightclub, change her name to Betty, and entertain several imperialist (white American) men, who make it obvious they view the Cuban woman as an object to acquire, possess, and exchange. Similar to the ways in which Yambaó finds pleasurable moments of abandon while dancing, María/Betty does the same.

The nightclub scene begins with a diagonally framed closeup of María/Betty. The stunning cinematography lights her forlorn face before the camera recedes and tracks her movement through the club from behind the bar. Women sit by the bar while couples dance in the background among shadows and light, offering a visual example of the racial binaries inherent in Cuba during this historic moment. Betty's friend approaches her and leads her to the table where three men sit. They pass by an overbearingly large statue of an African mask. Again, blackness looms over all the bodies present, just like the wall figures of African bodies looked over the cabaret audience when Caridad (in *Mulata*) performed.

One imperial man notices María/Betty's crucifix and comments on its size. Another offers to buy her a drink. María/Betty's ambivalent attitude magnifies the discomfort of this encounter within the libidinal racialized economy of a pre-Revolutionary Cuba. She refuses to look at any of the men. Instead, she directs her eyes downward. I read her gesture as one of apathy, not submission. When she pulls out a cigarette from her purse, two of the men light matches and offer them to her. One is off camera, the other has white hair. Her gaze remains detached, and she puts the cigarette back in her purse, refusing their performance of courtesy. The two lit matches stay in focus and in the frame for a beat before the flame on the left disappears from view. The man with the white hair holds his match, keeps it lit, moves it around slowly, and refuses to blow it out. Instead, he waits for it to get close to his fingers before he extinguishes it. These men may have flames of desire for her, with one of them stubbornly refusing to quell it, but María/Betty does not care. She remains stoic and emotionally unavailable. She will literally not fan those flames.

María/Betty's refusal prompts the man with the white hair to write down each woman's name on separate pieces of paper. If he cannot control María/Betty through his desire, he can control her by determining with whom she will spend the evening. The men draw the names and go dance with their respective women. María/Betty's "date" invites her to dance. Her body appears limp and passive as he leads her in a basic back-and-forth swing jazz step.

While every other dance partnership on the dance floor seems equally invested, (i.e., both male and female body maintaining an embodied relationship with one another, leading, following, improvising, exchanging weight and balance, *and* having fun), María/Betty and her dance partner go through the simple back-and-forth step. She appears wooden. He never lets go of her right arm as he pushes her back and forth. She follows complacently, but maintains the same expressionless face and limp, unstylized body language. She looks bored and ignores her partner's attempt at polite conversation.

Figure 3.22. Betty's expression begins to change as the *rumba* drums begin, in scene from *I Am Cuba*.

Suddenly, a random man grabs her and throws her to another man, who then throws her back to her original dance partner. They continue to toss her around violently from one man's arms to another. Back and forth. Back and forth. The man with the white hair grabs and drags her along the dance floor. She escapes, but runs into her original dance partner's arms, who grabs her again and continues to dance with her in the same back-and-forth swing step. This time, it is a faster and more urgent partnering, and María/Betty seems corporeally invested for a brief moment before she breaks free from him and runs away.

The jazz music with its insistent horns then stops and *rumba* drumming begins. This, I argue, signals for María/Betty a moment to find some peace and pleasure. The facial expression on María/Betty immediately changes from one of anxiety to relief (Figure 3.22). The rhythm brings a smile to her face, and she begins to sway (Figures 3.23 and 3.24). Up until now she had been stiff, vertical and upright. Her body was merely responding to the basic lead of her dance partner, with no embodied investment. Once the *rumba* begins, though, her hips ignite.

The camera shoots her from the waist up so we cannot see her hips moving, but we imagine their gentle sway below the frame. She rubs her

Figures 3.23 and 3.24. Betty's pleasurable reactions to the music.

temples, her head; she strokes her neck and arms. Her body struggles to do one thing, she struggles with it. She makes fists with both her hands and seems to hit herself on either side of her hips. Is she punishing her body for its embodied response to the African rhythms? Or, is this just another way to feel the rhythms and ensure she exists as a real embodied presence?

Just as she struggles free from being restrained and contained, the music shifts abruptly between the jazz music and the Afro-Cuban one. María/Betty continues her dance of self-expression while the crowd circles around her, chanting "Betty! Betty!! Betty!!!" The lighting at this particular moment intensifies the glow of their white faces—they appear spectral. The camera pans crowd in a full circle, and the large African mask statue is visible between the white chanting faces. Meanwhile, María/Betty continues to dance, eyes mostly closed or looking down, hips swinging and swaying, yet never shown on camera. She dances in front of and around the statue with a self-possessed abandon. In this moment, no men ogle at her or her crucifix. No men try to partner with her and toss her around like an object. She controls her body and its manifestation of rhythm and pleasure.

Although still a spectacle, her *mulata* body has not yet made the decision to claim the space of spectacle. In other words, while I read her dancing as a way for her to make an embodied statement of self-pleasure, resistance, and autonomy, her corporeality's history renders her a spectacle within the narrative structure of the scene. Nevertheless, María/Betty's brief reclamation of her body suggests the ways in which hip(g)nosis provides such opportunity. Although she must fulfill the terms of the sexual contract agreed upon for the evening (the subsequent scene shows her in bed with her dance partner), María finds a way to engage in pleasurable assertions with her body outside of the libidinal economy.

I do not position dance as exclusively a magical or transcendental space where material realities disappear. The body must still work to feel the embodied pleasure that could seem like transcendence. She still must use her body for a transactional purpose. Her body remains marked by the material conditions brought upon her by gender, race, and class. Her body, like Yambaó and Caridad's bodies, bears the historical weight of both *being* and often *having to enact* the tropes of *mulata*. However, their respective engagement with their dancing bodies during specific moments when their dancing bodies are being asked (or coerced) into performing the spectacle of *mulata* allows for a level of autonomy to emerge. They can negotiate to what extent their bodies can be spectacularized.

Caridad fully embraces becoming a cabaret star, thereby producing *mulata* spectacle through her labor as a cabaret performer. Yambaó moves between dancing for pleasure and dancing for spiritual or spell-casting purposes. Because she remains on the periphery of the plantation economy, she can choose to be among the enslaved and dance in their ceremonies, or she can roam free and excise pleasure from her liaisons with the master. María/Betty seems to have no choice in how, when, or why she dances. She appears resigned to her fate, as evidenced by her disembodied engagement with the imperial men sitting at the table. Not until the music shifts and she disentangles herself from their arms can María/Betty begin this dance of apparent self-expression, which leads to the cheers from the crowds.

María/Betty's improvisational dance combines frustration, liberation, and pleasure. In it, I see a manifestation of what Audre Lorde means when she writes about the erotic. Clearly, María/Betty is a fiction based on historical realities, but let's think about how she briefly claims that erotic aspect of herself. Lorde's statement is, "For the erotic is not a question only of what we do; it is a question of how acutely and fully we can feel in the doing."[32] How *we can feel in the doing*. That phrase speaks to the underlying questions in this book. In tracing these histories of *mulatas* through their bodies (and sometimes my own), I carve out a sense of *how* they felt doing what *they* did.

Feelings rarely appear in history books; facts overshadow or violently obliterate them. Feelings that belong to women, subaltern women, have passed through so many layers of representation, mostly at the hands of others who are speaking for those women. I think of the *mulata* concubine Joanna in Stedman's narrative as a classic example of this.[33] Yet, my identification of a way for the female subaltern to have a "voice" particularly through her body (even if it is through filmic representation) allows the pieces of the *mulata* lived experience fall into place. And it is here where her everyday history shines. As I watch the two-dimensional *mulata* characters dancing on screen, can I even approximate what it felt like for them to "acutely and fully" feel what they were doing? Further, what does analysis of filmic representations of *mulata* corporeality contribute to the history of *mulata* subjectivity, if at all? There are the limits of language and the many unspoken, non-filmic narratives out there that we can never know. However, this attempt at seeing how pleasure and religiosity frame an understanding of the *mulata* self provides a way to insert her experience into historical spaces that currently count her as objectified sensuality. Here, the complexity of her subjectivity appears when she dances briefly, vigorously, abruptly, sensationally, spiritually, and erotically.

LOS DEL BAILE (1965) AND SON O NO SON (1980)

I bring this chapter to a close by focusing briefly on moments that appear in two documentaries made after the Revolution. They diverge slightly from the chapter's topic—namely, the *mulata* and her relationship to blackness, spirituality, and pleasure. Nevertheless, while these two instances position the *mulata* in a public space where her dancing could function as spectacle, the way in which that dancing body appears on the screen and how it is filmed offers new considerations of the *mulata* body at those crucial moments in Cuban cultural history.

Although the documentary form functions as a mediated lens through which to consider how the *mulata* is represented, these films depict *mulatas* outside the prescribed narrative context, unlike the fictional films discussed earlier.

The opening frames of *Los del baile* (1965) cut between title and credits and a *mulata* dancing on a crowded outdoor dance floor.[34] She has a partner, but they never clasp hands or dance in an embrace. Instead, she moves independently yet aware of the camera and of the space around her. This post-Revolution outdoor space functions as a social site for everyday dance pleasures for and about the Cuban people. In line with the emerging nationalist rhetoric of a new socialist Cuba, the public spaces becomes space for solidarity. In *Los del baile,* many of those bodies in the public space are black, highlighting attempts by the new social order to make amends for years of colonial attitudes toward Afro-Cubans. In this different context, the *mulata* dancing pleasurably alone offers a new view of how a body might dance without giving power to the consuming tourist gaze. Instead, she dances spectacularly for herself while she belongs to a larger Cuban revolutionary community that finds solidarity in shared pleasure. She is not the consumable, commodified *mulata*; she is the self-sufficient *mulata* who emerges in synch with these new ideologies. She is one body among many dancing, and it is this collectivity that shifts how her body functions in this film.

Two things happen to me every time I watch the other documentary, *Son o No Son* (1980).[35] First, the sounds of Miguelito Cuñí and Felix Chapotín performing "El Carbonero" take me back to my childhood in New York City, where I would watch my Cuban father work through his nostalgia for his homeland by playing Cuban music really loud on Friday nights. This was one of the songs I remember hearing often. Second, my gaze always lands on a particular *mulata* in the film's crowd. While Cuñí and Chapotín are performing on an outdoor stage, singing their song about a charcoal seller, crowds of people dance on the open floor below. Multiracial Cuban bodies dance with one another, possibly symbolizing how music, dance, and collective pleasure promote nationalist sentiment and patriotism. They all seem to come together for the purpose of celebrating Cuban music, dance, and community.

In the crowd, a *mulata* wears plaid trousers and has her hair styled with two pony tails. It is not so much her outfit, hair, or way of dancing that strikes me, though. She dances no better or worse than the other bodies the camera sporadically focuses on. However, she continually catches my eye during the chorus (*"car-bon bon, car-bon bon"*) that makes up the *montuno* section of the song. As the rhythm of the *"car-bon bon"* continues, she pauses to highlight each iteration of the *"bon bon"* with a slight pulse of her hips, while her partner taps the rhythm on different parts of her body—first with his shoulder, then with his chest, and finally with his head. He gradually descends and crouches alongside her with outstretched arms, each *"bon bon"* announcing an opportunity for contact. His shoulder taps her hips. His chest taps her hips. His head taps her hips: one side, the other, her thigh, her calf, her ankle. Meanwhile, she rotates elegantly, providing a variety of contact points for him to punctuate the beat on her body with his head. She offers her body, and he accepts. This moment lasts no more than ten seconds, but within it resides a long and complex history.

In this scene I witness the historical contradiction between mind and body seamlessly resolving itself through quick, improvisational partnering. Hips and head must work together to materialize this pleasurable exchange (Figure 3.25). Neither one emerges more significant than the other. Together, they play with the rhythm. Together, their hips and head engage

Figure 3.25 The dialectic of the head and hip, in a scene from *Son o no Son*.

in a coherent partnering that pronounces an end to the mind's privilege over the body. Post-Revolution, this is a new type of Cuban embodiment that needs to spread—one that can work with the fraught racial history to find resolution through pleasurable negotiation between the constructed hierarchies that have sought to stay separate.

While this couple dances "innocently," a new type of *mulata* also emerges—one who must attend to the political responsibilities of the new Cuban revolutionary citizen, who defines herself beyond her hips, but who still can use them when necessary. As with the film's improvised duo, prolonged contact with the *mulata* body fades away; instead, brief contact becomes the new status quo. Her body needs to do other, more important things for the state. She cannot stay in one place, gyrate her hips, and invite multiple partnerings on the dance floor. Instead, the contact must be quick, brief, and efficient.

The 1980s in Cuba had brought about a stillness of the hips in favor of an active civic body. However, the subsequent collapse of the Soviet Union and its effect on Cuba stirred those hips once more. What type of hip choreographies did the changed economic condition bring about? What hip repertoire remained, and what new movement vocabulary developed? Chapter 4 examines the phenomenon of the *despelote* and its frenetic restlessness—as a means of survival.

INTERLUDE 3

Lost Baggage

Istanbul, January 1957

The pumpkin just finished cooking, and she breaks it into five pieces. She can still see the residue of cinnamon beneath her fingernails. This time she had to grate the sticks to make the powder. Back pain gnaws at her as she realizes she has been in the kitchen for almost three hours. One last *ebo* and finally her altar will be complete. Ochún required many things this time. As she rearranges the orange that had surreptitiously rolled away from the other four, Chelo Alonso, thinks about the promises she made to Ochún at the last toque. She has one left to fulfill.

She sings an Ochún canto to herself:

Òsun se're kété mi, owó
Òsun se're kété mi, owó
Omi dára o dára oge o
Òsun Wére kété mi, owó

Ochún make blessings without delay for me, money.
Ochún make blessings without delay for me, money.
Beautiful water, you are beautiful and ostentatious.
Ochún quickly without delay for me, money.[1]

That night in her dreams she hears her voice. She had fallen asleep crying. The voice calms her down; she couldn't imagine how she would find the money to replace her lost costumes, dresses, records, suitcase, or the $4,800 mink coat.

Tears ... crocodile tears that come as prayers of supplication awaken me ... asking me for money. No one can take what you earned away from you. It belongs to you and your sisters. My daughters, all of you, be firm, keep to your work. Strive, be tenacious. Use your charm if you must, enchant them on my behalf. Let them see your beauty that needs not eyes to be appreciated. Go, keep to your work.

A harrowing boat trip from Egypt to Greece had unsettled her.[2] She had slept on the deck of the small boat the entire journey. They had assured her that her bags would arrive in Istanbul with her. They did not. Somehow, during a layover in Cyprus, they disappeared. Two months later, she is still waiting for them to arrive. When should she give up?

The next morning she writes a quick letter to the editors at *Show* magazine in Havana. They love receiving news about her travels and adventures. She looks through a stack of photos recently taken of her in Egypt. She laughs at one in particular. *They will love this one*, she thinks. In it, she sits on a camel wearing one of her more revealing costumes. She leaned back and rested her head in her hands, thinking about the many pin-up poses popular back in Cuba. She chose not to wear her red heels. Instead, she kept her legs and feet encircled in seamed stockings. She made an extra effort to point her feet and extend her leg. *I have to get it as straight as the sides of the pyramids*, she kept telling herself.

> Face in profile, right leg not quite straight, left leg bent. Arms behind head. *Click.*
> Face to the camera, both legs bent forward. Eyes open. *Click.*
> Face to the side, chin down, both legs straight, sultry eyes, half smile. *Click.*
> Face to the side slightly, cheek resting on arm, left leg extended, foot pointed, right leg bent like a perfect triangle, eyes closed, upper lip pursed. *Click.*

They took several photos of her on the camel, but the last one proved her favorite (Interlude 3, Figure 1). She feels proud of her extension. She held her stomach in really tightly, and she had not eaten much the day before, in anticipation. Maybe that is why her lips look like that? *No matter*, she thinks. *They will love it in Cuba. So much work to look a certain way*, she thought. On their way back to the hotel, her entourage stopped quickly along the Nile. Their Muslim driver had to do his evening *sujud* (prostration), and thought it would be nice to show them a scenic point by the river.

Interlude 3, Figure 1. Detail from Chelo Alonso photograph that appeared in *Show* magazine, February 1957.

She walked alongside the river, and when no one was looking, she tossed five copper coins into it. In her head, she sang one of her favorite *cantos* to Ochún, still thinking about her lost luggage.

> *Iya mi ilé odò. Ìyá mi ilé odò*
> *Gbogbo àse*
> *Obí ni sálà máā wò e*
> *Ìyá mi ilé odò*
>
> My mother's house is the River.
> My mother's house is the River.
> All powerful
> Women that flee for safety habitually visit her.
> My mother's house is the River.[3]

The river babbled a little. Ochún always replies to her daughters.

OCHÚN WHISPERS BACK

I am the River. My sister is the sea. I dance with her. I lie next to her. I spill forth
into her. I lead you from her to me aboard ships with mermaids on the prow. She
leads the way. She rocks you. I lead you from my River Osogbo to the (Atlantic)
ocean, to the sea (Caribbean) to another River (Nile) and back to another sea
(Aegean and Meditteranean). All waters are mine and my sister. We flow to,
from, in and through each other. I swerve this way and that. I undulate through
and to a new place. My daughters, come to me. I am here for you whenever you
need me. I have never left you. Be calm, my daughters. Be calm.

That night after the photography session, she fell asleep early. Her body
hurt from the uncomfortable Jeep ride to get her to/from the location for
the photo shoot. No bombs dropped that evening.[4]

CANCIÓN DE CUNA/LULLABY BY OCHÚN

Yèyé yèyé mã wò'kun; mã yíyan yòrò

The Mother of mothers always visits the sea;
Always walking with a slow swagger to melt away.[5]

OCHÚN INTERRUPTS

My daughters walk, they map out space. They take up space. They use their
bodies, bodies I need to exist, bodies I bestow with grace, health, vibrancy . . .
bodies that work for me, venerating me. Their eyes sometimes are filled
with tears, and they cry. Their tears call me. Their tears connect many of
us. They also work, they sweat, they breathe, they move, they dance. Theirs
are bodies that both feel, and make you feel, make you sensate . . . experience
. . . express, re-dress. Use your bodies, think with it, feel with it. That is me.
Keep to your work, my daughters.

Still feeling groggy from last night's sleep, she decided to stay in her room
longer than usual. A pile of scripts from Rome lay on her desk. They had
been delivered the night before, while she was at Giza. She already knows
that most of the roles will involve veils, gold jewelry, and *danza orientale*.
She smiles at the realization that although she's not an expert, the producers want her anyway. *Sign of the Gladiator, Pirate and the Slave Girl*—these
titles remind her of bad romance novels her mother would read back home

in Camaguey, Cuba. Chelo thinks about having a proper speaking role one day, and these films could be the beginning. She heard that Italian cinema paid well. Maybe losing her fur coat proved fortuitous, after all. She would definitely not be able to wear it in Cuba, even though the *farandula* in Havana would love to see her in one for photographs. She rolls her eyes at the thought.

Now that she is in Istanbul with some regular performance work (headlining at the Kordor Blo, and then later at the Palais Hotel in Ankara), she figures she can go do some dance research. Who could teach her a little bit more about belly dance? She picks up the hotel phone and calls the concierge, asking about places to go see "authentic" *danza del vientre*. "We will get back to you, Signorina Alonso." For the rest of the afternoon she reads the scripts. Unenthused by the characters she will eventually portray, she sets the scripts aside. Instead, she practices arm and hip movements in front of a mirror. She hopes to learn some news ones after watching some performances while in Istanbul.

Mbe mbe máa Yèyé
Mbe mbe l'órò.

Exist exist continually Mother.
Exist exist in the tradition.[6]

I exist in many incarnations. When she decides to wear her gold bracelets and her brass rings, I am there. It's not allowed, they tell her. I don't care. I must be beautiful, I must be clean, clear, like the water. Look at her and you will remember me. When another one moves her body, shaking, shimmying, swaying her hips back and forth to transfixed and hip-notized eyes, I am there. Go, my daughters, make them see you. Make them love you. That way, they will see me, they will acknowledge me. They will understand what they have done. My daughters are everywhere—black, brown, copper, brass, gold, wheat, honey—beautiful, embellished, beloved, ornery, ornate, and honored. Make beauty. Never let them forget the work involved.

CODA

Chelo Alonso, born Isabella Garcia in Camaguey, Cuba, starred in nineteen films made in Italy from 1959 until 1969. Her most well-known film is the spaghetti Western *The Good, The Bad and The Ugly*. Ironically, she did not have a speaking part. Most of her films involved her dancing in

Orientalized costumes and playing an "exotic" slave girl or princess. This historicized fiction comes from a piece that appeared in *Show* magazine's February 1957 issue, which featured her photo on the camel. The picture and accompanying narrative haunted me for a while. I wondered how she struggled with the loss of her possessions.

What did that material loss mean to her as a working, traveling performer? Where did she receive emotional or spiritual comfort or support? I have no way of knowing if she was a devotee of Ochún. However, I imagine her seeking solace through the work of veneration. I also thought about her connection to Cuba and the Cuban entertainment scene's dependence on the labor of women like her. She was tasked with representing Cuba internationally, and I sense a national responsibility operating here. As its representative abroad, Alonso may have felt an urgency to honor the national imaginary of Cuba with stories about her life in foreign countries. To that extent, *Show* magazine functions as a rich archive for similar stories of these working, dancing women. Alonso's labor has been preserved in a ten-year archive of film, but what about the other women featured in *Show* magazine? When will their stories be written?

CHAPTER 4

Hip(g)nosis as Brand: *Despelote,* Tourism, and *Mulata* Citizenship .

*Tanto que la critican, pero la mulata es la que está salvando este país./*They criticize her so much, but it's the *mulata* who is saving this country.

An elderly Cuban woman walks casually down the street. Suddenly, she watches as a vivacious *mulata* in formfitting clothes, swinging hips and hair, breezes by. She stops to watch the spectacle of limbs and rhythm amble down toward the *malecón,* or seafront in Havana, and mutters the above statement out loud to herself. I have heard the preceding story told to me many times. As I have declared in the Introduction to this book, I am not interested in the veracity of such circulating stories in Cuba. I am more drawn to their rationale and why they have such cultural capital.

I always have questions when I hear them. How many others heard her utter these words? Did anyone agree? How many others thought the same but remained quiet? What did that particular *mulata* look like? I can continue, but more questions would detract from the significance of her declaration—and more important, the real question that should be asked: *How* is the *mulata* saving Cuba, if at all?

This story functions as a preamble to this final chapter, where I continue with the duet of the *mulata* and a Cuban social-dance form. In this chapter, the dance form is the *despelote,* a dance that emerged out of the *timba* music craze in Cuba of the late 1980s and early '90s. By linking the frenzy of the *despelote* with the *mulata* body in the 1990s, an economically traumatic moment in Cuban history, I demonstrate how the *mulata* continues to function as a visible, visceral commodity for a nation struggling with its shifting role in the transnational economy. This chapter traces the trajectory of the *mulata* from the 1960s and '70s, and into the '80s, when she became part of the new discourse of *la mujer revolucionaria*—the revolutionary woman who would act for and on behalf of the Revolution to improve Cuban society as a whole.

Despite a historical association with the *mulata* body and dance, the two decades after the Revolution witnessed a decline in social dance. It was not because Cubans stopped dancing altogether—they still managed to dance in private domestic spaces—but because the state issued regulations to control and, in most instances, prevent public social gatherings that involved dancing. The Castro Revolution closed major entertainment venues, such as the world-famous Tropicana nightclub, with an aim to redirect corporeal practices from kinesthetic pleasure to civic responsibility— namely, bodily activities that led to improvement in the social structure. Cuban bodies learned new techniques of corporeality: militarized, disciplined, and sometimes still modes of occupying space and working for the state. They volunteered, they marched in political rallies, they worked for the *zafra* (sugarcane harvests), and they even surveilled one another working for the neighborhood Committee for the Defense of the Revolution, or CDR. These activities conditioned their bodies to remain vigilant yet docile, productive yet passive.

I argue that the Cuban dictatorial regime contributed to the *despelote's* physicality: frenetic, loose limbs circulating in rhythmic bouts of self-expressive pleasure. The popularity of the music form *timba* and its corresponding dance, the *despelote*, the latter which literally means an unraveling, serves as a metaphor for the unraveling of not just the state's economy but also of the role of the *mulata,* reverting from citizen to commodity-citizen once more. I make a case for this seeming return to commodity as being a tense and contested one, where the *mulata* dancing *despelote* signifies the messiness, tension, and unresolved politics of national identity that Cubans negotiate on a daily basis.

The *mulata*-dancing-*despelote* phenomenon allows the social circulation of hip(g)nosis on a transnational level. Here, her hip(g)nosis solidifies into a national brand, if you will, particularly notable in a country where multinational corporate brands and advertisements are absent. By looking at specific moments in these last four decades of the Cuban Revolution that demonstrate either forcibly or subtly this significant shift from citizen to commodity-citizen, my interest here is not to set up a cause-and-effect rationale per se, but to excavate what the *mulata* body signifies post-Revolution and to expand upon it, particularly the changes in its meanings and its repositionings. Mapping this body will uncover how and to what extent specific associations of the *mulata* body, with a political-libidinal economy, serve the individual and the state in different ways.

I argue for some agency of the *mulata* within the current political-libidinal economy, as her agency can undermine the power of the Cuban state apparatus while simultaneously highlighting its tragedy. My intention is not to secure for the *mulata* a utopic space of constant and consistent agency through the use of her hips but, rather, to demonstrate how *mulata* corporeality partners with political-discursive forces to find moments of reclamation as commodity-citizen. A simplistic analysis that returns tragedy to the mulata (i.e., only being utilized for the purposes of the state apparatus' economic needs) prevents her from having a stake in *how* she can use her body's hip(g)nosis and its power as an international brand. Hip(g)nosis offers her power to assert a position (perhaps even as savior as the opening epigraph would suggest) in the new and ever changing iterations of the Cuban state.

THE FEDERACIÓN DE MUJERES CUBANAS AND THE FEMALE REVOLUTIONARY BODY

The Cuban government established the Federación de Mujeres Cubanas (FMC) in 1960, with the goal of addressing women's role in the new socialist regime. Its president, Vilma Espín, then wife of current Cuban President Raúl Castro, voiced the revolutionary discourse that favored the patriarchal associations of women with domestic affairs, national morality, and tradition favored by the new regime. Fidel Castro functioned as a benevolent patriarch that FMC would support and honor. The FMC promoted strong social supports for women in the form of literacy campaigns and work training programs. The new Cuban woman was one who attended to the needs of her family. She maintained the patriarchal structure of Cuban society particularly through traditional performances of femininity (self-sacrifice, as one of the more honorable virtues), yet she had moved beyond the domestic sphere into the public one.

With more access to the public, the new Cuban woman (regardless of race, even though historically it was the black and *mulatas* who had more access, as argued in chapter 1) not only created "poems, songs and chants in honor of Fidel Castro"[1] but also moved from the rural provinces to Havana so as to learn skills that would allow her to enter the wage-earning economy (specifically, in national hygiene and literacy campaigns). One such institution, the Ana Bentancourt Schools, established in 1960, taught the seamstress craft to women from the countryside.[2]

This interest in training women in activities of domestic femininity reinforced the paternalistic role of the state, while at the same time demonstrated its forward thinking in educating women for lives outside the traditional, though still valued, roles of wife and mother. That is, although women were expected to work, the domestic chores remained valued, as it was through wife and motherhood that women would produce the children necessary for the long-term success of the Revolution. As a 1962 document from the first Congress of the FMC attests:

> The tasks of our Revolution demand the incorporation of women into the work force. For this to happen it is necessary to provide women with a solution to their domestic problems, which pose an impediment in most cases to their involvement in the fundamental production chores that will conduce our fatherland to the path of progress.[3]

Nevertheless, tension arose between the idea of women as revolutionaries, employed outside the home, and that of women as caretakers and moral advocates inside the home. This resulted in implementation of the 1975 Family Code, which provided equal rights in the home in areas of "marriage, divorce, adoption, maintenance and responsibility for their children. Men are expected to share all the duties and responsibilities relating to the running of the household and the care of the children."[4] Moya Fábregas argues that although this legislation proved revolutionary for its time, effective enforcement didn't follow.[5] Traditional gender codes continued to inform how gender and sexuality functioned, especially in the emphasis on motherhood as the greatest aspiration for women. Even the logo of the FMC emphasized the maternal; a faceless (white) woman wears a military green uniform, carries a machine gun on her right shoulder, and firmly holds a baby in a blanket with her left arm (Figure 4.1). She is looking to the right, into the revolutionary future that the machine gun signifies, but her maternal role remains intact.[6]

The FMC continued its work most notably in areas of national literacy, hygiene, sexual education, rehabilitation of prostitutes, and skills training. The sexual activity of the young became a topic of considerable interest at FMC meetings.[7] In 1975, the report "Thesis on the Role of the Family in Socialism" critiqued the lack of sex education provided by parents, and thus the FMC began advocating for such education in the schools, but substantiated the mother to provide it as well.

To contrast the image of the universalized (white) Cuban woman of the FMC, I offer the image in Figure 4.2 to paint a more diverse picture of the women who were involved in or were used to publicize the

Figure 4.1. Iconography of a revolutionary maternal figure for the Federación de Mujeres Cubanas. From La Jiribilla Archive, appearing in Moya, "Una Aproximación."

Figure 4.2. Revolutionary women lifting their guns in solidarity. From La Jiribilla Archive, appearing in Moya, "Una Aproximación."

revolutionary effort. In this image, the predominantly black and *mulata* women lift their rifles in salute, a decidedly different gesture from that of the mother-*revolucionaria* one. Here, they have no time for swaddling infants; perhaps their husbands are taking care of that, waiting for them to return. Speculation aside, this second image allows a new *mulata* to emerge: one dressed in revolutionary fatigues, not ruffles; one standing in military salute, not leaning to one side with hand on hip, waiting to make another corporeal gesture. The circulating images of women post-1959 began to shift the focus from being mere sexualized woman/*mulata* to woman whose important function is to serve and support the Revolution's goals.

Nevertheless, Wilson (Luis Felipe Wilson Valera), a noted Cuban cartoonist whose work can be said to characterize much of Cuban social and popular culture during the 1960s , 70s and '80s, continued to make use of the sexualized image of the Cuban *mulata*. His series entitled *Las Criollitas* for *Palante* Magazine made use of the sensual corporeality of the *mulata* (and the *cubana*, in general): small waist, big hips and buttocks. Yet, although he portrayed the typified curvaceous *mulata* of the Cuban imaginary, she works for the *zafra* (the sugarcane harvest), she wears a military uniform, she teaches, and more important, she actively dismisses any objectification.

In one cartoon, the woman ignores the declarations of love that the drummer communicates through his rhythmic playing (Figure 4.3). Words seem unnecessary; rhythm is the language of romantic conquest. This is symbolized by the hearts coming out from his drum each time he beats it. The rhythm of the drum is just like the rhythm of his heart. It beats

Figure 4.3. From the series *Las Criollitas* by Wilson (Luis Felipe Wilson Valera) published in *Palante, Publicacíon Humorística De Cuba*. Palante started in 1961. Wilson began drawing for them in 1962 until his death in 2006.

faster for her. Her legs pound the pavement (*taconeando*, as they call it in Cuban slang), moving away from him at a steady and resolute pace. The hearts encircle her and, upon contact with her body, some of them explode, making faint "plop" sounds. Surely that's a disappointing outcome, yet his determination continues, made visible by quantities of hearts that envelope her. Despite all his efforts, her eyes remain closed and her chin raised. All that matters to her is moving away from him and getting to her destination.

Wilson's cartoon are reminders of how, despite the revolutionary zeal that empowers women outside the home and within the functions of government, the Cuban patriarchy maintained its stronghold on heteronormative courtship performance. This imagery circulated within the Cuban cultural imagination; though cloaked in revolutionary dogma, the purpose was quite different. Wilson's *mulatas* did not just dance, entertain, or serve imperialist desires, as they had historically done. Instead, they were implementing the new paradigm of female citizenry. The *mulata* is on a mission, and nothing will deter her.

By 1982, that idealized female body had emerged; it was a political one, participating in a variety of organizations. The FMC's book *Women: A Revolution Within a Revolution* presents the following description:

> Here she is: delegate to the Congresses of the Party or the Union of Young Communists, member of the National Assembly of People's Power, member of the Council of State or the Council of Ministers, or member of the Central Committee, a leading official in a ministry or the mass and social organizations.[8]

Through their participation in the FMC, Cuban women functioned as the moral educators of society.[9] It was this politically involved and socially aware woman whom respected feminist Germaine Greer sought to encounter when she visited Cuba in 1984 to attend the FMC's Fourth Congress. Her essay recounting that trip presents descriptions of the women she encountered, such as Vilma Espín (then president of the FMC), who "was hardly a charismatic speaker."[10] She describes some of the participants' reactions to a speech given by Fidel Castro:

> the women lept to their feet, waving the coloured nylon georgette scarves and matching plastic flowers they had all brought with them, pounding maracas, bongoes (sic), conga drums and cowbells, clapping their hands and singing fit to bust, *Para trabajar, para estudiar, para defender nuestra libertad! Firmes con Fidel! Firmes con Fidel!* [To work, to study, to defend our liberty. We stand firm with Fidel! We stand firm with Fidel!] Hips gyrated, scarves flashed, flowers wagged.[11]

In particular, my focus is on the comment about women's hips gyrating. How notable were the hip gyrations? Did they seem out of place for Greer, who may have been used to white First World feminists and their different ways of moving their bodies? Why an emphasis on their bodies at all? Greer continues to demonstrate her First World feminist perspective as she elaborates on the appearance of these Cuban women:

> Women whose bottoms threatened to burst out of their elasticized pants tottered round the exhibits on four-inch heels clutching their *compañeros* for support. Their nails and faces were garishly painted. Their hair had been dragged over curlers, bleached, dyed and coloured. Their clothes, including their brassieres, were all two or three sizes too small and flesh bulged everywhere.[12]

Greer's aesthetic judgments about the appearance of the Cuban women situate her within a particular kind of white middle-class feminism, in that she considers the colors, flesh, and corporeal unruliness noticeable. Greer's account speaks to how the aesthetics of the *mulata/cubana* had become an object for her to notice. I shall return to Greer and her aesthetic judgments shortly, but first let's take a quick trip to the ballet with her. She shares her experience:

> The first evening the delegates were taken to a ballet. They arrived stomping and chatting, sat chatting eagerly about the day's doings, and when the dancing had started and silence was finally imposed, a good proportion of them went straight to sleep, waking up only to applaud wildly. While exhausted *delegadas* slumbered around me, I watched Dionea, a man-eating plant composed of Josefina Menéndez and the *cuerpo de baile* to music by Villa-Lobos, as it ate three male dancers dressed as glittering mothy creatures, with horribly erotic gestures. This was followed by the world premiere of *Palomas*, a ballet choreographed by the Chilean exile Hilda Riveros, especially for the Fourth Congress of the FMC. The story ran straight down the party line; the dancers mimed birth, the mother mimed ecstatic admiration of her child. She was joined by her mate and mimed ecstatic admiration of him. They simulated spontaneous conjugal relations on the floor. She then went off for her militia training, and mimed something rather like kung fu in strict unison with the *cuerpo de baile*. Then she and her fellow soldiers were joined by their mates and mimed heterosexual fulfillment in unison.[13]

The dancing continues with Cuban ballet star Alicia Alonso (blind by this time) performing a *pas de deux* in which she "slid out of a lift and down Jorge Esquivel's nose, so that his eyes streamed with tears."[14] With the help of Greer's description, one can see how choreography/dance functions as an ideological representation of Cuban gender roles. The ballet choreographies of the traditional female roles such as mother and wife made these socially significant, yet the expectation of being in service to the revolutionary cause was made explicit with the dancer's portrayal of a militia member. As mentioned earlier, Cuban post-revolutionary femininity did not overtly dismiss the revered roles of wife and mother but, rather, made them the foundation from which the militia female body could emerge.

I find the use of ballet as a revolutionary pedagogic device interesting, for two reasons. First, by the 1980s, popular dance in Cuba had waned, owing to the closure of bars and clubs. Second, Cuban corporeality had never been associated with the rigid symmetry and erect spines of ballet, yet the disciplining factors of ballet mirror those of the military in producing a specific type of body: docile, erect, highly trained, and contained. In contrast, the pre-Revolution body was depicted as one of excess, rhythm, and feral unruliness. Thus, the dance form—ballet—functions as a metaphor for the state's desire to have docile female bodies who provide aesthetic and libidinal pleasure but must be trained and regimented for the fulfillment of state goals. Furthermore, the state's emphasis on ballet and docilization shifts the focus from the stereotypically rhythmic *mulata* to a female body aligned more closely with European ideals and aesthetics.

The juxtaposition of ballet dancers and audience members serves as a way to think about how black and brown women's bodies warrant containment. Whether that containment occurs in the discursive realm or the aesthetic one, it nevertheless restrains women's bodies and bodily excesses; the role of the *mulata* in the Cuban national and cultural imaginary, then, becomes a discourse about containment.

That Greer witnessed these fleshy "excesses" in the audience and memorialized them in her text illuminates the power of that excess to require words to describe it. Her words rest within a particular race and class register, yet they show that excess as something significant. In this context, excess emerges as a productive way of understanding what spills forth and rejects containment. It opens up a way to understand and experience the allure of these excessive and extravagant bodies, corporeality, flesh, and movements—yet, ironically, this concept of containable excess assuredly stems from a Euro-American imposition of value and taste.

Within Cuba, these excessive displays speak to paradoxical quotidian routines and dilemmas. They hide an economy in which scarcity forces one to choose between clothes or food, while providing a way of declaring one's individuality despite the state's control of the space and its imposition on individuality and freedom. The excess in its multiple forms (speech, manner, appearance) functions as a way to contest the limits of personal freedom that have been imposed upon Cubans by the state.

Gayatri Spivak writes about "the discourse of the clitoris . . . short-hand for women's excess in all areas of production and practice, an excess that must be brought under control to keep business going as usual."[15] In the case of these Cuban women, *mulata* or otherwise, their bodies, their gyrating hips and wiggling and jiggling buttocks, become the site where these excesses emanate. Cuban women danced (their "hips gyrated," as Greer wrote) and celebrated at these political functions as a way to socialize, because the 1970s and '80s had limited public spaces for social dancing. Actually, state regulations led to an explosion of gyrating hips and fleshy eruptions of excess. It took the form of *despelote,* which came about during the *timba* craze.

TIMBA AND THE RISE OF *DESPELOTE*

In the 1970s and '80s, dancing moved away from the public spaces of entertainment (cabarets, nightclubs, bars, diners) and to more intimate, private gatherings. The state's distrust of social gatherings that involved dancing had led to the closure of most bars, nightclubs, and dance halls. This was based on the idea that the places where people socialized and danced could become sites of anti-revolutionary behavior. Additionally, in 1973, Cuba had imposed a "cultural self-blockade," banning the broadcast of Anglo-American pop and folk music.[16] This also had a destructive effect on Cuban dance music, with many ethnomusicologists today considering it a veritable crisis, a dearth of *música bailable* in Cuba.[17] Thus, the desire for new words and new music gave rise to the *despelote.*

Basically, in the 1970s and '80s, Cuban music went into hibernation. Although the state promoted native cultural expressions based on *cubanía,* audiences preferred the *salsa romántica* coming from Latin America and pop music being brought secretly from the United States. Music journalist Rafael Lam insists that, despite the rise of Cuban groups such as Los Van Van and Irakere in the 1980s, interest in their music was mostly confined to the Afro-Cuban population. While other Cubans secretly consumed non-Cuban music, the black population remained aligned with black cultural expressions. Indeed, it was this loyalty to their culture that allowed NG La Banda to emerge as the international representative of Afro-Cuban music in the 1990s, thereby making blackness more visible in Cuban culture.

The *despelote* dance emerged as the corporeal response to *timba,* the latter a type of Cuban music developed by José Luis Cortés and his band NG

La Banda from 1988 onward. Cortés blended Cuban music such as the *son, guaracha, mambo,* and *rumba* into a new style—*timba*—that was representative of "a type of dance music rooted in barrio life."[18] In 1989, Cortés and NG La Banda toured the black barrios of Havana and spread their music in this unique way. Lam asserts that this "going back to the roots" assured NG credibility and a loyal fan base that would enable the spread of *timba* once Cuba became more dependent on tourism.

In 1991, NG La Banda was invited by Cubanacán, Cuba's tourist agency, to play a concert at Marina Hemingway, the largest marina in Cuba. Inportant for our topic in this book, it is also during this period from 1970 to 1990 that the association of the *mulata* with dance music waned in Cuba—that is, until the new sounds of *timba* began to circulate.

The Rise of Tourism and Reemergence of the *Mulata*

The year 1991 is a significant one for the promotion of Cuba as a tourist destination and also for the reemergence of the *mulata* as *sui generis* commodity. First, *Playboy* magazine's March 1991 issue featured photographs of alluring naked *cubanas* tempting visitors to an island that was off-limits to U.S. citizens. A visit to Cuba might even promise a happy ending; the article concluded with the photographer and one of his models falling in love. In essence, the potential for coupling in all of its variations emerged clearly in the pictorial and textual narrative.

Second, the August 1991 issue of *National Geographic* featured a Cuba in transition.[19] The first two images in the article showed strikingly distinct phallic images. The title page presented a shot of a missile erect and pointed skyward, as a soldier holds firmly to his machine gun. The dusky sky and fluorescent lighting on the military base blur his body and face. Though eerily out of focus, he is perhaps a metaphor for the uncertainty of the Cuban state at that time. The other image is of a Cuban flag hoisted above the construction of what would eventually become the Hotel Cohiba. Again, the tall building is reaching to the sky, the verticality of the flag on its rusty pole alludes to the phallic power of business and commerce.

Yet it is a third image in that second article that drew my interest. In this hazy nighttime photograph, a *mulata* is dancing in the center, with mostly dark-skinned black bodies surrounding her. The caption states that she has been photographed at a Santería ceremony as she dances for Afro-Cuban deity Babalú Ayé. Her arms reach way above her head, and one of her hands shows askew fingers. Her head leans back, and from the angle of the photograph, her eyes seem closed. She dances in ecstatic union with the rhythm.

This display of kinesthetic pleasure and spiritual communion furthers the myth of the escapist, liberatory, and sensual fantasies that the *mulatas* purportedly wield. The prospect of witnessing a *mulata* body in such a frenzy is a kind of advertising, however subtle.

These photo instances merge with the 1991 concert I am about to describe. Together, they are scaffolding for building a structure from which to situate the *mulata's* resurgence. At the Marina Hemingway concert, *mulatas* were contracted to dance and entertain international business guests, including foreign tourist companies and investors. At this private event, the *"imperio del mulataje"* (the empire of *mulata*-ness) welcomed them.[20] *Mulatas* accompanied NG La Banda on stage, and danced as a form of entertainment and advertisement. Rafael Lam states that many of these *mulatas* wound up in Europe as "the most expensive women in the world"; in order to have them, the men spent a lot of money on flights, hotel, clothing, and daily maintenance. I must note that Lam did not attend the *"imperio del mulataje"* event, but he shared his knowledge with me over a cup of strong Cuban coffee one January afternoon. Although this story functions as rumor, Lam's close friendship with Cortés lends credibility. I wish I could meet one of the women who danced at this event. Instead, I must imagine a scenario, not dissimilar to the scenarios I have been presenting in this book.

Using women as incentives to further political or economic goals is by no means new for any country. In Cuba, this tradition existed prior to the Revolution and continued so afterwards, despite assurances from the state that prostitution was no longer sanctioned. Cuban TV personality Hilda Rabilero offered some background information on how the Cuban government procured female entertainment, or "companionship," for these visiting dignitaries.[21] Her story highlights the degree to which women in the libidinal economy of Cuba received attention, depending on the female body telling the story.

Rabilero explained that an East German delegation headed by the former German Democratic Republic's general secretary, Erich Honecker, arrived in Cuba, and she was chosen to participate in a cultural event in his honor. Given her experience as a TV personality, she believed she would serve as mistress of ceremony. The generals organized a series of meetings with her, and she thought it strange that nobody else was invited to these clandestine meetings. When she attended one last meeting, she noticed that all of the artists invited for the occasion were women: *"Todas éramos mujeres, de las más bellas de la televisión. No había un solo artista masculino presente"*/We were all women, the most beautiful ones from television. There was not one single male artist present.

She was taken to the Habana Libre (the former Havana Hilton), and received instructions to "animate" the evening around the tables of the invited guests. In other words, she was to walk around, make small talk, smile, flirt—make the men feel welcome. One other woman performer, the well-known singer Farah María, became upset and asked who was going to accompany her on guitar, because she was there to sing, not to entertain men. A bodyguard tried to convince Rabilero to accompany Farah María on guitar, but she refused and the bodyguard responded, *"Para machos, nosotros sobramos"*/There are enough men here. In other words, you women are the entertainment.

Rabilera became upset as well, and as she admits, *"Salí llorando al balcón de aquel piso 25 del Habana Libre"*/I went to cry on the balcony on the 25th floor of the Havana Libre. Officials and other men in the vicinity admonished her patronizingly: *"No sé por qué te pones así, cuando nosotros fuimos a Alemania nos atendieron las mujeres más lindas del país"*/I don't know why you are acting like this. When we went to Germany we were courted by the most beautiful women there. Rabilero later left the television industry. She admits to having been traumatized by this event and felt shame: *"Me sentía como avergonzada de que cosas así pudieran pasar en una revolución supuestamente pura, digna"*/I felt almost ashamed that things like this could happen in a supposedly pure and dignified revolution.

As part of the greater genealogy of the *mulata/cubana* body and its association within a libidinal economy, Rabilero's story highlights the social circulation of the Cuban woman as sexual commodity. In this instance, her body functioned as a national signifier colluding with discourses about the availability of Othered women's bodies for consumption by European men. However, Rabilero's whiteness and her emotional reaction highlight, for this project, the ways in which racialized gender required different types of performances and interactions. Given the historical predominance of the black and *mulata* woman as sexual commodity, Rabilero's public shock and outrage demonstrate her privileged position within the state.

Many *mulatas* do not have the same ability to show their displeasure or disapproval at being treated as mere sexual object. Unlike many *mulatas*, Rabilero had the ability to say no to such advances or expectations; her economic well-being did not depend on providing such favors. But what about the *mulatas* at the Marina Hemingway? How did they deal with sexist comments or advances? Had some of them eaten before they arrived? Or, were they waiting to finish their dancing to be able to eat something remarkably different or even to eat at all, given the scarcities during this *periodo especial*?

When Cuban state companies (e.g.,Cubanacán) began using the sensual *mulata* iconography in tourist advertisements in the 1990s, the Federation of Cuban Women issued the following statement:

> Part of the present tourist and commercial adverts employ women as simple object of advertisement with aims and interests similar to those of lowest-quality advertising in capitalist countries. . . . The stereotype of the *rumbera* and sensual mulata is enduring, and sometimes does not bear any relation with the product object of the advert.[22]

Although there exists some critique of the use of the *mulata* in claiming that the stereotype sometimes has nothing to do with the product being sold, the statement nevertheless functions in collusion with the government; it agrees that the idea of the *mulata* as sensual, dancing corporeality endures. In other words, why spoil a good thing? Why not engage the *mulata* citizen as a citizen in service to the Cuban tourist economy?

Shannon Bell, in writing about the politico-libidinal economy of socialist Cuba, has said, "it is argued that the FMC's purpose is more that of representing government policy to women than of representing women to the government."[23] Should this be the case, then the lack of severe criticism on the part of the FMC for state (ab)use of the *mulata* stereotype comes as no surprise, particularly during Cuba's economic crisis. Indeed, use of the *mulata* as a commodity for foreign capital continues.

The *Despolete* Emerges

After the success of the *mulata* campaign at Marina Hemingway and with the rising popularity of *timba*, new salsa clubs began to open. Greater tourism necessitated new spaces to capture the flow of capital in all its forms: libidinal, aesthetic, cultural, and economic. Places such as the Casa de la Música in Miramar, Palacio de la Salsa in the Hotel Riviera, the Turquino in the Habana Libre Hotel, and La Cecilia (a restaurant with an open-air salon for dancing) attracted tourists, music aficionados, and foreign music-industry executives. The decision to maintain two levels of peso (convertible to dollars and nonconvertible) made these dollar-only tourist enclaves cost-prohibitive for most Cubans, even *mulatas*, whom some would argue existed as the raison d'etre for Cuban tourism. Those *mulatas* who did get into these places found ways to *resolver*, or solve their currency predicament. Once inside, willing and able male (Euro-American) tourists would provide the *mulatas* with beverages, food, company, and more important, the possibility of a future relationship that would help alleviate the daily scarcity and other problems during the *periodo especial*.

The legibility of the *despelote* through the theorization of hip(g)nosis demands a socio-historical engagement with the dancing body's every day. In this case, history does not so much repeat itself but, rather, provides an outline that bodies can vigorously blur, obfuscate, or perhaps even erase. Erasure seems quite hopeful in this instance, especially since the need for the *mulata* to enact predetermined gendered and racialized choreographies for money and other capital supercedes the need for her to completely resist and re-choreograph her body into the status quo.

Undoubtedly, *timba* and *despelote* revolutionized social relations and interactions in Cuba in both micro- and macropolitical ways. The dance form encouraged solo dancing, with virtuosic displays of hip rotations and torso undulations that tapped into the European/North American male tourists' fantasies about the sexual, sensual Cuban *mulata*. The *despelote* allowed the *mulata* dancing body to set the parameters for the transactional relationship that developed from these nocturnal dance encounters, especially since at this time both parties' desires were well known: his to be coupled, hers to ameliorate her personal economic circumstances. Her hips, therefore, became the battleground for the transaction; mythologized mobilized hip-notic hips that render witnesses speechless and still.

The words of performance studies scholar Awam Amkpa seem appropriate here. He suggests that black bodies (black diasporic bodies) have been spoken for. As a result, said bodies must "learn to textualize the mythologies, the grand truths and moralities, and the other is to learn how to deconstruct them."[24] Hip(g)nosis allows the *mulata* to engage in just that—a dance between the sexualized and mythologized choreographies of race and gender that typify her existence in the cultural imaginary of Cuba. How might she deconstruct said mythologies, or at the very least, have them work for her?

DANCING AND THEORIZING THE *DESPELOTE*

The word *despelote* can possess a variety of meanings. As a noun, it can be translated to mean "mess." As a verb, *despelotar* can mean "to strip, undress." And *despelotarse* (the reflexive) means "to undress oneself." It also contains the word *pelota* or ball. I think of a soccer ball, for example; on the outside, a skin of sewn leather, but if you toss a ball that is falling apart, the skin is broken and the fabric stuffing unravels. This is what I envision with the word *despelote*—an unraveling, not just of fabric but also of lives, social conditions, and codes of conduct. It's an economic unraveling, the stripping away of excess control, of surveillance. It's also a stripping away of something familiar and comfortable in exchange for something unknown; and with it, an unraveling of expectations so that practicality seeps in, making it easier to deal with misfortune and stress. *Despelote* is a dance of frenzy, freedom, and financial need. It began during a time marked by uncertainty, and it continues as a practice. Frenzy for the rhythm, the music, *despelote* allows for hip(g)nosis to function as a source of pleasure—pleasure in shaking the excess free and making it visible. *Despelote* lures through its presumed chaos and lack of control. The hips and hair are whipping around like ecstatic limbs shaking off the discursive tragedy, and trying to shake off the economic one, as well.

Pleasure in the enactment of *despelote* becomes a type of revolutionary act. Move and shake off the uncertainty. Enjoy the process. Make room for new things to have to shake off. There will always be things to get rid of, to revolt against, to feel, to be angry about, to contest, to suppress. How can the hips move in new ways to shake off the excess? To shake it off pleasurably? What choreographic and corporeal attributes does *despelote* possess that renders it such a powerful tool of hip(g)nosis? I highlight the ways in which *despelote* articulates a Cuban corporeal structure of feeling, informed by hip(g)nosis, but more overcome by the challenges of the transnational economy.

Improvisation is crucial in many dances of the African diaspora, and I classify the *despelote* within this framework. Just as Cubans must improvise measures to *resolve* their daily challenges concerning transportation, work, food, and political uncertainty, the *despelote* improvises through codified movements that the dancing body can put together in personal ways. As a way of dancing to the *timba*, *despelote* differs from standard salsa partnering. In fact, *despelote* requires no partnering, and often looks best when danced alone—alone by a *cubana* who closes her eyes and lets the rhythm affect her corporeal response to it.

While the dance form has heteronormative implications, especially if she dances with a man mobilizing representational strategies of a sexualized nature, my focus remains on the *cubana* dancing alone; engaging in corporeal pleasure on her own shifts the significance of the form from one of self-pleasure to one couched in heteronormativity and the fulfillment of male desire.

Hips and pelvis trace circles over bent knees with legs slightly wider than shoulder width apart. Arms can be lifted to mid-torso or way up above her head. They must not be rigid, for rigidity would counter the overall kinesthetic objective of the *despelote*—to rhythmically flail and gyrate along to the exigencies of the complex rhythms of *timba*. Here are Randy Martin's musings on the concept of a social kinesthetic: "We could say that all of these body techniques are decentered in the sense that they are no longer inspired by the heavens and enlightenment but by the ground itself, which becomes a source for all manner of bodily practices and intelligence and therefore *practice itself* becomes something that must be figured out, worked through, made legible."[25]

I wonder—legible for whom? And, what would be the epistemologically specific tools to make it legible? Clearly, the legibility depends on the importance of being read and the ways in which the reading creates power relations. Within this framework, *despelote* exists inside a Cuban social kinesthetic as part of hip(g)nosis, yet the ground where *despelote* springs forth is one that grapples with decolonization, displacement, and decentering. Cuba is haunted by its Spanish colonial past, where hierarchies of race imprinted themselves on all forms of social relations. How, then, to read what a *mulata's* hips are doing without summoning the colonial gaze that renders such hips, as Céspedes told us in the beginning, "semi-savage"?[26]

The legibility of *despelote* does not necessarily depend on a witness's experience of it. As an embodied act, it exists whether or not it is witnessed. I am interested in how the *despelote* becomes a corporeal pleasurable response by the body doing it; nevertheless, its legibility has rendered *despelote* an attractive and venerable force in Cuban social and international relations.

The frenzied *mulata*, moving with abandon, hair disheveled, legs spread apart while she pulses her torso and breasts, signifies a desire for coupling. And this presumed (yet historically validated) desire becomes appropriated and circulated by the state through its tourist economy. However, I suggest that this unravelling of the body—the *mulata* body, the Cuban *mulata* body—articulates the current unsteadiness of the ground on which she dances. Staying still here is not a matter of survival, moving is. The body must move and must move quickly to survive—to *resolver*, the Spanish verb that echoes through quotidian conversations about daily predicaments: food, money, water, employment, and transportation. What economic options might Cuba have if no dancing brown and black women were available for First World male dalliances? Are the exigencies of white male desire the catalysts for such frenzy? Or, have these bodies (and bodies with libidinal forces in general) always had the need for release, frenzy, and rhythmic pleasure? If the latter, then how do the contacts and collisions between differently raced, classed, and gendered bodies materialize the complexities of colonial and contemporary desire? How might one decolonize desire?

In inserting the *despelote* into the larger framework of critical dance studies, I make the case for this dance phenomenon as a corporeal expression of a shifting *Cubanidad*. As a defining popular dance form of contemporary Cuba, *despelote* and the hip(g)nosis it can transmit allow for a way to think about the impact that material conditions and tourism have on the Cuban body. The dizzying, frenetic jerking of *despelote* partners with the constant circulation of those hip-notizing hips, those seemingly disparate mobilizations of body parts moving away from one another yet coming together, always together because the spine's strength permits the unraveling to transform into a refiguring, a refiguring of the body faced with new challenges.

Racialized discourse continues to exist in Cuba, especially when it concerns music and dance. The *despelote*, which emerged from black barrio social-dance activity, met resistance to its legitimacy as a dance style. This resistance stems from the binary of high and low culture in Cuba, where high culture alludes to Europeanist legacies and low culture pertains to anything that is either popular and/or black. Cristy Dominguez, lead choreographer for Cuban television, began using *despelote* choreography on national television, thereby legitimizing the *despelote* by tracing a genealogy of Cuban corporeal expressivity. As an important popular entertainment choreographer with a long history of dance practice and involvement, her pronouncement silenced those who were quick to dismiss *despelote* as a banal dance of lascivious abandon.

Thus, partly through Dominguez's legitimation, *despelote* gained popularity. The dance became more public and more visible; tourists arrived wanting to take lessons created teaching and performing opportunities for Cubans. Additionally, it began to appear on Cuban stage shows. In its codification, *despelote* joins other dances from Cuban's popular dance repertoire—for example, *rumba, cha-cha-chá,* and *mambo*—which circulate as choreographic signatures of a Cuban corporeality. It's a consumable choreography, to be sure, yet one that relies on physical and lived experience to emerge, circulate, and endure.

Rather than address the tourism and re-commodification of the *mulata* as continuation of the "tragic *mulata*" narrative, and allow for this to stand in for the overall tragedy of the misuse and abuse of the Cuban *mulata*, I suggest that the new macro-politics of tourism necessitates new ways of being and acting in the Cuban everyday. This need to *resolver* and *estar en la lucha*/to be in the struggle becomes evident in the way the body dances the *despelote*. Not that *despelote* exists as the only response to the Cuban situation, but this dance—and dance in general—provides an opportunity to witness how bodies react to social and ideological shifts at particular historical moments. The Cuban *mulata* shaking her body, *despeloteandose*/unraveling of herself for herself, for agency, forbids the tragedy of the *mulata* at the mercy of the Cuban condition to stick to her body. Her body is moving too fast for this to occur.

The tragedy is not that Cuba continued its fetishization of the *mulata* myth after the collapse of the Soviet Union had destroyed the Cuban economy, but that the ways in which the discourse surrounding *despelote* during its inception failed to see how history, pleasure, and tactics of resistance emerged from the bodies practicing this dance style. The African legacy in Cuba continues to shape the ways in which bodies move and respond to the amalgamation of African, Caribbean, and European rhythms on the island and so evident in the Cuban musical repertoire. The acknowledgment of pleasure requires an urgency, especially when the *periodo especial* took over Cuban life. *Despelote* offered a way to move the body in pleasurable manifestations that has nothing to do with waiting hours on a queue for a bus, scrounging for something to eat, or enduring a daily diet of tomatoes with sugar, as was rumored to be so during the *periodo especial*.[27] In the Cuban context, the politics of making and unmaking identities, of winding up and unraveling, attests to the ways bodies make do, as Michel De Certeau has famously written. These Cuban *mulata* bodies "make do": pumping, primping, pulsating, and preening. Stillness is not an option.

As dance is a direct expression of corporeal practices, then it cannot be fully excluded from the ideological inscriptions that play upon it through the politics of representation. Enter the *despelote* and its ability to unravel and make visible the precarious conditions of its creation. Despite the efforts of the government to delegitimize the sex industry and dissolve its association with a pre-Castro Cuba, the devastating economic effects of the *periodo especial* saw the country pick up an old script. The *despelote* almost requires a theory of measured chaos to partner with it. Actually, to partner with it would do it a disservice. The *mulata* who dances *despelote* must remain unfettered and unpartnered; *despelote* loses its significance otherwise. Similarly, although *despelote*, like other Africanist dance forms such as krumping, twerking, or the wine, emerges from a specific lived condition, where does its urgency as a choreographed tactic go when it risks commodification through dance workshops or even music videos? As dances that speak to that tenuous space between pleasure and liberation, the historical legacy of these bodies moving and doing it cannot be dismissed. Likewise, what feels like pleasure and liberation for black and brown dancing bodies can become an invitation for pleasure through objectification. This legacy of transactional gazing refuses to go away, yet we can complicate, historicize, and rupture the transaction when we understand the conditions that necessitated that body to move and choreograph like that in the first place. So, this is the battle between the visible and the invisible that I face as I complete this project. How will the *mulatas* in Cuba today negotiate their *mulata*-ness? It seems easy to adopt the historical choreography of *mulata*-ness and wield hip(g)nosis, because everything else in their everyday lives proves complicated. Finding pleasure in the unbearable, untenable, or intolerable becomes a revolutionary act both physically and politically. To hip-notize with her "acrobatic hips"—what fun she can have.

Conclusion, or Rear Endings

I have divulged my distaste for endings, mostly because they warrant a kind of grieving period, or at least a courageous detachment: letting go of something in order to produce something else, something new. Part of this project stems from a personal attempt to learn how to move my hips. I struggled with an inability to move my hips to express what they have needed to say and speak about my family, and about its relationship to a circum-Atlantic history of miscegenation and diasporic hauntings. I have attempted to make my hips limber, agile, to find a fluency of their own. This project has given language to that possibility.

How do I end these stories of hips that constantly circulate, revolve, and barely stop? The stories move along a continuum of time and space, sometimes changing direction, speed, and rhythm; sometimes as a tactic of survival; sometimes for pleasure and sometimes for the pleasure of being watched, yet always as an assertion of bodies and their presence. This requires some celebratory moment to match the spectacle of hip(g) nosis. Perhaps I should put a big yellow bow (Ochún would love that) on my butt to draw attention to the *mulata's* hips? Hips that throughout this book have outlined an alternative way to view the history of this land and the water mass of the black Atlantic, which I renamed the hip-notic torrid zone? This torrid zone interrupts the straight lines of ship paths cross the ocean, and the linear progression of modernity based on the cargo of those ships. It interrupts with water spirals, with ripples. The ripples expand outward, making circular movements—just like those of the dancing *mulata*—that blur and complicate the ways in which history functions and is remembered.

I have excavated the *mulata* sign through the activities of *mulátas* and their use of hip(g)nosis in the nineteenth century as participants in plaçage or concubinage in New Orleans and Havana, as domestic servants in plantation economies, and as dancers on stages in Havana. In the twentieth century, the *mulata* continued to populate the stages of Havana and wields hip(g)nosis globally: on stages in Egypt, Turkey, the former Czechoslovakia, Italy, Mexico, and the United States, featuring Ninón Sevilla, La Karula, Lalín Lafayette, Mayda Limonta, Chelo Alonso, and Carmen Curbelo. And lastly, hip(g)nosis helps us understand how the Cuban *mulata* reconfigured herself to meet the new pressures of the 1990s Cuban tourist economy.

Hip(g)nosis serves as a way to understand how the *mulata* can enact a response to the trope of tragedy associated with her body's history. As a brand, it can circulate among different bodies, regardless of their cultural affiliation with Cuba's history, as I have delineated in this book. In other words, the power and pleasure in hip-notizing with hip(g)nosis need not be the exclusive domain of *mulata* bodies. However, there's a deep responsibility in its enactment and its witnessing—sometimes a painful responsibility. We might avoid it, perhaps in order to *not* have to feel our complicity wherever we may lie along the spectrum of power relations. And witnessing could be about more than just consumption. It requires a deep historical engagement so that certain stories need not be repeated—yet they do, they will, and this is why I dislike endings; they promise finality, a resolution to many things that still continue.

The hips want to take us out. Let's see what they have to say:

The Spanish word for "hip" is *cadera*. Upon closer examination, the word *cadera* has a cognate with the Latin word *cathedra*, or "seat." The Real Academia Española (Royal Spanish Academy), the "seat" of power for the Spanish language, explains:

Cadera: Del lat. cathedra, asiento, silla, y este del gr. καθέδρα

From Greek, the word moved to the Latin. In Latin, the word *cathedra* led to *cathedral*. Many seats lie inside the cathedral: hard ones, ornate ones, the ones where bishops and other members of a patriarchal church wield their powers by sitting on their seat of power. From this seat of power, they took away the power of the *cadera*—women's *caderas,* especially—and everything that lies within and around them. But, these *caderas,* my *caderas* are *catedráticas* (another cognate). A *catedrática/o* is one who sits at a university and teaches/disseminates knowledge. There seems to be much power coming from sitting, from being on a seat. But what about the power of moving? Of moving your "seat"?

I do not like to remain still for too long. My power lies in my ability to move. To move you. To move you into different states of being. To move you to know my history. To know your history. To know how they are continually intertwined. My hip rotations tie them together, continually. I am rolling them together, entwining them. They do not form tight knots, but they are tightly knotted. How do we proceed, then? How can we?

Do you want to just sit there on your *asiento* and be hip-notized?

I can enjoy that if I want.

Do you want to know more? Shall I tell you more? Shall I show you more?

I can do that, too.

I can do many things. I know many things. Let me share them with you; I am, after all, full of knowledge. *La catedrática de las caderas* (a hip scholar, a scholar of the hips). I like that. I like that a lot.

NOTES

PROLOGUE

1. Behar, *The Vulnerable Observer*, 140.
2. Clifford Geertz, quoted in Behar, *The Vulnerable Observer*, 5.

INTRODUCTION

1. De Céspedes, quoted in Lane, *Blackface Cuba*, 180.
2. Rich. "Notes Towards a Politics of Location."
3. *Habitus* is a term attributed to sociologist Pierre Bourdieu.
4. *Sab*, by Gertrudis Gomez de Avellaneda, and *Cecilia Valdes*, by Cirilo Villaverde, use the trope of the tragic *mulata* or *mulato*. The series of lithographs used for tobacco packaging, called *Vida y Muerde de la Mulata*, features a tragic *mulata* narrative as well. See Summer, *Foundational Fictions*, for analysis of *Sab*. For the lithographs, see Kutzinski, *Sugar's Secrets*.
5. A large bibliography on the historical significance of the Cuban *mulata* already exists. Among such titles listed are Lane, *Blackface Cuba*; Kutzinski, *Sugar's Secrets*; Bost, *Mulattas and Mestizas*; Diaz, *The Virgin, The King and the Royal Slaves of El Cobre*; and Thomas, *Cuban Zarzuela*.
6. Moore, *Nationalizing Blackness*, moves through those rich twenty years in Cuba's history to demonstrate how the nation reinvigorated its identity by turning its attention to the once marginal people and cultures with African origins. Primarily focusing on the musical development of Afro/Cubanismo, Moore maintains certain constants throughout, the *mulata* being the one crucial to this study.
7. Daniel, *Dance and Social Change*; Moore, *Nationalizing Blackness*; and Lane, *Blackface Cuba*, among others spend considerable time analyzing the development of the *danzón* as the national dance of Cuba and what that meant to Cuban racial and national identity. I'm more interested in how these dances became embodied and conflated with a *mulata* body, both then operating analogously as signifiers of the Cuban nation.
8. Moore, *Nationalizing Blackness*, 58.
9. Dance anthropologist Yvonne Daniel, *Rumba*, describes the *rumba* in the following manner: "The rhythm was hypnotic.... Their movements brought my attention to the very subtle undulations from the lower spine. The undulations flowed upward and laterally through the sea of bodies.... The basic footwork appeared like a touch to the side and a return to normal standing position, repeated on alternating sides. In reality, there was a small, weighted push of one foot to the side and a step in place with the same foot, alternating from one side to the other.... No knees were straightened; all male and female bodies were slightly

lowered in a forward tilt (about a forty-five degree hip flexion), responding to the rhythmic pulse of the *claves*. The rhythm acted like an injection that affected the body deeply and traveled upward through the spine, laterally through the hips, and forward and backwards in the chest, creating sensuous polyrhythms within the body" (2–3).

10. For an ethnographic analysis of the Cuban *rumba* and its three variations, *rumba guaguancó, rumba yambú,* and *columbia,* refer to Daniel's *Rumba.*

11. Daniel, *Rumba,* 18. Daniel provides rich historical information on the African "origins" of *rumba.*

12. Moore, *Nationalizing Blackness,* 186.

13. Moore, *Nationalizing Blackness,* 99.

14. Although Cuba still considers *danzón* its historically national dance, *danzón* has in fact traveled, gained popularity, and become endemic to Veracruz, Mexico, where weekly outdoor *danzón* events are held. During one of my visits to Havana, I attended the International Danzón Festival, where the majority of dancers and competitors were, indeed, from Mexico. Watching several folkloric companies do their renditions of the *danzón,* I noticed that they were dancing a subtle version of the *son,* not the *danzón* (this can be seen by the way the woman moves her hips and the paths the couple makes). In my view, the couples from Veracruz represented the more historical Cuban *danzón.* Since the Revolution, *rumba, son,* and Yorùbà praise dances receive more national attention.

15. Cuban actress and *rumbera* Ninón Sevilla began a long and successful career in Mexican *cabaretera* films, even though her family was against this type of career for her. She was white, and *rumberas* were considered to be either lower class and/ or *mulata* in Cuban cultural productions. Her *cabaretera* debut was in 1946. Cuban scholar Reynaldo González, *Cine Cubano,* has an entire chapter on Ninón's career and her place in the *cabaretera* genre.

16. Ruf's article, "Qué linda es Cuba!," examines how the famous nightclub idealizes the *mulata* for Cuba. She mentions Miguel Barnet's book, *La canción de Raquel* about a German-Hungarian dancer (with "gypsy" features) who made a career dancing the *rumba* and "perfecting the mannerisms" of the Cuban *mulata* at the Alhambra from the 1910s to the 1920s (Ruf, 87). The film *La Bella del Alhambra* is based on Barnet's book and was directed by his brother. This commentary suggests how the practice of corpo-*mulata* operates. Lowinger and Fox, *Tropicana Nights,* offers a more nostalgic, romanticized view of the nightclub. Lowinger uses Ofelia Fox's account to glamorize and sanitize the underlying race, gender, and class tensions inherent in pre-Revolutionary Cuba. Lam, *Tropicana,* offers a post-Revolutionary look at the nightclub.

17. Piedra, "From Monkey Tales to Cuban Songs," 107.

18. Hartman, *Scenes of Subjection,* 51.

19. Hartman, *Scenes of Subjection,* 57.

20. *Figurantes* are the women who do not necessarily dance on the stage or around the audience. Instead, they are dressed alike and walk around the cabaret space, sometimes near the audiences.

21. I thank one of my anonymous readers for this clear turn of phrase.

22. Foster, ed. *Corporealities,* 1995; Srinivasan, 2012, De Frantz, "Black Beat Made Visible"; Scott, "A Fala que Faz,"; Savigliano, *Tango and the Political Economy;* Cooper Albright 2007.

23. Desmond 29.

24. Fanon, *Black Skin, White Masks,* 112.

25. My intent in joining these geographic locations under the rubric of hip(g)nosis is to demonstrate how bodies, set into signifying processes through histories of colonization and all of its machinations, operate as systems and sources of analysis. In turn, a more productive understanding of the legacies of colonialism and its disturbing processes of racialization emerge.

26. Scott, "Articulations of Blackness."

27. See Susan L. Foster, "Choreographies of Protest" *Theatre Journal* 55:3, October 2003, 395-412; Martin, *Critical Moves;* and Desmond, *Meaning in Motion,* for examples of the body as a site of resistance and declarative statement through protests, nationalization of folk dances, and choreographic techniques, among others.

28. Díaz, *The Virgin, the King.*

29. Badejo, *Osun Séégesi*; Farris Thompson, *Flash of the Spirit;* Murphy and Sanford, *Òsun Across the Waters;* Oweyumi, *The Invention of Women.*

30. Craig Ramos, phone conversations with author, October 1 and November 2, 2006, and March 3, 2006; Craig Ramos, email correspondence with author, October 1–2, 2005. Other Ifa consultants tell me there is no road "Yeyé Móoro" with which they are familiar. According to several of them, "Yeyé Móoro" may be a variation of another avatar called Pasanga or it may have been a praise name used only during ceremonial rites to call or praise Ochún, and then through time it developed into this "avatar" widely circulated in Cuba.

31. Badejo, *Osun Séégesi* 182.

32. Mason and Edwards, *Black Gods*, 315.

33. In Yorúbà culture, the word *amewa* (knower of beauty) represents someone "who looks for the manifestation of pure artistry"; Farris Thompson, *Flash of the Spirit,* 5. This *amewa* would locate beauty in the middle ground—that is, in something or someone who isn't too beautiful or too ugly, too big or too short, for example. So, Òsun's hyperbolic beauty levels off when she labors so that others may be beautiful or have (material, spiritual) beauty.

34. Some of her ghastly attributes include diseases of the blood and genitals. She cuts off the ability to feel, care, and to love (Mason and Edwards, *Black Gods,* 316). By labor in this instance, I mean others such as her followers, must perform *ebos*, or gifts for her so that she is fulfilled and doesn't invoke her "wrath."

35. This claim specifically pertains to the Judeo-Christian ethical paradigm.

36. Stoler, *Along the Archival Grain,* 21.

37. Savigliano, *Nocturnal Ethnographies*, 21.

38. Fraser Delgado and Muñoz, *Everynight Life,* plays a significant role in how I think about the social dancing done by Latino bodies.

39. Braidotti, *Nomatic Subjects*, 14.

40. Some books include Hopkinson, *The Salt Roads*; Ferré, *Maldito Amor*; Cliff, *Abeng*; Conde, *Winward Heights*; Jones, *Corregidora*; Allende, *Island Beneath the Sea* and Tademy, *Cane River.*

41. I thank Anita Gonzalez, who turned me onto the idea of rumor after a Black Performance Theory performance I did in Santa Barbara, 2011.

42. The idea of a historian being rogue comes from De Certeau, The *Writing of History*, 7.

43. White, *Speaking with Vampires,* provides a methodological foundation for this book, as it considers how rumors, gossip, and storytelling articulate a lived "truth." In her book, White examines the circulation of rumors and their effect on those that circulated them. She argues that historical facts emerge from social

truths, just as social truths develop from readings of historical facts (34). Thus, her study is not so much about whether vampires really did exist in colonial Africa, but about how the Africans, in their attempt to construct a reality that made sense to them, spoke about vampires as a way of understanding the repressive colonial framework. White uses "the imaginings of the migrants, the farmers, the women who lived alone in Nairobi's townships" to question how one can write a colonial history (34). Ultimately, White is thoughtfully considering the place oral and written evidences have in historical reconstruction (51).

44. This is informed by Kamala Visweswaran, who states, "when the historian can depict neither past nor future, chronologies are destabilized, and temporality itself is subject to suspension, signalling a suspended temporality, a repudiated nation. The subject speaks betwixt and between time and spaces" *Fictions of Feminist Ethnography*, 69.

45. Allport and Postman, 162, 170.

46. Gema Guevara's "Inexacting Whiteness," argues that the almost white *mulata* literary figure was positioned as the figure that could whiten Cuba as the nation sought to establish a monolithic racial identity.

47. Among Cuban studies scholars, concepts centered around Cuban-ness or terms such as *cubanía, Cubanidad, lo cubano,* and *cubanismo* provoke rich discourse. Such work includes Quiroga's *Cuban Palimpsests;* Hernandez-Reguant, "Multicubanidad"; Pérez, *On Becoming Cuban;* Fernandez and Betancourt, *Cuba, the Elusive Nation.*

48. Cooper Albright, 2007, 7–8.

49. Kutzinski's *Sugar's Secrets* analyzes the potency of this lithograph series and how it addressed the racial anxieties that the *mulata* body caused in nineteenth-century Cuba.

50. I thank Victor Fowler for drawing my attention to these two films. His analysis of these films as historical examples of Cuban dance on screen appears in Blanco Borelli, *Oxford Handbook of Dance and the Popular Screen.*

51. I thank Christina McMahon and Rashida Braggs for their cooperation, patience, and collaboration on our performance of "The Search for True North."

52. Pollock, "The Performative 'I.'"

CHAPTER 1

1. Mason, *Orin Orisa*, 316.

2. Madison, "The Labor of Reflexivity," 129.

3. I use the Spanish spelling of the term when I focus on the *mulata* in Cuba and Spanish New Orleans. When I write about French New Orleans, I use *mûlatresse*. When I mention said corpo-real in Jamaica, I use the term *mulatta* or *mulatto woman*.

4. See Kutzinski *Sugar's Secrets* for numerous examples of mulata poetry that both exalts and demeans the *mulata* and her hips or buttocks.

5. Paul Gilroy's *The Black Atlantic* and Joseph Roach's *Cities of The Dead* establish how this geographical area played a significant role in the conceptualization of black diasporic performance histories. I highlight the feminized space of the diaspora through the hips of the *mulata* and the different labors women of color have had to do and endure, given the histories of slavery, colonialism, and patriarchy in these locations.

6. Here I would like to address the work that Jayna Brown's *Babylon Girls* does in rethinking the concept of transatlantic modernity through the traveling, singing,

and dancing bodies of black women performers in the early twentieth century. Brown's extensive research frames these women's bodies against literature and drama, European primitivism, and colonialism (2). By so doing, Brown troubles the epistemologies that situate the body and performance outside of history making and demonstrates how the transatlantic movement of black expressive cultures undergirds any discussion of modernity. This type of analytical work is crucial to the study of transatlantic black performance and influences my own thinking of the *mulata* as a transnational actor moving with and through her hips.

7. These languages are primarily spoken in the Caribbean and in North and South America.

8. Amalia L. Cabezas writes extensively on sex work in Cuba and the Dominican Republic in her monograph, *Economies of Desire: Sex and Tourism in Cuba and the Dominican Republic*. Other publications include her "Discourses of Prostitution: The Case of Cuba," in *Global Sex Workers: Rights, Resistance, and Redefinitions*, ed. Kempadoo; and her "On the Border of Love and Money: Sex and Tourism in Cuba and the Dominican Republic" in *Labor versus Empire: Race, Gender, and Migration*. Her work specifically looks at the history, market, and participants in this phenomenon. Performance artist/activist Coco Fusco has also written on the *jineteras* in Cuba, see her "Hustling for Dollars."

9. Anglo-Caribbean historian Trevor Burnard questions most American slavery scholarship that only examines sexual relationships between women of color and white men as merely exploitative:

The pronounced differences in the treatment of the Caribbean and North American experiences of enslaved women or free women of African descent are striking, given the existence of similar power relationships between white men and black women in both regions. (85)

Some of these differences include the following: greater influence of feminist thought in North American slave historiography; greater historical and contemporary acceptance of interracial sexual relations in the Caribbean than in the United States; the absence in North America of the concept of an intermediate racial category of mulatto, since existence of mulatto class of "browns" with greater privileges and higher status than blacks is a distinctive feature of Caribbean society, both during and after slavery (101n17). Although not denying the violence and exploitation that occurred, Burnard comments that in the Caribbean, historians tend to view interracial relationships more positively. Refer to Burnard's chapter on Thistlewood and his slave lover, Phibbah, in Gaspar and *Beyond Bondage*, where he quotes from Edward Cox (1984) and Barbara Bush (1990), other historians of Caribbean women, to qualify his argument about the "less exploitative" relationships between Caribbean slaves, mulattos, and their white masters.

10. In Gaspar and Hine's, *Beyond Bondage*, the various authors voyage throughout the Americas and situate these women in different economic positions (p. x).

11. In her essay "Victims or Strategists? Female lodging-house keepers in Jamaica," Paulette A. Kerr presents how the *mulatto* woman mobilized her identity within the political economy of colonization. For the Jamaican *mulatto* woman, the keeping of lodging-houses and taverns was "one of the few means of economic and possibly social independence for women during and after slavery" (198).

12. Monique Guillory's dissertation, "Some Enchanted Evening on the Auction Block," does comparative analysis between historical accounts, fictional representations, and ephemera from the era of the quadroon balls. She makes the claim that although the events were sumptuous in their production, they were merely

a fancier version of the auction block. Lisa Ze Winters's dissertation, "Specter, Spectacle and the Imaginative Space," examines both the quadroon balls of New Orleans and the signare balls in Senegal as a way to rethink the *mulata* as a relevant diasporic actor.

13. Cundall, quoted in Sharpe, 45.
14. Cocuzza, "The Dress of Free Women," 82.
15. Cocuzza, "The Dress of Free Women."
16. The term "epidermal reality" comes from Anna Beatrice Scott's work on blackness, race and carnival in Brazil. See *A Fala que Faz*.
17. Hazard, 167.
18. Mason, *Orin Orisa*, 375.
19. Òsun is the Yorùbà spelling. Ochún is the Cuban spelling. I differentiate between the two to demonstrate how this deified energy force is understood in these cultural contexts, and how Cuban Ochún developed differently.
20. Farris Thompson, *Flash of the Spirit*, 80.
21. Mason, *Black Gods*, 101.
22. Mason, *Black Gods,* 99.
23. During the nineteenth century in Cuba, Yemayá (Ochún's sister, and other water goddess) came to represent dark beauty, while Òsun represents honey-colored beauty. Yorùbà scholar John Mason states that Yemayá contains qualities of another African deity, Mamí Wàtá (pidgin English for "Mother of the Water") (Mason *Olóòkun*, 56). Mamí Wàtá, similar to Òsun, procures gifts and wealth to her followers. The *mulata,* as a product of Africa and Europe, benefited from the mobility and access afforded to lighter-skinned bodies. Mason corroborates by writing that "[i]n the Americas, this position [being mulata] allowed for greater facility of movement in the procuring of wealth and position. Òsun's traditional role as Ìyálóde (titled mother who deals with external affairs/strangers) sets the New World stage for the *mulatta*/Òsun/Màmí Wàtá/child of whites to step into the role" (Mason, *Black Gods*, 55).
24. Mason, *Orin Orisa*, 317. For information about the variety of avatars, see Cabrera, *Yemayá y Ochún*.
25. Kutzinski's *Sugar's Secrets* and Lane's *Blackface Cuba* trace the development of the *mulata* archetypes that circulated in Cuba by the end of the nineteenth century.
26. Badejo, *Òsun Séégesi*, 177.
27. Mason, *Black Gods*, 98.
28. Hanger, *Bounded Lives*, 46.
29. Mason, *Orin Orisa*, 361.
30. Dance scholar Susan Leigh Foster's "Choreographies of Gender" aims to naughtily disturb, disrupt, and contribute to the fields of feminism, dance, and performance studies. For her, a dissection of choreographic strategies in dance enables a clearer understanding of the intention behind the dance. Her adamant suggestion to examine gender as a form of choreography stresses the significance of how bodies both create and resist culturally specific coded meanings. She writes, "To analyze gender as choreography is to acknowledge as systems of representation the deeply embedded, slowly changing rules that guide our actions and that make those actions meaningful. Not biologically fixed but rather historically specific, these rules are redolent with social political, economic and aesthetic values . . . connect[ing] that body to other cultural orchestrations of identity" (29).

31. See Guillory, "Under One Roof: The Sins and Sanctity of the New Orleans Quadroon Balls."
32. See http:// www.rosetterochon.com , accessed May 5 2006, for details on how one of her homes is being renovated to become a museum. Wikipedia also features a long biography of her under the heading of *plaçage*, notable *placées*.
33. Villaverde, quoted in Guevara, "Inexacting Whiteness," 124.
34. Chasteen, "A National Rhythm," 63.
35. Merlin, quoted in Chasteen, "A National Rhythm," 63.
36. The other two danced events in *Cecilia Valdés* are a black-tie dance and a dance for the Spanish peninsular aristocrats, respectively. These two were homogenous dance environments where minimal, if not nonexistent, contact between races and different social classes predominated.
37. González, *Cine Cubano*, 206.
38. De Certeau explains that "strategies are actions, which, thanks to the establishment of a place of power, elaborate theoretical places" while "tactics are procedures that gain validity in relation to the pertinence they lend to time"; De Certeau, *The Practice of Everyday Life*, 38. He contends that strategies and tactics volley between the roles that space and time afford one or the other. Strategies depend on having an established location as the locus of power, while tactics find moments within the historical progression of power and time to insert their "guileful ruses." Theoretically, strategies and tactics operate as distinctly separate spheres of influence. That is, one emerges, the strategy, as more triumphant than the other thereby establishing what we come to understand as the ideological status quo: patriarchy, logos, transnational capitalism.
39. Guillory, "Some Enchanted Evening," 27.
40. Guillory, "Some Enchanted Evening," 28.
41. Sullivan, quoted in Li, "Resistance, Silence and Placées," 94.
42. Didimus, quoted in Li, "Resistance, Silence and Placées," 94.
43. The inspiration for these two letters stems from the historical records gathered in both Martinez Alier, *Marriage*, 1974 and Clinton and Gillespie, *The Devil's Lane*. Both volumes examine the relationships between free women of color, men and the juridical systems in Spanish New Orleans and Cuba. Kimberly Hanger's "Coping in a Complex World," examines court records where many free women of color sought legal or honorable remuneration for their rights. I take complete creative licence in imagining this character and story of Maria Garcia Granados, but I am attendant to the historical records that exist to provide a context.
44. These two last names are my great-grandmothers' last names, respectively.
45. Mason, *Orin Orisa*, 372.

INTERLUDE 1
1. I say skin color because race can be a porous term in a miscegenated country such as Cuba. Nevertheless, *blanco, negro,* and *mulato* maintain their specific historically contingent currencies when linked to social class and privilege.
2. Chasteen, *National Rhythms*, and Lane, 2005.
3. González Mandri, *Guarding Cultural Memory*, 67.
4. Excerpt from Alfonso Camín, "La mulata Candelaria," in Kutzinski, *Sugar's Secrets*, 173.
5. Johnson, *Soul to Soul,*11.

CHAPTER 2

1. At the time of this writing, the relations between Cuba and the United States have normalized. New travel and trade regulations have been set in place since January 2015. In April 2015, President Obama met with Cuban president Raúl Castro at the Summit of the Americas. This was the first time the heads of state of the United States and Cuba met since 1961 when ties between the countries were severed. On July 20, 2015, the Embassy of Cuba in Washington, D.C. was officially opened after fifty-four years. The Cuban flag was raised in a formal ceremony which solidified diplomatic relations between the two countries.
2. Stein, "All Havana Broke Loose," 340.
3. *Paraiso bajo las estrellas,* or "paradise beneath the stars," is one of the more common nicknames given to the Tropicana.
4. I do not mean to suggest that only this group of people experiences nostalgia, nor do I want to imply nostalgia is a banal affect. Instead, I hope to articulate how this specific affect shapes the kinds of memories and memorializations that happen in books, magazines, and other cultural materials about a pre-Castro Cuba, particularly those produced outside of Cuba.
5. Stoler, *Along the Archival Grain*, 187.
6. The majority of stories told to me involved Marlon Brando's desire to see El Chori's show. Brando was a fan of Cuban music and was learning how to play the *conga.*
7. Visweswaran's *Fictions of Feminist Ethnography* features a chapter in which the subject of the ethnography refused to speak with the author. Visweswaran adroitly analyzes the silence as part of a larger discourse on politics, power, and refusal.
8. White, *Speaking with Vampires*, 55.
9. Bhabha, *Nation and Narration*.
10. Lena Hammergren, "Many Sources, Many Voices," asks "how do we conceive of sources and what can we make of them?" (20) when considering a dance historiographic project. She elaborates on the multiple ways to tell a dance history, citing intertextuality to highlight history's multiple voices (27).
11. The scenario comes from Diana Taylor's *The Archive and The Repertoire*. The idea of practiced-space is from De Certeau's "Spatial Stories," in *The Practice of Everyday Life*.
12. Perna, *Timba,* features significant information on the Cuban government's post-Revolution activities to monitor public dancing and nocturnal entertainment activities.
13. Jesus Blanco Aguilar's *80 Anos del son y soneros* provides a copious list of the *academias de baile,* with their names and/or locations.
14. Here I am thinking about Visweswaran's *Fictions of Feminist Ethnography,* in which she articulates how ethnography involves the act of fictionalizing encounters.
15. He uses the word *mulatona,* for "mulata." The addition of the *ona* suffix literally increases the size of the *mulata*. Rather than just translate it as "big mulata," I see the use of the suffix as a way to really corporealize the *mulata* by having her body occupy significant space, regardless of actual size. In its hyberbole, the *mulata* body becomes more visceral.
16. José Galiño, "Academias de Baile."
17. Robin Moore's *Nationalizing Blackness* delves into the history of this music revolution in early-twentieth-century Cuba.

18. Guayaberas are the shirts worn by men in warmer Latin American climates. They are usually made of cotton or linen, and can have either long or short sleeves. They are notable for the four pockets and the embroidered details in the front.

19. Galiño, "Academias de Baile."

20. Galiño, "Academias de Baile."

21. Cabezas, *Economies of Desire*, 117.

22. Authors such as Smith and Padula, *Sex and Revolution*; Randall, *Cuban Women Now*; and Lewis, Lewis, and Rigdon, *Four Women* offer testimonies of women who were rehabilitated by the Revolutionary government.

23. Fernandez Robaína, 76–77.

24. Cabezas, *Economies of Desire*, 43.

25. Serpa, *Contrabando*, 93–94.

26. Martin, *Technologies of the Self.*

27. Serpa, *Contrabando*, 92.

28. Serpa, *Contrabando*, 97.

29. Serpa, *Contrabando*, 97.

30. By *cubanía* I am referring to nationally specific and circulating gestural choreographies of Cuban-embodied identity.

31. I am influenced by the work of Cindy Garcia, "Don't Leave me Celia," and her subsequent book *Salsa Crossings*. In her excellent ethnography of the salsa dance scene in Los Angeles, Garcia pays particular attention to the relationships women have with one another in the spaces off the dance floor.

32. Serpa, *Contrabando,* 99.

33. Robin Moore's *Nationalizing Blackness* features some information about the *academias de baile* that he also collected through oral history (98–99).

34. Many well-known musicians and singers passed through Los Jóvenes del Cayo. These included Pérez Prado, Celia Cruz, Blanca Rosa Gil, Felix Chapotín, and Miguelito Valdés, among others.

35. Portelli, 36.

36. Cuba featured many orchestras performing live on the radio station. The orchestras would go to Radio Progreso, for example, and record sessions on a regular basis to be aired nationally.

37. Steedman, "Something She Called a Fever," 1159; Also see Steedman, *Dust.*

38. Orujuela Martinez, *History of El Son*, 22.

39. For an account of El Chori's life told anecdotally, Cuban journalist Rafael Lam's article "El Chori, King of the Timbal in Marianao Beach" is a good example.

40. In my interviews with both men and women who knew about *academias de bailes*, social dancing, and nightlife stories, the recurring narrative was indeed that many of these public-dancing women desired to marry a nice man who would take care of them so they would no longer have to dance (or do other things) for money.

41. Here I am referencing Benedict Anderson's *Imagined Communities* (198), who writes about Jules Michelet as a historian who performs an act of resurrection in sifting through the dusty archives to revive the dead and their desires. Carolyn Steedman also spends some considerable time engaging with Michelet's process in her wonderful book on archives, called *Dust*.

42. Gordon, 8.

43. Clifford, 36.

44. DeFrantz and Gonzalez, *Black Performance Theory*, 12.

CHAPTER 3

1. In film studies, this scene is well regarded because of its clever and almost seamless editing technique. The scene lasts about seven minutes and there are eight edits, which are hardly noticeable.

2. This comes from the Rodgers and Hart song "Bewitched, Bothered and Bewildered." I am also playing on the English translation of *Yambaó* to *Cry of the Bewitched* and the effects that watching dancing *mulata* hips have on observers.

3. Ernesto Caparrós, director, *Tam Tam o el Origen de la Rumba* (Tam Tam or the Origin of the Rumba), 1938.

4. Benitez Rojo, *The Repeating Island*, 20.

5. Orta, "*Cubanizando a Hollywood* Bohemia," 36–37, 57–58.

6. Orta, "*Cubanizando a Hollywood* Bohemia."

7. Jill Lane makes a similar argument in her work on the smoking *habaneras*, the clay figurines popular in contemporary Cuban tourist markets. According to Lane, the Habaneras have Lethean dimensions in that they "perform a similar operation on the past, literally forgetting the revolution in favor or reviving the colonial past." See Lane, "Smoking Habaneras," 31.

8. Lane, Kutzinski, *Sugar's Secrets,* and Arrizón, "Race-Ing Performativity through Transculturation." engage in the trope of the *mulata de rumbo* as part of the Cuban imaginary's portrayal of the public, mobile *mulata.*

9. Gilberto Martínez Solares, director, *Mulata*, 1954 [DVD distributed by Tekila Films].

10. Ninón passed away in Mexico on January 1, 2015, after living there for most of her life. To a certain extent, her *cubanía* and her hip(g)nosis enabled her celebrity status outside of Cuba. It is difficult to say whether she would have achieved such celebrity status had she remained in Cuba; their film industry was not as developed as that of Mexico's in the 1940s–'50s, and Ninón's looks or talent were not considered extraordinary enough for the Cuban cinema then. González's chapter on Ninón in *Cine Cubano* delves into further detail and speculation on her career.

11. Ramos, Craig. personal communication with author, Los Angeles, CA March 3, 2006.

12. González, *Cine Cubano,*106.

13. Foucault, *Discipline and Punish,* 93.

14. Alfred B. Crevenna, director, *Yambaó* produced by Rubén Calderón and Alberto López, Cinematográfica Calderon, SA, 1957.

15. DeFrantz, "Black Beat Made Visible," 66.

16. IMDB Movie Summary, http://www.imdb.com/title/tt0049968/plotsummary.

17. I base my analysis on two film versions of *Yambaó*: an English-dubbed version produced by Psychotronica in 1996, and a black-and-white 1957 version available on YouTube at https://www.youtube.com/watch?v=hfK6DQZyoTw [accessed July 22, 2015].

18. VCI Entertainment, *Psychotrónica, Volume 3: Mermaids of Tiburón/Cry of the Bewitched*. DVD, 2008.

19. Perez, *Slaves, Sugars, and Colonial Society,* and Mintz, *Sweetness and Power,* contextualize life on the sugar plantations and the economic power the sweet white powder wielded during the plantation economy.

20. I have chosen to call the enslaved bodies "slaves" in accordance with characters depicted in Cuba's teatro bufo: *esclavo, mulata, gallego, gallega, calesero.*

21. See Contreras, "Yo conocí a Beny Moré," and Lam, *La Engañadora Vive en La Habana,* as well as Lam, *La Leyenda de las Mulatas del Fuego* . These sources relate how La Karula was "the only woman" to dance the *Columbia* with daggers in her hands. Because Rodney had created Las Mulatas del Fuego, and then went on to choreograph *Yambaó,* it is my contention that it was La Karula's initial choreography that inspired the one for the film.

22. Srinivasan, *Sweating Saris,* particularly chap. 3.

23. By surrogation, I reference the concept put forth by Roach, *Cities of the Dead.*

24. Foucault. "Nietzsche, Genealogy, History," 143.

25. Murphy, *Working the Spirit*; Ramsey, 1997; Dayan, "Erzulie," Drewal.

26. Voudou is a dance of the spirit, a system of movements, gestures, prayers, and songs in veneration of the invisible forces of life; Murphy, *Working the Spirit,*10. These invisible forces, or *loas*, need a physical body to materialize and experience the life of the *serviteur*, without whom the practice of voudou would be impossible. Voudou implies a reciprocal relationship between *serviteur* and *loa*. In simple terms, they need each other.

27. I want to thank Ramón Rivera-Servera and Laura M. Gutierrez for pointing out the possibility of a queer reading in this exchange between Ninón Sevilla and Olga Guillot.

28. Yvonne Daniels, *Dancing Wisdom*, 137.

29. In Sharpe's *Ghosts of Slavery,* she analyzes the case of Joanna, the *mulata* mistress of Captain Stedman (British soldier stationed in Surinam during late eighteenth century) in order to complicate the precarious relationships between white men and their *mulata* concubines. The domestic arrangement, while outwardly demonstrating ease, belies the tensions, coercions, mimicries, and unstable power positions in these relationships. I situate Yambaó's relationship within this historical nexus as a way framing it ina significant context and not as an isolated event of mere desire between a woman of color and a white man.

30. Mikhail Kalatozov, director, *I am Cuba/Soy Cuba.* Produced by Bela Friedman, Semyon Maryakhin and Miguel Mendoza, ICAIC and Milestone Films, 1964.

31. Once ties with the United States were severed in 1961, Cuba turned to the Soviet Union for a variety of partnerships.The USSR agreed to finance the film as it was a chance to promote socialism on an international scale. The movie was not successful with Cuban or Soviet audiences, and it was only in the mid 1990s when it received renewed interest due to endorsements from American directors Francis Ford Coppola and Martin Scorsese. The film is widely recognized for its many innovations in cinematography.

32. Lorde, *Sister Outsider,* 54.

33. John Gabriel Stedman was a professional soldier who, in 1772, went to live in Surinam, South America and penned a book based on his daily journals while there. *Narrative of a Five Year's Expedition Against the Revolted Negroes in Surinam* (1806[1796]) featured Joanna, a mulatta slave, his concubine. The reader gets to know her through his writings about her. Thus, her subjectivity is mediated through him. Sharpe (2002) analyses the racial and gender dynamics in their relationship.

34. Nicolás Guillén Landrián, director. *Los del Baile*. Eduardo Valdés, producer. ICAIC, 1965.

35. Julio García Espinosa, director. *Son. . .o no son*. Guillermo García, producer. ICAIC, 1980.

INTERLUDE 3

1. Mason, *Orin Orisa*, 375.
2. Chelo Alonso was in Egypt during the Suez Crisis of 1956. She left from Egypt for Istanbul by boat via Cyprus and Greece.
3. Mason, *Orin Orisa*, 361.
4. She explains in her letter to *Show* Magazine about the bombings in Egypt during the Suez Crisis of 1956.
5. Mason, *Orin Orisa*, 372.
6. Mason, *Orin Orisa*, 374.

CHAPTER 4

1. Moya Fabregás, "Cuban Women's Revolutionary Experience," 70. Her article provides much of the information in this section. I am indebted to her excellent evaluation of the role of women during this crucial period in Cuban history.
2. Moya Fabregás, "Cuban Women's Revolutionary Experience," 70.
3. Moya Fabregás, "Cuban Women's Revolutionary Experience," 71.
4. As cited in Cuba Solidarity web page document "Women in Cuba", 9.http://www.cuba-solidarity.org.uk/faqdocs/WomenInCuba.pdf, accessed August 3, 2012.
5. Moya Fabregas, "Cuban Women's Revolutionary Experience," 73.
6. Moya. "Una Aproximación."
7. Smith and Padula, 174.
8. Federation of Cuban Women, *Women*, 53.
9. Moya Fabregas, "Cuban Women's Revolutionary Experience," 69.
10. Greer received this response: "'She doesn't have to impress us,' answered one of the delegates. 'We know her. She is our Vilma'"; Greer, *Madwomen's Underclothes*, 256. Throughout her essay, Greer seems aware of her First World feminist positioning and makes it explicit that she is judging the Cuban women from this perspective. At one point she admits, "I abandoned my posture of superiority and let myself be impressed." (258). By considering the discursive as performative, Greer's act of abandonment may only be textual, yet it shows how feminism is fraught with cultural and geographic divides.
11. Greer, *Madwomen's Underclothes*, 257.
12. Greer, *Madwomen's Underclothes*, 255.
13. Greer, *Madwomen's Underclothes*, 258.
14. Greer, *Madwomen's Underclothes*, 258.
15. Spivak, "Subaltern Studies," 82.
16. Perna, *Timba*.
17. Perna, *Timba*; see his chapter "Música bailable under the Revolution, 1959-1989," which traces the effects of the Revolution on dance music during this period.
18. Perna, *Timba*, 61.
19. Peter I. White, "Cuba at a Crossroads." *National Geographic 180*, no. 2 (August 1991).
20. Rafael Lam, personal communication. Havana, Cuba January 2011.
21. Hilda Rabilero, interview with, available at http://baracuteycubano.blogspot.com.es/2007/03/en-contacto-con-hilda-rabilero.html, accessed April 26, 2012.
22. Statement issued by FMC, Memorias del VI Congreso de la FMC, 1995, quoted in Perna, *Timba*, 210.
23. Bell, "The Political-Libidinal Economy," 346.
24. Amkpa, "A State of Perpetual Becoming," 82.
25. Martin, "Toward a Decentered Social Kinaesthetic," 77–78.
26. De Céspedes quoted in Lane, 180.

27. Several Cubans have told me that they survived on a diet of tomatoes and sugar. One Cuban even demonstrated how he dipped his tomatoes in sugar and ate them. Other stories include using Chinese condoms as cheese substitutes on pizza, making pots and pans out of aluminum billboards, and eating cats. I do not question the validity of these stories as they are a way to interpret the trauma of the *periodo especial* and its abysmal scarcity.

WORKS CONSULTED

Allende, Isabel. *Island Beneath the Sea*. New York: Harper Collins, 2009.

Allport, Gordon and Leo Postman. *The Psychology of Rumor*. New York: Henry Holt and Co., 1948.

Amkpa, Awam. "A State of Perpetual Becoming: African Bodies as Texts, Methods, and Archives." *Dance Research Journal* 42, no. 1 (Summer 2010): 83–88.

Anderson, Benedict. *Imagined Communities: Reflections on the Origins and Spread of Nationalism*. London: Verso, 1991.

Aparicio, Frances R., and Susana Chávez-Silverman, eds. *Tropicalizations: Transcultural Representations of Latinidad*. Hanover: University Press of New England [for] Dartmouth College, 1997.

Arbery, Glenn Cannon. "Victims of Likeness: Quadroons and Octoroons in Southern Fiction." *Southern Review* 25 (1989): 52–71.

Arondekhar, Anjai. "Without a Trace: Sexuality and the Colonial Archive." *Journal of the History of Sexuality* 14, no.1–2 (January-April 2005): 10–27.

Aróstegui, Natalia Bolívar. *Los orishas en Cuba*. Cuidad de Panama: Mercie Ediciones, 2005.

Arrizón, Alicia. "Race-Ing Performativity through Transculturation, Taste and the Mulata Body." *Theatre Research International* 27, no. 2 (2002): 136–52.

Arrizón, Alicia. "Transculturation and Gender in U.S. Latina Performance." *Theatre Research International* 24 (1999): 288–94.

Arrizón, Alicia, and Lillian Manzor, eds. *Latinas on Stage*. Berkeley, CA: Third Woman Press, 2000.

Aubry-Kaplan, Erin. "Back Is Beautiful." *Salon*, July 1998, available at http://archive. salon.com/ent/feature/1998/07/cov_15feature.html.

Badejo, Deirdre. *Osun Séégesi, The Elegant Deity of Wealth, Power and Femininity*. Trenton, NJ: Africa World Press, 1996.

Baker, Houston A., Jr. "Caliban's Triple Play." In *"Race." Writing and Difference*, edited by Henry Louis Gates Jr. and Kwame Anthony Appiah, 381–95. Chicago: University of Chicago Press,1986.

Barnet, Miguel. *Canción de Raquel*. Barcelona: Libros del Asteroide, 2012.

Barrera, Magdalena. "Hottentot 2000: Jennifer Lopez and Her Butt." In *Sexualities in History*, edited by Kim M. Phillips and Barry Reay, 407–20 New York & London: Routledge, 2002.

Barthes, Roland. "The Discourse of History." Translated by Richard Howard. In *The Rustle of Language*, 127–40. Berkeley: University of California Press, 1989.

Barthes, Roland. *Image-Music-Text*. New York: Hill and Wang, 1977.

Barthes, Roland. *Mythologies*. Translated by Annette Lavers. New York: Farrar Strauss & Giroux, 1972.

Barthes, Roland. *Writing Degree Zero*. New York: Hill and Wang, 1968.

Beckels, Hilary. *Centering Woman: Gender Discourses in Caribbean Slave Society*. Princeton, NJ: Marcus Weiner, 1999.

Behar, Ruth. *The Vulnerable Observer: Anthropology That Breaks Your Heart*. Boston: Beacon Press, 1996.

Bell, Shannon. "The Political-Libidinal Economy of the Socialist Female Body: Flesh and Blood, Work and Ideas." In *Women and Revolution: Global Expressions*, edited by M. J. Diamond, 339–55. Dordrecht: Kluwer Academic Publishers, 1998.

Beltrán, Mary C. "The Hollywood Latina Body as Site of Social Struggle: Media Constructions of Stardom and Jennifer Lopez's 'Cross-over Butt.'" *Quarterly Review of Film and Video* 19 (2002): 71–86.

Benítez Rojo, Antonio. *The Repeating Island: The Caribbean and the Postmodern Perspective*. Translated by James E. Maraniss. Durham, NC: Duke University Press, 1996.

Berzon, Judith. *Neither White nor Black, the Mulatto Character in American Fiction*. New York: New York University Press, 1978.

Bhabha, Homi, ed. *Nation and Narration*. New York: Routledge, 1990.

Blanco Aguilar, Jesus. *80 Años del son y soneros en el Caribe*. Caracas: Fondo Editorial Tropicos, 1992.

Blanco Borelli, Melissa. ed. *The Oxford Handbook of Dance and the Popular Screen*. New York: Oxford University Press, 2014.

Bordo, Susan. *Unbearable Weight: Feminism, Western Culture, and the Body*. Berkeley: University of California Press, 1983.

Bost, Suzanne. *Mulattas and Mestizas: Representing Mixed Identities in the Americas, 1850-2000*. Athens: University of Georgia Press, 2003.

Bradiotti, Rosa. *Nomadic Subjects*. New York: Columbia University Press, 1994/2011.

Brandon, George. *Santería from Africa to the New World*. Bloomington: Indiana University Press, 1993.

Brown, Jayna. *Babylon Girls: Black Women Performers and the Shaping of the Modern*. Durham, NC: Duke University Press, 2008.

Buck-Morss, Susan. *Dialectics of Seeing*. Cambridge, MA: MIT University Press, 1989.

Burnard, Trevor. "'Do Thou in Gentle Phibia Smile' Scenes from an Interracial Marriage, Jamaica, 1754–86" in *Beyond Bondage: Free Women of Color in the Americas* edited by Gaspar, David Barry and Darlene Clark Hine, 82–105. Urbana and Chicago: University of Illinois Press, 2004.

Bush, Barbara. *Slave Women in Caribbean Society, 1650-1838*. Bloomington: Indiana University Press, 1990.

Butler, Judith. *Gender Trouble: Feminism and the Subversion of Identity*. London: Routledge, 1990.

Cabezas, Amalia L. "Discourses of Prostitution: The Case of Cuba" in *Global Sex Workers: Rights, Resistance and Redefinition* edited by Kamala Kempadoo, 79–86. New York: Routledge, 1998.

Cabezas, Amalia L. "On the Border of Love and Money: Sex Tourism in Cuba and the Dominican Republic" in *Labor versus Empire: Race, Gender and Migration* edited by González, Gilbert G., Raúl Fernández, Vivian Price, David Smith and Linda Trinh Võ, 108–18. New York: Routledge, 2004.

Cabezas, Amalia L. *Economies of Desire: Sex and Tourism in Cuba and the Dominican Republic*. Philadelphia: Temple University Press, 2009.

Cabrera, Lydia. *Yemayá y Ochún*. Madrid: C.R.,1974.

Cámara, Madeline. "La Mulata, Cuerpo-Símbolo De La Cultura Cubana." *Monographic Review/Revista Monográfica* 15 (1999): 121–29.

Cámara, Madeline. "La Mulata, Un Cuerpo Sin Voz En La Cultura Cubana." *Palabra y el Hombre: Revista de la Universidad Veracruzana* 109 (1999): 75–81.

Cámara, Madeline. "Ochún: Una Metáfora Incompleta En La Cultura Cubana." *South Eastern Latin Americanist* 42, nos. 2–3 (1998): 21–28.

Cámara Betancourt, Madeline. "Between Myth and Stereotype: The Image of the Mulatta in Cuban Culture in the Nineteenth Century, a Truncated Symbol of Nationality." In *Cuba, the Elusive Nation: Interpretations of National Identity* edited by Damian and Madeline Cámara Betancourt Fernandez, 100–15. Gainesville: University Press of Florida, 2000.

Carbonell, Walterio. "Birth of a National Culture." In *AfroCuba: An Anthology of Cuban Writing on Race, Politics and Culture*, edited by Pedro Perez Sarduy and Jean Stubbs, 195–203. Melbourne: Ocean Press, 1993.

Cashion, Susan V. "Educating the Dancer in Cuba." In *Dance: Current Selected Research*, vol. 1, edited by Lynnette Y. Overby and James H. Humphrey, 165–87. New York: AMS Press,1989.

Chasteen, John Charles. "A National Rhythm: Social Dance and Elite Identity in Nineteenth-Century Havana." *Critical Studies: Music, Popular Culture, Identities* 19, no. 1 (August 2002): 55–73.

Chasteen, John Charles. *National Rhythms, African Roots: The Deep History of Latin American Popular Dance*. Albuquerque: University of New Mexico Press, 2004.

Chatterjea, Ananya. *Butting Out: Reading Resistive Choreographies through Works by Jawole Willa Jo Zollar and Chandralekha*. Middletown, CT: Wesleyan University Press, 2004.

Chavez, Rebeca, director. *Con Todo Mi Amor, Rita*. Havana: Instituto Cubano de Arte e Industria Cinematográfica, 2000.

Cheung, Floyd D. "Les Cenelles and Quadroon Balls: Hidden Transcripts of Resistance and Domination in New Orleans, 1803–1845." *Southern Literary Journal* 29, no. 2 (1997): 5–16.

Clair, Drake, St. *Black Metropolis: A Study of Negro Life in a Northern City*. Chicago: University of Chicago Press, 1993.

Clément, Catherine. *Opera, or the Undoing of Women*. Translated by Betsy Wing. Minneapolis: University of Minnesota Press, 1988.

Cliff, Michelle. *Abeng*. New York: Penguin, 1984.

Clifford, James. *The Predicament of Culture: Twentieth Century Ethnography, Literature and Art*. Cambridge: Harvard University Press, 1988.

Clinton, Catherine, and Michelle Gillespie. "Caliban's Daughter: The Tempest and the Teapot." *Frontiers: A Journal of Women's Studies* 12, no.2 (1991): 36–51.

Clinton, Catherine, and Michelle Gillespie, eds. *The Devil's Lane: Sex and Race in the Early South*. New York: Oxford University Press, 1997.

Cocuzza, Dominique. "The Dress of Free Women of Color in New Orleans, 1790–1840" *Dress* 27 (2000): 78–87.

Cohen, Jeff. "Cuba Libre," Playboy (March 1991): 69–75, 157–158.

Condé, Maryse. *Land of Many Colors; Nanna-Ya*. Translated by Nicole Ball. Lincoln: University of Nebraska Press, 1999.

Condé, Maryse. *Windward Heights*. Translated by Richard Philcox. New York: Soho Press, 2003.

Contreras, Felix. "Yo conocí a Beny Moré," unpublished manuscript.

Coombes, Rosemary. *The Cultural Life of Intellectual Properties: Authorship, Appropriation, and the Law*. Durham, NC: Duke University Press, 1998.

Cooper, Carolyn. *Noises in the Blood: Orality, Gender, and the "Vulgar" Body of Jamaican Popular Culture*. Durham, NC: Duke University Press, 1995.

Cooper Albright, Anne. *Traces of Light: Absence and Presence in the Work of Loïe Fuller*. Middletown, CT: Wesleyan University Press, 2007.

Couch, R. Randall. "The Public Masked Balls of Antebellum New Orleans: A Custom of Masque Outside the Mardi Gras Tradition." *Louisiana History* 35, no. 4 (1994): 403–31.

Dagan, Esther A., ed. *The Spirit's Dance in Africa: Evolution, Transformation and Continuity in Sub-Sahara*. Westmount, Quebec: Galerie Amrad African Arts Publications, 1997.

Daly, Ann. *Done into Dance: Isadora Duncan in America*. Middletown, CT: Wesleyan University Press, 1995.

Daniel, Yvonne. *Dancing Wisdom: Embodied Knowledge in Haitian Vodou, Cuban Yoruba, and Bahian Candomblé*. Bloomington: University of Illinois Press, 2005.

Daniel, Yvonne. *Rumba: Dance and Social Change in Contemporary Cuba*. Bloomington: Indiana University Press, 1995.

Dayan, Joan. "Erzulie: A Woman's History of Haiti." *Research in African Literatures* 25, no.2 (1994): 5–32.

De Certeau, Michel. *The Practice of Everyday Life*. Translated by Steve Rendall. Berkeley: University of California Press, 1984.

De Certeau, Michel. *The Writing of History*. New York: Columbia University Press, 1988.

DeFrantz, Thomas. "African American Dance—Philosophy, Aesthetics, and 'Beauty.'" *Topoi* 24 (2005): 93–102.

DeFrantz, Thomas. "Black Beat Made Visible." In *Of the Presence of the Body: Essays on Dance and Performance Theory*, edited by André Lepecki, 64–81. Middletown, CT: Wesleyan University Press, 2004.

DeFrantz, Thomas. *Dancing Many Drums: Excavations in African American Dance*. Madison: University of Wisconsin Press, 2002.

DeFrantz, Thomas, and Anita Gonzalez, eds. *Black Performance Theory*. Durham, NC: Duke University Press, 2014.

De la Campa, Román. *Latin Americanism*. Minneapolis: University of Minnesota Press, 1999.

De La Torre, Miguel A. "Ochún: [N]Either the [M]Other of All Cubans [N]or the Bleached Virgin." *Journal of the American Academy of Religion* 69, no.4 (2001): 837–61.

DeLauretis, Teresa. *Alice Doesn't: Feminism, Semiotics, Cinema*. Bloomington: Indiana University Press, 1984.

DeLauretis, Teresa. *Technologies of Gender: Essays on Theory, Film, and Fiction*. Bloomington: Indiana University Press, 1987.

Dent, Gina, ed. *Black Popular Culture*. Seattle: Bay Press, 1992.

Derrida, Jacques. *Specters of Marx: The State of the Debt, the Work of Mourning, and the New International*. Translated by Peggy Kamuf. New York: Routledge, 1994.

Desmond, Jane, ed. *Meaning in Motion: New Cultural Studies of Dance*. Durham, NC: Duke University Press, 1997.

DeVere Brody, Jennifer. *Impossible Purities: Blackness, Femininity and Victorian Culture*. Durham, NC: Duke University Press, 1998.

Diamond, M. J., ed. *Women and Revolution: Global Expressions*. Dordrecht: Kluwer Academic Publishers, 1998.

Díaz, María Elena. *The Virgin, the King, and the Royal Slaves of El Cobre: Negotiating Freedom in Colonial Cuba, 1670–1780.* Stanford, CA: Stanford University Press, 2000.

Diggs, Irene. "Color in Colonial Spanish America." *Journal of Negro History* 38 (1953): 403–27.

Dinerman, Margaux Eve. "St. Lazarus: Myth, Song and Dance." Master's thesis, UCLA, 1994.

Doane, Mary Ann. *Femmes Fatales.* New York: Routledge, 1991.

Drewal, Henry John, and Margaret Thompson Drewal. *Géléde: Art and Female Power among the Yoruba.* Bloomington: Indiana University Press, 1983.

Elam, Harry J. Jr., and Kennell Jackson, eds. *Black Cultural Traffic: Crossroads in Global Performance and Popular Culture.* Lansing: University of Michigan Press, 2005.

Fajardo Estrada, Ramón. *Rita Montaner: Testimonio de una época.* Havana: Casa de las Américas, 1997.

Falola, Toyin, and Matt D. Childs, eds. *The Yoruba Diaspora in the Atlantic World.* Bloomington: Indiana University Press, 2004.

Fanon, Frantz. *Black Skin, White Masks.* New York: Grove Press, 1967.

Farris Thompson, Robert. *Flash of the Spirit: African & Afro-American Art & Philosophy.* New York: Vintage Books, 1983.

Fauley, Lynn Emery. *Black Dance 1619–Today.* 2nd ed. Princeton, NJ: Princeton Book Company Publishers, 1988.

Fausto-Sterling, Anne. "Gender, Race and Nation: The Comparative Anatomy of 'Hottentot Women' in Europe 1815–1817." In *Deviant Bodies: Critical Perspectives on Difference in Science and Popular Culture*, edited by Jennifer Terry and Jacqueline Urla, 19–42. Bloomington: Indiana University Press, 1995.

Federation of Cuban Women. *Women: A Revolution with the Revolution.* Havana: ORBE Publishing, 1982.

Fernández, Damian, and Madeline Cámara Betancourt, eds. *Cuba, the Elusive Nation: Interpretations of National Identity.* Gainesville: University Press of Florida, 2000.

Fernández Retamar, Roberto. "Adios a Caliban." *Casa de las Américas* 33, no.191 (1993): 116–22.

Fernández Retamar, Roberto. *Caliban and Other Essays.* Minneapolis: University of Minnesota Press, 1989.

Fernández Robaina, Tomás. *Historias de Mujeres Públicas.* Havana: Editorial Letras Cubanas, 1998.

Ferré, Rosario. *Maldito Amor y Otros Cuentos [Sweet Diamond Dust].* New York: Vintage Books, 1998.

Ferré, Rosario. *Papeles De Pandora.* Lincoln: University of Nebraska Press, 1991.

Flores-Peña, Ysamur. "Overflowing with Beauty: The Ochún Altar in Lucumí-Aesthetic Tradition." In *Òsun Across the Waters: A Yoruba Goddess in Africa and the Americas*, edited by Joseph M. Murphy and Mei-Mei Sanford, 113–27. Bloomington: Indiana University Press, 2001.

Foster, Susan. "Choreographies of Gender." *Signs* 24, no.1 (1998).

Foster, Susan, ed. *Choreographing History.* Bloomington: Indiana University Press, 1995.

Foster, Susan, ed. *Corporealities.* New York: Routledge, 1995.

Foucault, Michel. *Archeology of Knowledge.* Translated by A. M. Sheridan Smith. New York: Pantheon, 1972.

Foucault, Michel. *Discipline and Punish: The Birth of the Prison.* Translated by Alan Sheridan. New York: Vintage, 1977.

Foucault, Michel. "Nietzsche, Genealogy, History." In *Language, Counter-Memory, Practice: Selected Essays and Interviews*, edited by D. F. Bouchard. Ithaca: Cornell University Press, 1977.

Foucault, Michel. *Technologies of the Self: A Seminar with Michel Foucault*. Edited by Luther Martin. Boston: University of Massachusetts, 1998.

Frasier Delgado, Celeste, and José Esteban Muñoz, eds. *Everynight Life:Dance and Culture in Latin/o America*. Durham, NC: Duke University Press, 1997.

Fraunhar, Alison. "Re-Visioning the Mulata in Cuban Visual Culture 1880–2000." PhD diss., University of California, 2005.

Fraunhar, Alison. "Tropics of Desire: Envisioning the Mulata Cubana." *Emergences* 12, no.2 (2002): 219–34.

Fusco, Coco. "Hustling for Dollars" *Ms*. Magazine, September-October, 1996, 62–70.

Fusco, Coco, ed. *Corpus Delecti: Performance Art of the Americas*. London: Routledge, 2000.

Fusco, Coco. "Jineteras En Cuba." *Encuentro de la Cultura Cubana* 4, no. 5 (1997): 53–64.

Galiño, José. *"Academias de baile."* Unpublished essay.

Galiño, José, and Lourdes Prieto. *Daniel Santos: Para Gozar La Habana*. Documentary, 2004.

Gallagher, Patrick. "Cuba: Ariel or Caliban?" *Torre de Papel* 3, no.3 (1993): 5–19.

García, Cindy. "Don't Leave Me Celia: Salsera Homosociality and Pan-Latina Corporealities." *Women and Performance: A Journal of Feminist Theory* 38 (November 2008): 199–213

García, Cindy. *Salsa Crossings: Dancing Latinidad in Los Angeles*. Durham, NC: Duke University Press, 2013.

García Canclini, Nestor. *Cultural Híbridas: Estratégias Para Entrar y Salir De La Modernidad*. Mexico City: Grijalbo, 1989.

Gaspar, David Barry, and Darlene Clark Hine, eds. *Beyond Bondage: Free Women of Color in the Americas*. Urbana and Chicago: University of Illinois Press, 2004.

Gates, Henry Louis, Jr. *Figures in Black: Words, Signs, and The "Racial" Self*. New York: Oxford University Press, 1988.

Gikandi, Simon. "Race and Cosmopolitanism." *American Literary History* 14, no. 3 (2002): 593–614.

Gikandi, Simon. *Writing in Limbo: Modernism and Caribbean Literature*. Ithaca, New York: Cornell University Press, 1992.

Gilliam, Angela. "The Brazilian Mulata: Images in the Global Economy." *Race and Class* 40, no.1 (1998): 57–69.

Gillman, Susan. "The Mulatto: Tragic or Triumphant? The Nineteenth-Century American Race Melodrama." In *The Culture of Sentiment: Race, Gender and Sentimentality in Nineteenth-Century America*, edited by Shirley Samuels. 221–243. New York: Oxford University Press, 1992.

Gilroy, Beryl. *Stedman and Joanna—a Love in Bondage: Dedicated Love in the Eighteenth Century*. New York: Vantage Press, 1991.

Gilroy, Paul. *Against Race: Imagining Political Culture Beyond the Color Line*. Cambridge: Harvard University Press, 2000.

Gilroy, Paul. *The Black Atlantic: Modernity and Double Consciousness*. Cambridge, MA: Harvard University Press, 1992.

Gilroy, Paul. *Small Acts: Thoughts on the Politics of Black Cultures*. London: Serpent's Tail, 1993.

Gold Levi, Vicki, and Steven Heller. *Cuba Style: Graphics from the Golden Age of Design*. Princeton, NJ: Princeton Architectural Press, 2002.

Gomez de Avellaneda y Arteaga, Gertrudis. *Sab and Autobiography.* Translated and edited by Nina Scott. Austin: University of Texas Press, 1993.

González, Reynaldo. *Cine Cubano: Ese Ojo Que Nos Ve.* San Juan: Editorial Plaza Mayor, 2002.

González Mandri, Flora María. *Guarding Cultural Memory: Afro-Cuban Women in Literature and the Arts,* Charlotte: University of Virginia Press, 2006.

González Pagés, Julio César. *En busca de un espacio: Historia de mujeres en Cuba.* Havana: Editorial de Ciencias Sociales, 2003.

Gottschild, Brenda Dixon. *Digging the Africanist Presence in American Performance and Other Contexts.* Westport, CT: Greenwood Press, 1996.

Gould, Virginia. "In Full Enjoyment of Their Liberty: The Free Women of Color in the Gulf Ports of New Orleans, Mobile and Pensacola, 1769–1860." PhD diss., Emory University, 1991.

Greer, Germaine. *Madwomen's Underclothes: Essays and Occasional Writings, 1968-1985.* London: Picador Books, 1986.

Griffin, Farah Jasmine. "Textual Healing: Claiming Black Women's Bodies, the Erotic and Resistance in Contemporary Novels of Slavery." *Callaloo* 19, no.2 (Spring 1996): 519–36.

Guevara, Gema R. "Inexacting Whiteness: Blanqueamiento as a Gender-Specific Trope in the Nineteenth Century." *Cuban Studies* 36 (December 2005): 105–128.

Guillory, Monique. "Under One Roof: The Sins and Sanctity of the New Orleans Quadroon Balls" *in Race Consciousness: African-American Studies for the New Century* edited by Jackson Fossett, Judith and Jeffrey A. Tucker, 108–118. New York: Routledge, 2004.

Guillory, Monique. "Some Enchanted Evening on the Auction Block: The Cultural Legacy of the New Orleans Quadroon Balls." PhD diss., New York University, 1999.

Hammegren, Lena. "Many Sources, Many Voices." In *Rethinking Dance History.* Edited by Alexandra Carter, 20–31. New York: Routledge, 2004.

Hanger, Kimberly S. *Bounded Lives, Bounded Places: Free Black Society in Colonial New Orleans, 1769–1803.* Durham, NC: Duke University Press, 1997.

Hanger, Kimberly S. "Coping in a Complex World: Free Black Women in Colonial New Orleans." In *The Devil's Lane: Sex and Race in the Early South,* edited by Catherine Clinton and Michelle Gillespie, 218–231. New York: Oxford University Press, 1997.

Hartman, Saidiya. *Scenes of Subjection:Terror, Slavery and Self-Making in Nineteenth Century America.* Oxford: Oxford University Press, 1997.

Hazard, Samuel. *Cuba with Pen and Pencil.* Oxford: Signal Books Ltd, 2007 (1871).

Hernandez-Reguant, Ariana. "Multicubanidad." In *Cuban and The Special Period,* edited by Ariana Hernandez-Reguant 69–88. New York & London: Palgrave MacMillan, 2009

Hopkinson, Nalo. *Salt Roads.* New York: Grand Central Publishing, 2004.

Jameson, Frederic. *The Prison House of Language.* Princeton, NJ: Princeton University Press, 1972.

John, Suki. "The Técnica Cubana." In *Caribbean Dance from Abakua to Zouk,* edited by Susanna Sloat, 73–78. Gainesville: University Press of Florida, 2002.

Johnson, Walter. *Soul to Soul: Life Inside the Antebellum Slave Market.* Cambridge, MA: Harvard University Press, 2001.

Jones, Gayl. *Corregidora.* Boston: Beacon Press, 1987.

Jordan, Stephanie, and Dave Allen, eds. *Parallel Lines: Media Representations of Dance.* London: John Libbey, 1993.

Kerr, Paulette A. "Victims or Strategists? Female Lodge Keepers in Jamaica." In *Engendering History: Caribbean Women in Historical Perspective*, edited by Verene Shephard, Bridget Brereton, and Barbara Bailey, 197–212. New York: St. Martin's Press, 1995.

Kristeva, Julia. *Powers of Horror: An Essay on Abjection*. Translated by Leon Roudiez. New York: Columbia University Press, 1982.

Kutzinski, Vera M. *Sugar's Secrets: Race and the Erotics of Cuban Nationalism*. Charlottesville and London VA: University Press of Virginia, 1993.

Kwan, Kevin. *I Was Cuba: Treasures from the Ramiro Fernandez Collection*. San Francisco: Chronicle Books, 2007.

Lam, Rafael. La Engañadora Vive en La Habana. Available at http://www.salsapower. com/Editorials/la-enganadora-habana.html [Accessed on 20 July 2015].

Lam, Rafael. "La Leyenda de las Mulatas de Fuego." In *Música Cubana No. 3*. Unión de Escritores y Artistas en Cuba (UNEAC) Publication, 1999.

Lam, Rafael. " El Chori, King of The Timbal at Marianao Beach" Available at http://www.salsapower.com/Editorials/el-chori-the-king-of-the-timbal-at-marianao-beach-el-chori-rey-del-timbal-en-la-playa-de-marianao.html>> [Accessed 11 July 2015]

Lam, Rafael. *Tropicana: A Paradise under the Stars*. Havana: Editorial José Martí, 1999.

Lane, Jill Meredith. *Blackface Cuba, 1840-1895*. Philadelphia: University of Pennsylvania Press, 2005.

Lane, Jill Meredith. "Smoking Habaneras, or A Cuban Struggle with Racial Demons." *Social Text* 28, no. 3 104 (Fall 2010): 11–37.

Leal, Rine. *Teatro Bufo, Siglo XIX: Antología*, vol. 1. Havana: Letras Cubanas, 1975.

Lewis, Oscar, Ruth M. Lewis, and Susan M. Rigdon, eds. *Four Women: Living the Revolution, An Oral History of Contemporary Cuba*. Bloomington: University of Illinois Press, 1978.

Li, Stephanie. "Resistance, Silence and Placées: Charles Bon's Octoroon Mistress and Louisa Picquet." *American Literature* 79, no. 1 (2007): 85–112.

Lorde, Audre. *Sister Outsider: Essays and Speeches*. New York: Ten Speed, 1984.

Lowinger, Rosa, and Ofelia Fox. *Tropicana Nights: The Life and Times of the Legendary Cuban Nightclub*. Orlando, FL: Harcourt, 2005.

Madison, D. Soyini. "The Labor of Reflexivity." *Cultural Studies <-> Critical Methodologies* 11, no. 2 (2011): 129–138.

Manning, Susan. "Black Voices, White Bodies: The Performance of Race and Gender in How Long Brethren." *American Quarterly* 50, no.1 (1998): 24–46.

Manzanas Calvo, Ana Maria. "What Does It Mean to Be Caliban? Visions of 'Other' in the Tempest and Afro-American Slavery." *Confronto Letterario: Quaderni del Dipartimento di Lingue e Letterature Straniere Moderne Dell'Universitá di Pavia* 12, no. 23 (1995): 149–62.

Marrero, Teresa. "Scripting Sexual Tourism: Fusco and Bustamante's STUFF, Prostitution and Cuba's Special Period." *Theatre Journal* 55 (2003): 235–50.

Martin, Luther, ed. *Technologies of the Self: A Seminar with Michel Foucault*. Amherst: University of Massachusetts Press, 1998.

Martin, Randy. *Critical Moves: Dance Studies in Theory and Politics*. Durham, NC: Duke University Press, 1998.

Martin, Randy. "Toward a Decentered Social Kinaesthetic." *Dance Research Journal* 42, no. 1 (Summer 2010):77–80.

Martínez Alier, Verena. *Marriage, Class and Colour in Nineteeth Century Cuba: A Study of Racial Attitudes and Sexual Values in a Slave Society*. London: Cambridge University Press, 1974.

Martínez Echazábal, Lourdes. *Para Una Semiótica de la Mulatez*. Madrid: Porrúa Turanza, 1990.

Mason, John, and Gary Edwards. *Black Gods: Spirituality in the New World*. New York: Yoruba Theological Archministry, 1998.

Mason, John, and Gary Edwards. *Olóòkun: Owner of Rivers and Seas*. New York: Yoruba Theological Archministry, 1996.

Mason, John, and Gary Edwards. *Orin Orisa: Songs for Sacred Heads*. New York: Yoruba Theological Archministry, 1992.

McClintock, Anne. *Imperial Leather: Race, Gender and Sexuality in the Colonial Conquest*. New York: Routledge, 1995.

McNeill, Tamara. "The Politics of Identity and Race in the Colored Creole Community: The Gens De Couleur Libre in Creole New Orleans, 1800–1860." *Berkeley McNair Journal*, available at http://www.mcnair.berkeley.edu/UGA/OSL/McNair/94BerkeleyMcNairJournal/02_McNeill.html.

Meduri, Avanthi. "Western Feminist Theory, Asian Indian Performance, and a Notion of Agency." *Women & Performance: A Journal of Feminist Theory* 5, no. 2 (1992): 90–103.

Mena, Luz. "Stretching the Limits of Gendered Spaces: Black and Mulatto Women in 1830s Havana." *Cuban Studies* 36 (December 2005): 87–104.

Mendieta Costa, Raquel. "Exotic Exports: The Myth of the Mulatta." In *Corpus Delecti: Performance Art of the Americas*, edited by Coco Fusco, 43–54. London: Routledge, 2000.

Mintz, Sidney. *Sweetness and Power: The Place of Sugar in Modern History*. New York: Penguin, 1995.

Mohammed, Patricia. "'But Most of All Mi Love Me Browning': The Emergence in Eighteenth and Nineteenth Century Jamaica of the Mulatto Woman as the Desired." *Feminist Review* 65 (Summer 2000): 22–48.

Moore, Robin D. *Nationalizing Blackness: Afrocubanismo and Artistic Revolution in Havana, 1920–1940*. Pittsburgh: University of Pittsburgh Press, 1997.

Morazan, Ronald R. "Quadroon Balls in the Spanish Period." *Louisiana History* 14 (1973): 310–15.

Morejón, Nancy. "Cuba and Its Deep Africanity." *Callaloo* 28, no.4 (2005): 933–51.

Morejón, Nancy. *Fundación De La Imagen (Ensayos)*. Havana: Editorial Letras Cubanas, 1988.

Morúa Delgado, Martín. *Sofía*. Havana: Instituto Cubano del Libro, 1972.

Moruzzi, Peter. *Havana Before Castro: When Cuba Was A Tropical Playground*. Layton, UT: Gibbs Smith, 2008.

Moya, Isabel. "Una Aproximación desde el enfoque de género a la situación y condición de la mujer en el proceso de la Revolución Cubana." *La Jiribilla: Revista de Cultura Cubana* 3–9 (January 2009), available at http://www.lajiribilla.cu/2009/n400_01/400_05.html#_ftn14, accessed July 4, 2012.

Moya Fábregas, Johanna I. "The Cuban Woman's Revolutionary Experience: Patriarchal Culture and the State's Gender Ideology 1950-1976." *Journal of Women's History* 22, no. 1 (2010): 61–84.

Murphy, Joseph M. *Working the Spirit: Ceremonies of the African Diaspora*. Boston: Beacon Press, 1994.

Murphy, Joseph M., and Mei-Mei Sanford, eds. *Òsun Across the Waters: A Yoruba Goddess in Africa and the Americas*. Bloomington: Indiana University Press, 2001.

Negrón-Muntaner, Frances. "Jennifer's Butt" *Aztlán* 22, no.2 (1997): 181–95.

Nichols, Grace. "The Battle with Language." *Caribbean Women Writers: Essays from the First International Conference*, edited by S. R. Cudjoe, 283–289. Wellesley: Calaloux Publications, 1990.

Olmstead, Frederick Law. *The Cotton Kingdom: A Traveler's Observations on Cotton and Slavery in the American Slave States*. New York: Alfred A. Knopf, 1953.

Orejuela Martínez, Adriana. *El Son No Se Fue de Cuba: Claves Para Una Historia 1959–1973*. Havana: Editorial Letras Cubanas, 2006.

Orta, Sergio. "Cubanizando a Hollywood Bohemia." In "Hollywood in Havana: Film Reception and Revolutionary Nationalism in Cuba Before 1959," by Megan J. Feeney, PhD diss., University of Minnesota, 2008.

Ortiz, Fernando. *Etnia Y Sociedad*. Havana: Editorial de Ciencias Sociales, 1993.

Oyewumi, Oyeronke. *The Invention of Women: Making an African Sense of Western Gender Discourse*. Minneapolis: University of Minnesota Press, 1997.

Parker, Andrew, ed. *Nationalisms and Sexualities*. New York: Routledge, 1992.

Paternostro, Silvana. "Dancing Their Way out of Poverty." *Marie Claire*, October 2003, 114–20.

Pérez Jr., Louis A. *On Becoming Cuban: Identity, Nationality and Culture*. Chapel Hill: University of North Carolina Press, 1999.

Pérez Jr., Louis A. *Slaves Sugars and Colonial Society: Travel Accounts of Colonial Cuba 1801–1899*. New York: SR Books, 1992.

Pérez Firmat, Gustavo. *The Cuban Condition: Translation and Identity in Modern Cuban Literature*. New York: Cambridge University Press, 1989.

Pérez Sarduy, Pedro, and Jean Stubbs, eds. *Afro Cuba: An Anthology of Cuban Writing on Race, Politics and Culture*. Melbourne: Ocean Press, 1993.

Perks, Robert, and Alistair Thomson, eds. *The Oral History Reader*, 2nd ed. New York: Routledge, 2006.

Perna, Vincenzo. *Timba: The Sound of the Cuban Crisis*. Aldershot: Ashgate, 2005.

Phelan, Peggy. *The Ends of Performance*. New York: New York University Press, 1998.

Phelan, Peggy. *Unmarked:The Politics of Performance*. London: Routledge, 1993.

Piedra, José. "From Monkey Tales to Cuban Songs: On Signification." In *Sacred Possessions:Vodou, Santería, Obeah, and the Caribbean*, edited by Margarite Fernández Olmos and Lizabeth Paravisini-Gebert, 122–50. New Brunswick, NJ: Rutgers University Press, 1997.

Piedra, José. "Hip Poetics." In *Everynight Life: Dance and Culture in Latin/o America*, edited by Celeste Frasier Delgado and José Esteban Muñoz, 93–140. Durham, NC: Duke University Press, 1998.

Pollock, Della. "The Performative I." *Cultural Studies, <-> Critical Methodologies* 7 (2007): 239–55.

Portelli, Alessandro. "What Makes Oral History Different" in *The Oral History Reader*, 2nd Edition. Edited by Robert Perks and Alistair Thomson, 36–42. New York: Routledge, 2003.

Portuondo Zúñiga, Olga. *La Virgen De La Caridad Del Cobre: Símbolo De Cubanía*. Santiago de Cuba: Editorial Oriente, 1995.

Pratt, Mary Louise. *Imperial Eyes: Travel Writing and Transculturation*. London: Routledge, 1992.

Pravaz, Natasha. "Performing Mulatice: Hybridity as Identity in Brazil." PhD. diss., York University, 2002.

Quiroga, José. *Cuban Palimpsests*. Minneapolis: University of Minnesota Press, 2005.

Randall, Margaret. *Cuban Women Now*. Kitchener-Waterloo: Women's Press Dumont Press Graphix, 1974.

Reid, Michelle. "The Yoruba in Cuba: Origins, Identities, and Transformations." In *The Yoruba Diaspora in the Atlantic World*, edited by Toyin and Matt D. Childs Falola, 111–29. Bloomington: Indiana University Press, 2004.

Rich, Adrienne. "Notes Towards A Politics of Location" Conference Keynote, June 1,1984. Published in *Women, Feminist Identity and Society in the 1980s*. Edited by Diaz-DioCaretz, Myriam and Iris Zavala. Amsterdam: John Benjamins Publishing Company, 1985.

Roach, Joseph. *Cities of the Dead:Circum-Altantic Performance*. New York: Columbia University Press, 1996.

Rodríguez Monegal, Emir. "The Metamorphoses of Caliban." *Diacritics* 7 (1977): 78–83.

Rojas, Maria. *Women in Pre-Colonial Nigeria*. Blog, August 17, 2006, available at http://www.postcolonialweb.org/nigeria/precolwon.html.

Ruf, Elizabeth. "Qué Linda Es Cuba! Issues of Gender, Color, and Nationalism in Cuba's Tropicana Nightclub Performance." *Drama Review* 41, no.1 (1997): 86–105.

Sánchez, Marta E. "Caliban: The New Latin American Protagonist of the Tempest." *Diacritics* 6, no.1 (1976): 54–61.

Sangster, Joan. "Telling Our Stories: Feminist Debates and the Use of Oral History." *Women's History Review* 3, no. 1 (1994): 5–28.

Savigliano, Marta. *Tango and the Political Economy of Passion*. Middletown, CT: Wesleyan University Press, 1995.

Savigliano, Marta. "Nocturnal Ethnographies: Following Cortázar in the Milongas of Buenos Aires." *Trans: Revista Transcultural de Música*, Issue 5, 2000. Available at: http://www.sibetrans.com/trans/articulo/245/nocturnal-ethnographies-following-cortazar-in-the-milongas-of-buenos-aires [accessed on July 12, 2014]

Schwartz, Rosalie. *Pleasure Island, Tourism and Temptation in Cuba*. Lincoln: University of Nebraska Press, 1997.

Scott, Anna Beatrice. "Articulations of Blackness in Salvador Bahia, Brasil." Paper presented at Blackness in Global Contexts: Reflections on Experiences of Blackness from a Transnational Perspective, University of California Davis, 2002.

Scott, Anna Beatrice. *A Fala Que Faz Words That Work: Power, Performance, Blackness, and Carnaval in Salvador, Brazil 1968–1998*. Saarbrücken: VDM Verlag Dr Müller, 2010.

Scott, Anna Beatrice. "Dance." In *Culture Works: The Political Economy of Culture*, edited by Richard Maxwell, 107–30. Minneapolis: University of Minnesota Press, 2001.

Serpa, Enrique. *Contrabando*. La Habana: Editorial de Arte y Literatura, 1977.

Sharpe, Jenny. *Ghosts of Slavery: A Literary Archeology of Black Women's Lives*. Minneapolis: University of Minnesota Press, 2003.

Shephard, Verene, Bridget Brereton, and Barbara Bailey, eds. *Engendering History: Caribbean Women in Historical Perspective*. New York: St. Martin's Press, 1995.

Shohat, Elie. *Unthinking Eurocentrism*. New York: Routledge, 1994.

Smith, Lois M., and Alfred Padula. *Sex and Revolution: Women in Socialist Cuba*. New York: Oxford University Press, 1996.

Sollors, Werner. *Neither Black nor White yet Both: Thematic Explorations of Interracial Literature*. New York: Oxford University Press, 1997.

Spivak, Gayatri Chakravorty. "Can the Subaltern Speak?" In *Marxism and the Interpretation of Culture*, edited by C. and L. Grossberg Nelson, 271–311. Urbana: University of Illinois Press, 1988.

Spivak, Gayatri Chakravorty. *A Critique of Postcolonial Reason: Towards a History of the Vanishing Present*. Cambridge, MA: Harvard University Press, 1999.

Spivak, Gayatri Chakravorty. "Subaltern Studies: Deconstructing Historiography." In *Other Worlds: Essays in Cultural Politics*. New York: Metheun, 1987.

Srinivasan, Priya. *Sweating Saris: Indian Dance as Transnational Labor*. Philadelphia: Temple University Press, 2012.

Stearns, Marshall. *Jazz Dance: The Story of American Vernacular Dance*. New York: Schirmer Books, 1979.

Stein, Jean. "All Havana Broke Loose." *Vanity Fair*, September 2011.

Steedman, Carolyn. *Dust: The Archive and Cultural History*. New Brunswick, NJ: Rutgers University Press, 2001.

Steedman, Carolyn. "Something She Called a Fever: Michelet, Derrida, and Dust." *American Historical Review* 106, no.4 (October 2001): 1159–80.

Stevens-Arroyo, Anthony M. "The Contribution of Catholic Orthodoxy to Caribbean Syncretism: The Case of La Virgen De La Caridad Del Cobre in Cuba." *Archives des Sciences Sociales des Religions* 117 (January–March 2002): 37–58.

Stoler, Ann Laura. *Along the Archival Grain: Epistemic Anxieties and Colonial Common Sense*. Princeton, NJ: Princeton University Press, 2009.

Sublette, Ned. *Cuba and its Music: From the First Drums to the Mambo*. Chicago: Chicago Review Press, 2004.

Summer, Doris. *Foundational Fictions: The National Romances of Latin America*. Berkeley: University of California Press, 1991.

Summers, Doris. "Cecilia No Sabe, O Los Bloqueos Que Blanquean." *Revista de la Crítica Literaria Latinoamericana* 19, no. 38 (1993): 239–48.

Tademy, Lalita. *Cane River*. New York: Grand Central Publishing, 2002.

Taylor, Diana. *The Archive and the Repertoire: Performing Cultural Memory in the Americas*. Durham, NC: Duke University Press, 2003.

Taylor, Diana, and Juan Villegas, eds. *Negotiating Performance: Gender, Sexuality, and Theatricality in Latin/O America*. Durham, NC: Duke University Press, 1994.

Thomas, Helen, ed. *Dance in the City*. New York: St. Martin's Press, 1997.

Thomas, Helen. *Dance, Gender and Culture*. New York: St. Martin's Press, 1993.

Thomas, Susan. "Lo Más Femenino De Los Géneros: Gender, Race, and Representation in the Cuban Zarzuela, 1927–1944." Ph.D diss., Brandeis University, 2002.

Thomas, Susan. *Cuban Zarzuela: Performing Race and Gender on Havana's Lyric Stage*. Urbana: University of Illinois Press, 2009.

Thompson Drewal, Margaret. *Yoruba Ritual: Performers, Play, Agency*. Bloomington: Indiana University Press, 1992.

Thorpe, Edward. *Black Dance*. New York: Overlook Press, 1990.

Ugwu, Catherine, ed. *Let's Get It On: The Politics of Black Performance*. London: Institute of Contemporary Arts, 1995.

Vaughn, Alden T. "Caliban in the 'Third World': Shakespeare's Savage as Sociopolitical Symbol." *Massachusetts Review* 29, no. 2 (1988): 289–313.

Vicent, Mauricio. "Bailando hasta la eternidad." *El Pais Semanal*, May 24, 2013, available at http://elpais.com/elpais/2013/05/23/eps/1369328253_930790.html, accessed August 15. 2014.

Villaverde, Cirilo. *Cecilia Valdés O La Loma Del Ángel*. Havana: Instituto Cubano del Libro, 1972.

Visweswaran, Kamala. *Fictions of Feminist Ethnography*. Minneapolis: University of Minnesota Press, 1994.

White, Luise. *Speaking with Vampires: Rumor and History in Colonial Africa*. Berkeley: University of California Press, 2000.

White, Peter I. "Cuba at a Crossroads." *National Geographic* 180, no. 2, August, 1991.

Williams, Claudette M. *Charcoal and Cinammon: The Politics of Color in Spanish Caribbean Literature*. Tallahassee: University Press of Florida, 2000.

Williams, Linda. "Film Body: An Implantation of Perversions." *Ciné-Tracts* 12 (Winter 1981): 19–35.

Williams, Lorna. "From Dusky Venus to Mater Dolorosa: The Female Protagonist in the Cuban Antislavery Novel." In *Woman as Myth and Metaphor in Latin American Literature*, edited by Carmelo Virgillo and Naomi Lindstrom, 121–35. Columbia: University of Missouri Press, 1985.

Winters, Lisa Ze. "Spectacle, Specter and the Imaginative Space: Unfixing the Tragic Mulatta." PhD diss., University of California Berkeley, 2005.

Wynter, Sylvia. "Beyond Miranda's Meanings: Un/Silencing the 'Demonic Ground' of Caliban's 'Woman.'" In *Out of the Kumbla: Caribbean Women and Literature*, edited by Carole Boyce Davies and Elaine Savory Fido, 355–72. Trenton, NJ: Africa World Press, 1990.

INDEX

Numbers in *italics* indicate images.